EVALUATION AND
MEASUREMENT TECHNIQUES
FOR DIGITAL
COMPUTER SYSTEMS

Prentice-Hall
Series in Automatic Computation

George Forsythe, editor

MATHISON AND WALKER, *Computers and Telecommunications: Issues in Public Policy*
MCKEEMAN, et al., *A Compiler Generator*
MEYERS, *Time-Sharing Computation in the Social Sciences*
MINSKY, *Computation: Finite and Infinite Machines*
NIEVERGELT, et al., *Computer Approaches to Mathematical Problems*
PLANE AND MCMILLAN, *Discrete Optimization: Integer Programming and Network Analysis for Management Decisions*
PRITSKER AND KIVIAT, *Simulation with GASP II: a FORTRAN-Based Simulation Language*
PYLYSHYN, editor, *Perspectives on the Computer Revolution*
RICH, *Internal Sorting Methods Illustrated with PL/1 Programs*
RUSTIN, editor, *Algorithm Specification*
RUSTIN, editor, *Computer Networks*
RUSTIN, editor, *Data Base Systems*
RUSTIN, editor, *Debugging Techniques in Large Systems*
RUSTIN, editor, *Design and Optimization of Compilers*
RUSTIN, editor, *Formal Semantics of Programming Languages*
SACKMAN AND CITRENBAUM, editor, *On-Line Planning: Towards Creative Problem-Solving*
SALTON, editor, *The SMART Retrieval System: Experiments in Automatic Document Processing*
SAMMET, *Programming Languages: History and Fundamentals*
SCHAEFER, *A Mathematical Theory of Global Program Optimization*
SCHULTZ, *Digital Processing: A System Orientation*
SCHULTZ, *Spline Analysis*
SCHWARZ, et al., *Numerical Analysis of Symmetric Matrices*
SHERMAN, *Techniques in Computer Programming*
SIMON AND SIKLOSSY, editors, *Representation and Meaning: Experiments with Information Processing Systems*
STERLING AND POLLACK, *Introduction to Statistical Data Processing*
STOUTEMYER, *PL/1 Programming for Engineering and Science*
STRANG AND FIX, *An Analysis of the Finite Element Method*
STROUD, *Approximate Calculation of Multiple Integrals*
STROUD AND SECREST, *Gaussian Quadrature Formulas*
TAVISS, editor, *The Computer Impact*
TRAUB, *Iterative Methods for the Solution of Polynomial Equations*
UHR, *Pattern Recognition, Learning, and Thought*
VAN TASSEL, *Computer Security Management*
VARGA, *Matrix Iterative Analysis*
WAITE, *Implementing Software for Non-Numeric Application*
WILKINSON, *Rounding Errors in Algebraic Processes*
WIRTH, *Systematic Programming: An Introduction*

EVALUATION AND MEASUREMENT TECHNIQUES FOR DIGITAL COMPUTER SYSTEMS

MANSFORD E. DRUMMOND, Jr.

Systems Development Division
International Business Machines Corporation

Adjunct Professor
The University of Texas at El Paso

PRENTICE-HALL, INC.

ENGLEWOOD CLIFFS, NEW JERSEY

Library of Congress Cataloging in Publication Data

DRUMMOND, MANSFORD E.   1930–
    Evaluation and measurement techniques for digital
computer systems.

    Bibliography: p.
    1. Electronic digital computers—Evaluation.
I. Title.
QA76.5.D74   621.3819'52   72–8858
ISBN 0–13–292102–2

10 9 8 7 6 5 4 3 2 1

Printed in the United States of America

PRENTICE-HALL INTERNATIONAL, INC., *London*
PRENTICE-HALL OF AUSTRALIA, PTY. LTD., *Sydney*
PRENTICE-HALL OF CANADA, LTD., *Toronto*
PRENTICE-HALL OF INDIA PRIVATE LIMITED, *New Delhi*
PRENTICE-HALL OF JAPAN, INC., *Tokyo*

1734463

To my wife, Jean

PREFACE

Because of the complexity of digital computer applications, methods of evaluation and measurement are becoming more important to the user and the designer of the systems. Where once a simple examination of "add time" or "record rate" was satisfactory, more sophisticated techniques are now needed. In approaching the subject, some degree of discipline is required. Various users and designers have their own criteria of "goodness" with some overlap and confusion in terminology.

The purpose of this text is to supply some guidance and information about the basic techniques used in evaluation and measurement. The material presented should be sufficient to allow analysts to perform simple but meaningful investigations into the activity of a system.

Chapter 1 identifies potential users of evaluation and measurement information. It also distinguishes between the two primary areas of performance; availability and work capability.

Chapter 2 provides a brief history of the relationships between design and use of systems and the requirements of evaluation and measurement.

Chapter 3 concentrates on the evaluation of central processing units (CPU's). Comparative and absolute evaluations are identified. Techniques for evaluating CPU's are demonstrated along with sensitivity to variables.

Chapter 4 introduces the system approach through the use of formula timing, profile conversion, and synthetic techniques. The concept of *relative systems throughput* is introduced.

Chapter 5 is a brief introduction to the field of simulation techniques as applied to the evaluation of computers. Advantages and disadvantages of various types of simulation are explored.

Chapter 6 is a brief note on data acquisition. Its purpose is to set the stage for hardware and software measurement techniques.

Chapter 7 presents the elementary forms of programmed measurement techniques. The two primary types of "intercept" and "sample" routines are discussed.

Chapter 8 presents various forms of hardware monitoring techniques and their capability to obtain system information.

Chapter 9 discusses methods of presenting the results of evaluation and measurement investigations. It concentrates on methods for the analyst to use to transmit results to the nontechnical audience.

Chapter 10 brings together the various techniques both of evaluation and measurement, as they are applied to particular problems.

The manuscript has been used in both industrial and university courses. The intention of this work is also to provide a reference text on evaluation and measurement techniques to be used wherever computers are installed. The intended audience covers the span of individuals from the detail designer to the business management of computer installations.

I am very indebted to several people involved in the preparation of this text. It was Professor Gerald Estrin, University of California, Los Angeles, who first caused me to undertake the work and also provided guidance concerning the scope of the text. Colleagues at IBM, especially Harold Heath of the IBM Systems Research Institute, have provided many suggestions as a result of using the manuscript for courses in the company. I would also like to thank the many students who made suggestions for improvement. Last, but not least, my thanks to Mrs. Dorothy Lewis for typing the bulk of the manuscript.

MANSFORD E. DRUMMOND, Jr.

Santa Cruz, California

CONTENTS

1 EVALUATION AND MEASUREMENT

It is worthwhile to distinguish between the two words "evaluation" and "measurement." Reference to a dictionary indicates that evaluation is the ascertaining of the *value* of a subject, while measurement is the ascertaining of the *extent* of a subject. One need not utilize measurement in the evaluation of a subject, but it is a direct and useful method. Other tools to aid in evaluation are formula projections and mathematical models, both analytic and simulative. Executing a measurement or an analysis will produce a result. The determination of how good the result is, or what value it has is the evaluation.

In the early days, a computer was accepted because it could perform work which would not otherwise be performed, especially in the time required. Very often, the presence of the system was more important than any investigation into its relative capabilities. Of course, we had comparisons such as one computer doing the work of one thousand graduate mathematicians with desk calculators. If we had investigated the relative efficiency of that comparison, the result could well have been that it was doing the work of only five hundred well trained high school graduates who were very proficient with desk calculators. (We still see comparisons of a computer doing the work of "ordinary" people. Keep in mind that all the computers in the world cannot do the work of even one *extraordinary* person.) With the growing complexity of computers and the various options available to a user, evaluation techniques must be employed in all phases of procurement and use.

The basic reason for performing an evaluation or measurement is to determine how best to design, install or improve the operation of a computing system. We should recognize, however, that various individuals have limited resources or competence to execute an improvement. We shall therefore examine the potential users of evaluation and measurement.

1.1. USERS OF EVALUATION

The simplest method of distinguishing between users of evaluation is the familiar classification of manufacturers and customers. This, however, may be misleading. After all, within a manufacturer's company, there are people who have all of the attributes of a customer; and within a customer's organization, there are people who have all of the attributes of a manufacturer. A better classification would be between the developer of a product and the user of a product. In this classification, a developer would be someone (group or individual) who is creating a facility, either a device, a programmed routine, or both, for someone else to use. A user would be one who uses the results of development in an optimum fashion to perform his primary function. From the developer's point of view, various activities require evaluation input. Examples are given as follows:

Planning: Determination of advantages and disadvantages of alternative plans.

Development: Determination of such items as hardware/software tradeoffs, i.e., what items should be implemented in equipment and what items should be implemented in programmed routines.

Testing: Determination of the product's meeting its broad intended objectives (hardware and/or software).

Sales: Determination of the product's meeting individual user requirements.

Installing: Determination of optimum system generation for a particular set of requirements.

Optimization: Determination (usually on a continuing basis) of system modification to enhance performance.

From the user's point of view, examples of activities in which evaluation can play an active part are as follows:

Procurement: Determination of relative values of various proposals of products.

Installing: Determination of optimum system generation for his requirements.

Optimization: Determination (usually on a continuing basis) of system modifications to enhance performance.

Scheduling: Allocation of system resources to the various demands placed on the system.

Accounting and   Determination of information for cost distribution to
Control: the subsequent users of the system and planning future
workload on the system.

There are two of the examples which are shared between the developer and the user: installation and optimization. These activities are typically conducted as joint ventures with each side contributing specialized knowledge to the solution of discovered problems. It is naturally to the interest of both parties that the system perform as efficiently as possible.

The primary consideration in establishing the requirements of an evaluation is in the level of detail required for a decision process. The extremes in the level of detail required are exemplified by considering on one hand an individual who is designing circuitry or microcode for a component of a system where timing sensitivities are expressed in terms of nanoseconds; and on the other hand, an individual who is concerned with distributing a month's system time to the users of the system, where the timing sensitivity is expressed in tenths or hundredths of an hour. (Later we shall see that the distribution process must take into account very small increments of time.) At this point, one may question whether the function of accounting and control is properly within the field or definition of evaluation. The mere act of distribution would require only measurement facilities. Whether an evaluation takes place is up to the installation. If an analysis is made of the distribution data as well as the act of distribution, then evaluation takes place.

At any particular time, an individual may be concerned with one of three levels of requirements for evaluation. These levels broadly indicate the amount of detail and level of sensitivity which are required by the user. They are not intended to be precise classifications, but rather generic definitions of design points for evaluation. The three levels are the gross level, the job level, and the intra-job level.

The gross level of requirement is one in which the result of the evaluation is to represent the widest possible application area. This level would generally be used by individuals who wish to characterize the potential performance of a product on a very wide basis. This type of evaluation is typically used in the developer's planning, development, and testing cycle and in the user's acquisition phase. The requirement of broad representation is naturally an attribute of a general purpose computer. The general purpose computer is intended to perform well in a wide spectrum of applications in many different situations. The assessment of its performance must take into consideration this broad spectrum. When a user is evaluating a potential computer for a possible acquisition, he also tries to take into account a spectrum of applications representing the work that he is performing in a single installation.

Within the application spectrum, there could be applications which represent the old classical cases of scientific and commercial computing as well as other special cases such as high usage of a particular compiler. The primary problem in applying the results of a gross evaluation to any particular installation is that the assumed application base may bear absolutely no resemblance to any particular environment. For example, there may be a requirement to assess the performance of all compile activity within a single installation. Although the result would be valid for the installation as a whole, the result may not apply to an individual's particular compile job.

The job level requirement is one in which the result of an evaluation is to represent the performance of a product on a particular job or class of job. A particular job such as a hydrocode or pipe stress analysis or insurance rating may be classical of a particular field of computer application. Evaluation of typical representatives of the class would indicate the system's performance for the field of interest. The user of the system is interested in individual jobs so that he can schedule or allocate the system for major work. During the acquisition phase, this type of evaluation is very popular in that it is the basis of the "benchmark" problem. This will be described later under "Choice of Data."

The intra-job level requirement is normally used by the developers of products and sometimes by individual users who are optimizing major individual applications. The intention here is to determine which system facilities are used by a particular application. The determination would be done in such a way as to high-light the critical factors of the job. In this way those items which can effect the best performance pay off can be examined for possible improvement. If, for example, the critical element in an application is the speed of data transmission for a particular auxiliary storage unit (as opposed to access time or other possible attributes), then a storage element with the highest data transmission speed would probably produce the best performance increase with the least increase in cost.

1.2. CLASSES OF EVALUATION

There are two primary classes of performance calculations; namely, availability and work capability. Availability is an expression of how much time a system (or part of a system) is in a state such that it can be used for productive purposes. Work capability is an expression of what a system is capable of performing while it is in a state that can be used for productive purposes. Although the calculations for these two attributes are generally independent, they may be taken together in a total systems evaluation.

There is yet another class of evaluation, which is basically outside the scope of this text; human factors evaluation. This field of study is concerned with the interaction of an individual with the computing process. Ease of use is a prime consideration in this field. Some factors will be considered in the section on interactive systems.

1.2.1. Availability

Availability is an expression of the amount or proportion of time that a system is operative for its intended purpose. There are two additional concepts that have an effect of availability: *reliability* and *repair time*.

Reliability is an expression which is the *probability* of the system being in an operative condition to perform its intended function. This calculation is for a specified period of time, the period of interest.

Repair time is that amount of time required to bring the system back into an operative condition following the occurrence of an error. It includes diagnosis, fault location, fault correction, and confirmation time. Depending on the criticalness of the failed unit, repair time may become either scheduled or unscheduled maintenance time. (*Serviceability* is a field of study designed to reduce repair time of failed units.)

These three concepts are joined together by the following:

(a) the mean time between failure, or its reciprocal, the error rate, of a unit;

(b) the time to repair a unit; and

(c) the period of planned operation of the unit.

The relationships are demonstrated below.

Availability may be expressed in absolute terms or as a percentage. When the expression is in absolute terms, it is usually called good available time. A simple calculation of good available time (GAT) is as follows:

$$GAT = \text{Total Time} - \text{Maintenance Time}.$$

Total time is generally considered to be that time that the system has power turned on. On the other hand, one can imagine a power-on time of say 10 hours with a scheduled shift time of only 8 hours. In this case, total time would be 8 hours. That is the total time the system is allocated for any purpose whatsoever. If the total time was 24 hours, and the maintenance time was four hours, the good available time would be 20 hours. This is an example of a simple calculation of good available time; however, in actual practice there are many more factors to be calculated. First of all, maintenance usually comes in two parts, scheduled and unscheduled.

Scheduled maintenance generally includes the time to do repair on units that were previously determined to be in error but not critical to the operation, i.e., deferred maintenance; preventive maintenance on those units which have a somewhat predictable failure rate based on previous history; and scheduled updating of the system to avoid possible future problems. Scheduled maintenance is a term which is fairly self-descriptive. It is work which can be scheduled ahead of time on a reasonably expected basis. The schedule varies from installation to installation, and may be daily, weekly, and/or monthly.

To understand the activities during scheduled maintenance, consider the following examples. If during normal operation, a tape drive were to become inoperative due to failure, one of three things could happen. Either a replacement could be used, or the application would have to cease operation, or another alternative could be that some other application not requiring the tape drive could be put onto the system. Assume that a replacement is available, and the application could be recovered so that work could continue. At this point the system is producing work but the tape drive that failed is not part of the process. Maintenance could take place on the unit at that time, but to fully checkout the drive, there may be a requirement to use the main system. Whether a matter of convenience or a matter of necessity, the maintenance on that unit can be *deferred* until a later time. Usually this later time is during the next scheduled maintenance period.

Preventive maintenance is intended to avoid the possibility of failure during operation. It is essentially the same as performing normal scheduled service on an automobile. Through constant use, especially with mechanical items, a device may slowly be getting out of adjustment. Reading mechanisms tend to become clogged with dust or other foreign material. In the case of electronic components, there may be heat buildup in certain areas that accelerate the failure of some components. Given guidelines to probable failure, preventive maintenance can be performed on a scheduled basis to minimize an error's occurring during a critical operation.

Updating of a system differs from deferred maintenance in that it is a change to the system rather than an adjustment or repair (even by replacement) to the system. As an example, in the case of an electronic component, replacing a transistor or other logic element that is expected to go bad because of heat buildup is preventive maintenance. To modify the system so as to eliminate the heat buildup itself would be a change or update of the system. The intention of an update is to eliminate a probable failure or the need for a particular preventive action.

Unscheduled maintenance, on the other hand, is that time when the machine *must* be allocated for maintenance because some unit of the system must be repaired *at that time* so that the system can perform *any* intended function. An obvious intention is to reduce unscheduled maintenance to near-zero time and maintenance in general to a low level, i.e., improve the availability of the system.

There are many approaches to improving the availability of a system; three of them are reliable units, redundant units, and the concept of partial failure. A unit is a device which is generally considered to be in one "box" or frame. Exceptions to this are typified by two independent core storage units housed in one frame with only the power supply common, or two tape drives in the same frame with only the power supply common.

The first way is totally within the realm of the manufacturer, that is, to "build reliability" into the various components of the system. This not only includes the practice of using basic components of high reliability, such as transistors and other elements; the use of redundant components within the unit; but also includes the recognition that some errors may be of a temporary or transient nature. This latter factor influences the design of such concepts as error correction and error retry in system components.

When we consider a component within a unit, there are generally two functions which have an adverse effect on its reliability, speed of operation and loading effects. Typical relationships are shown in Figure 1.1. As the required speed of a component increases, its reliability decreases.

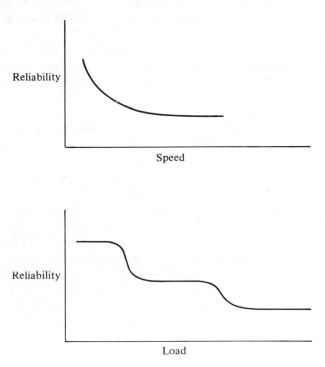

Fig. 1.1   Reliability vs. speed and load.

Similarly, as the load or activity on the component increases, its reliability decreases. (The particular shapes of the curves are hypothetical.) Therefore, to increase reliability as a function of speed, either the speed must be reduced or some other technology, usually more expensive, must be utilized. To increase reliability as a function of load, less load must be put on any individual component. This implies that more components must be used to achieve the same loading function. This also tends to increase the cost.

The creation of basic componentry which operates at higher speeds with greater loads at a high level of reliability is a continuing improvement in the state of the art. Fortunately, great strides have been made in almost all fields of basic technology.

The second method of improving system availability is within the realm of the user, that is, redundancy of critical units. Although we may think that redundancy is used principally in well known "real time" systems, it is in fact quite popular with normal business applications. An example would be an installation that required a large number of magnetic tape drives at all times in its work. If an installation required, say, 16 units, it may very well have 18 or more units installed just to ensure that the necessary number of units are available when needed. This, of course, adds to the cost of the system. Its only justification is that it is economically feasible in light of the work to be performed.

The third way to achieve higher availability is a method of approach which is reached between the manufacturer and the user. This approach involves using the remainder of the system, i.e., the collection of components not in error, to do part of the work while a component is taken out for maintenance. In a way, it is analogous to an installation rescheduling work around a unit that just went down. Other work which does not need that unit is performed. The primary difference is that the computer system itself does the rescheduling, performs the work which can be performed and, if part of its capabilities are needed for the repair of the unit which fails, concurrently provides such service. Various names have been given to this type of operation, such as "fail soft," "partial degradation," and "graceful degradation." Evaluation of the availability of this type of environment can become extremely complex because of the many job and environment dependencies. Simulation techniques are generally employed to assess the availability of such systems.

One of the more simple methods of calculating reliability is given here. These calculations are based on the assumption that the reliability of the system is calculated during the particular period of "useful life."

Components have the characteristic of going through three phases:

Burn in
Useful life
Wear out

"Burn in" is that period of time just after manufacture that a component is first activated. For the general installation, we will ignore this period since manufacturers generally "pre-burn" components where necessary.

"Useful life," which is self-descriptive, is that period of time which is of most interest to the users of equipment who do not perform their own maintenance. This is the time which we will be concerned with. We shall see later on that "useful life" is a much greater time than expected operational time.

"Wear Out" is that time where the component begins to degrade its performance following its useful life. For most computers, preventive maintenance is used to replace those components which begin to come near to the end of their useful life.

During useful life, reliability is primarily affected by random errors. These errors may be expressed as occurring in a Poisson distribution. As such, the formula for the reliability of a unit may be expressed by the exponential formula

$$R(t) = e^{-t/m},$$

where $R(t)$ is the reliability during the time t;
     m is the mean time between failure for the unit;
     t is the period of time of interest.

Naturally, m and t are expressed in the same units of time. From the above formula, we see that for a given mean time between failure, the reliability of a unit varies (exponentially) with the period of interest. If the period of interest is one month's operation, 176 hours, then to obtain a high reliability, we would expect to see the mean time between failures several orders of magnitude greater than 176 hours. The reason for this expectation is that if the mean time between failures is on the order of the period of interest, i.e., m nearly equals t, then we have a reliability of approximately 0.36. In other words there's only a 36% chance that the system will run without failure during the month's operation. In this simple calculation, error rates due to switching the system on and off are assumed to be included in the mean time between failures over the period of 176 hours.

As noted before, the mean time between failure for a unit during its useful life is established by the designers of the unit. In order to maintain a particular mean time between failure, the unit must be properly maintained. In the calculations which follow we shall assume that proper maintenance is performed. If it is not, then the mean time between failure will degrade over time. Furthermore, we shall assume that the period of interest is held constant for all calculations, say 1000 hours. As noted before, all failure rates due to switching equipment on and off are assumed to be included in the failure rate over 1000 hours. (This assumes some "normal" usage during that period.)

Under these conditions, we shall express the reliability of a unit as r, which is its probability of operating successfully during the 1000 hour period.

When two or more units are connected so that they must *all* be in operation for the system to function, we call that a *series* connection.

In Figure 1.2, we have a CPU, its processor storage, and a data path to input/output. For the system to operate, all three must operate correctly.

Fig. 1.2   Series reliability.

The equation for a series connection is the product of the reliability of each component. So, if we have *n* components, the reliability of operation of the system (*s*) is

$$s = \prod_{i=1}^{n} r_i.$$

Consider the simple case of a central processing unit operating with just its processor storage unit. If the CPU has a reliability of 0.95 and the processor storage unit has a reliability of 0.90, the combined reliability is 0.95 × 0.90, or 0.86. In other words, over our period of interest, the two units will have an 86 percent probability of working together without failure.

If units are connected in *parallel*, the system has the characteristic that it *will* operate unless *all* of the components fail. If any one of the components are operative, the system is operative.

In Figure 1.3, we see the case where either one of two disk files are suffi-

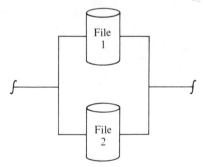

Fig. 1.3   Parallel reliability.

cient to keep the system in operation. The equation for this calculation is defined in terms of total failure. If *r* is the probability of successful operation, then $1 - r$ is the probability of failure. For a parallel system to fail, we have the equation

$$1 - s = \prod_{i=1}^{n} (1 - r_i).$$

Solving for s, we have the equation of successful operation

$$s = 1 - \prod_{i=1}^{n} (1 - r_i).$$

This is the simple equation for any *one* of the parallel units to be in operation for the system to be operational. Consider the simple case of having two disk files, each having a reliability of 0.75, with the requirement that if either one is operating, the subsystem will operate. This subsystem reliability is calculated as

$$s = 1 - (1 - 0.75)(1 - 0.75) = 0.94.$$

For m out of n units operating in parallel, we resort to a truth table of 2^n entries. (This is equivalent to the method of binomial expansion of reliability.) The method is to form the truth function whenever the total number of entries of the n possible units equals or exceeds the m required units, perform a reliability product, and then sum the reliability of each true entry. Let us take the example of having three disk file complexes available with the requirement that we must have two of the three available to do the required work. Assume that each file complex has a reliability, r. The truth table is shown in Figure 1.4.

Entry	Units 1 2 3			2/3 in Operation
1	0	0	0	0
2	0	0	1	0
3	0	1	0	0
4	0	1	1	1
5	1	0	0	0
6	1	0	1	1
7	1	1	0	1
8	1	1	1	1

Fig. 1.4 Truth table for two out of three units.

We see that the entries 4, 6, 7, and 8 meet the requirement of satisfying the required number of units. The reliability of each entry is calculated by performing the product of the probability of failure for each *zero* entry and the probability of success for each *one* entry. In this example, we therefore have the reliability expressions as shown in Figure 1.5.

Entry	Units 1 2 3	Reliability Expression	Combined
4	0 1 1	$(1-r)*(r)*(r)$	$r^2 - r^3$
6	1 0 1	$(r)*(1-r)*(r)$	$r^2 - r^3$
7	1 1 0	$(r)*(r)*(1-r)$	$r^2 - r^3$
8	1 1 1	$(r)*(r)*(r)$	r^3

Fig. 1.5 Reliability for each entry

Summing the results of each true entry, we have the reliability of the sub-system expressed as

$$s = 3r^2 - 2r^3.$$

If the reliability of each file complex is 0.75, we calculate the reliability of the subsystem for the two out of three case as

$$s = 3(0.75)^2 - 2(0.75)^3 = 0.84.$$

A system will generally consist of combinations of series and parallel related units. To calculate the reliability of the system, we will reduce each parallel structure to a single entry in the series, and then calculate the reliability by the series formula. Consider a systems configuration as given in Figure 1.6. This shows the total number of units available to perform work.

A particular application may require the central processing unit, the processor storage unit, one channel, one disk control unit, one disk file, one tape control unit, and two tapes. The reliability diagram is shown in Figure 1.7.

The relative physical position in this diagram has no meaning. It is simply in the same sequence as the statement of required units.

Assume that we have the following reliability factors of the various components:

Central Processing Unit	0.95
Processor Storage	0.90
Channel	0.85
Disk File	0.75
Disk Control Unit	0.85
Tape Unit	0.75
Tape Control Unit	0.85.

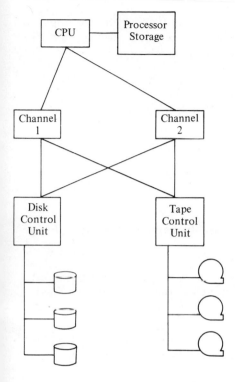

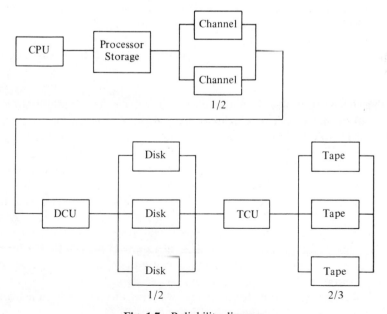

Fig. 1.6 Total units in system configuration.

Fig. 1.7 Reliability diagram.

There are three nets which must be reduced from parallel form for input to a series calculation; the channel net, the disk net, and the tape net. The channel net reduces on a one out of two formula which is

$$r(c) = 1 - (1 - 0.85)(1 - 0.85) = 0.9775.$$

The disk file net reduces on a one out of three formula to

$$r(d) = 0.9844.$$

The tape net reduces on a two out of three basis to

$$r(t) = 0.8438.$$

We now have a completely serialized reliability diagram as shown in Figure 1.8.

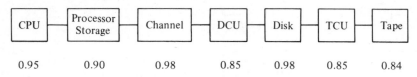

Fig. 1.8   Serialized reliability diagram.

The reliability of the total system is now calculated on the series formula of the product of the individual reliabilities, namely;

$$r(s) = 0.95 \times 0.90 \times 0.98 \times 0.85 \times 0.98 \times 0.85 \times 0.84$$
$$= 0.50$$

The simple examples given above are indicative of the reliability of a unit for a failure not to occur which causes it to stop performing its intended function. However, there are many techniques employed which try to overcome the outright failure. In the case of magnetic recording devices, whether tape or disk type, error detection and error correction codes are employed so that a temporary or transient failure will not cause a complete outage of the unit. Also, the ability to check data as it is written onto the media is utilized. Similarly, electronic devices employ techniques which allow them to retry the operation which failed. Programming systems are organized to overcome the temporary occurrence of failure in a unit. These techniques increase the reliability of units in the system by reducing the number of failures which cause an outage of the unit.

To calculate repair time for a system, we return to the mean time between failure and repair time for the individual units.

The number of errors (N) for a system of n units over t hours is given by the formula

$$N = \sum_{i=1}^{n} \frac{t}{m_i},$$

where m_i is the mean time between failure of the ith unit.

For each unit, there is an (average) repair time, T. The repair time for the system over the period of interest is given by

$$T_s = \sum_{i=1}^{n} \left(\frac{T_i}{m_i}\right)t,$$

where T_i is the repair time for the ith unit

T_s is the repair time for the system (over the period of interest t).

In order to break the repair time between scheduled and unscheduled maintenance, we can perform two calculations, one for the units that could fail and have their repair time deferred and one for those units which would cause a system outage. However, a conservative approach would be to do the calculation assuming any failure would result in a system outage.

This brief section on availability was to introduce the reader to some of the basic concepts. It is recommended that to pursue the subject, one should do further study. Bazovsky's *Reliability Theory and Practice* (Prentice-Hall, Inc., 1961) is an excellent text on the subject.

1.2.2. Work Capability

The calculation of work capability can take many forms. Again, the calculation can be absolute or comparative. The three most popular parameters of work capability are job time, throughput, and response time. Job time is a calculation of how long a system will take to perform an intended operation. This criterion is usually applied to jobs which tend to be discrete such as a sort job, a compile job, or a file update job. Throughput is an expression of the *processing rate* of a system, usually expressed as jobs per hour, transactions per minute, or some other parameter. For example, if card processing rate is the critical parameter of an application, then a system's throughput may be expressed as a card rate. The term can be applied loosely to any number of other attributes. In the 1950's throughput was sometimes used to indicate a relative performance factor between two systems. Because of the wide diversity of use and diversity of spelling, the phrase "relative systems throughput" is presented later in the text.

Response time is almost always expressed in absolute terms. This is a phrase which requires further definition depending upon the context of the evaluation. In terminal oriented systems, it generally refers to the amount of time that the computing system takes to react to various transactions from the terminal. In other real-time systems, response time can indicate the time it takes to identify, load, and execute a critical function. Although no response to the activating source is required, there could be a requirement to finish the processing of the critical program within some specified time. Response time calculations must be well defined within the context of their intended use.

Within the general concept of response time, there is the particular attribute of *turnaround* time. This phrase is generally used with batch-oriented systems. It is an expression of the time it takes from the submission of a job to be performed to the time when the results of the computation are available. Within the concept of turnaround there are the two subsidiary concepts of *system turnaround* and *application turnaround*. System turnaround is considered to be that time from the submission of a job at the computation center to the time it is available from the computation center. Application turnaround is the time from when a programmer is ready to submit his job until he has usable results back at his work station in order to proceed with his work. The difference in these two definitions is generally the time that it takes to transport a job between a programmer's work station and the computation center. If preparation of the job, such as key punching of programs and data, is required external to the computation center, then that activity would be part of the application turnaround and not the system turnaround time. In Figure 1.9, there is indicated the relationship between application and system turnaround time.

To understand the importance of these concepts, let us examine the make-up of system turnaround time. In Figure 1.10, there is indicated the component parts of system turnaround time based on an older method of processing batch jobs. This involved the use of "off-line" equipment for the preparation of input to the main computing system and the use of off-line equipment for the preparation of output for the user. Although this type of processing was introduced in the early 1950's, it has remained and probably will remain prevalent for many installations.

At Point 1 in Figure 1.10, the originating programmer or job requester hands his keypunched program deck and associated data to the dispatcher in the computation center. In return, he is given a piece of paper or a stub card or some other means of identification for his job. The function of the dispatcher is to log in the job under some system that can identify its progress through the computation cycle. At Point 2, the input is generally checked for accounting information to see that proper billing may be made to the project under which the programmer is operating. Also at this point, various other determinations may be made, such as the type of priority this particular job has in relation to the rest of the work which must be processed through the system. Based on these examinations, the job is either returned to the request-

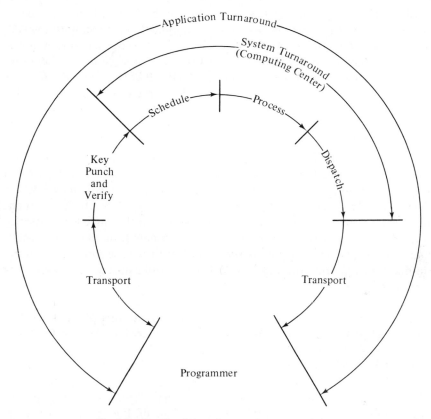

Fig. 1.9 Application and system turnaround time.

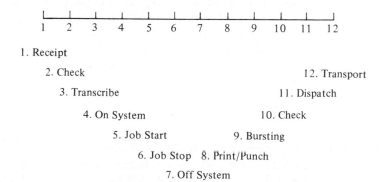

Fig. 1.10 Elements of system turnaround.

er for failing to meet some criterion, or assigned to a batch of jobs for processing. Of course, if the job has a high enough priority, it becomes a batch of one, for immediate processing. Batch assignment occurs on both the type of job and a time-of-day criteria. Type of job usually is based on the language family in which the program is written. Typically, these would be the native compiling languages of the system: ALGOL, BASIC, COBOL, COGO, FORTRAN, JOVIAL, PL/1, or some other language. The time-of-day criterion is literally that; when a certain time occurs, say three o'clock, all jobs presently assigned to the batch are transported to the next stage for the transcription process.

At Point 3 there is the transcription process, usually from punched card to high density magnetic tape. Extremely high priority jobs may bypass this stage and be fed into the computing system in whatever media may exist for them, whether punched cards, punched paper tape, or low density magnetic tape. After the transcription process, the resulting reel of tape is transported to an input station of the main computing system. Although high density magnetic tape is the most popular end result of the transcription process, we do find transcription onto other high density media such as removable disk files.

At Point 4, the (assumed) magnetic tape reel containing a series of jobs is mounted onto a drive attached to the system. At this point, the job is considered to be under the control of the computer, itself. Up to this time, it has been under manual or semi-manual control.

At Point 5, the job's processing requirement are initiated by the computer, and at Point 6, the requirements are completed.

At Point 7, the output media, usually magnetic tape, is removed from the computing system for off-line processing. The off-line process occurs at Point 8, usually in the form of printing results. Variations of output may be the punching of results into punched card or punched tape, or the plotting of results for further analysis. At Point 9, there is the bursting of paper and other activities to separate the individual jobs from the batch processing. At Point 10, the individual jobs are checked for both logistic control and accounting control so that they will be ready for dispatching at Point 11. At Point 12, the job is dispatched either to a courier or to a pick-up point for the requester. The purpose of interactive systems is to overcome this mode of operation.

1.2.3. Component Characteristics

The intention of a system evaluation is to combine the contributions of each system component in such a way as to reflect its effect on the processing of applications. However, there are times when these individual components require evaluation in themselves without regard to any system's environment.

The assessment of a component's availability is usually in terms of error incidence and repair times. An example of this information might be as follows:

Scheduled maintenance:	2 hours/month
Mean time between failures:	700 hours of operation
Unscheduled repair time:	2 hours

It is important to realize that the expression of mean time between failures is based on a probability calculation. Furthermore, this calculation is based on a large number of units, and therefore is the expectation for the class as a whole. Any particular unit may have a higher or lower error incidence. Any particular unit would probably have different characteristics depending on the age of the unit. Recognizing these qualifications, this type of assessment is generally of greater use to the developer of products rather than to individual installations. It does, however, provide to installation management a guideline as to a reasonable expectation of the availability of individual units.

A simple way to approximate availability information for this unit is to examine the availability of the unit over a period of 700 hours. If we consider that four months of single shift operation is about 700 hours (704 hours), we see that we should expect to have eight hours of scheduled maintenance. In addition, we can expect one unscheduled interruption during that time which would probably take two hours. During the 700 hours, we can therefore expect the unit to be not available for ten hours. This implies reliability on the order of 0.99 (690 hours divided by 700 hours). Of course, this is only an expectation. As is the case with all probability studies, any particular unit can fail at any particular time with varying amounts of time to repair. However, with that particular unit as a member of a large class of products, this calculation will provide an estimate.

The assessment of a component's work capability usually takes one of two forms; a listing of primary characteristics, and/or the calculation of a "figure of merit." The listing of primary characteristics is generally provided along with other public information made available at the time of announcement of the product. For products which have functions that are well defined and with somewhat regular performance characteristics, the expression is quite simple. For example, a line printer's capability could be expressed as "1000 lines per minute." If, on the other hand, the speed of the printer was sensitive to the number of characters printed on each line, a performance range may be indicated or some maximum capability may be expressed. An example of this could be the expression "up to 1500 lines per minute." When applying a unit's capability to a particular installation, sensitivity of critical characteristics would be taken into account. For example, each job proposed for printing would be examined so that the expected performance for the printer could be better assessed. The more complex devices generally have multiple characteristics listed. Magnetic tape drives would have character transmission rate and start/stop times listed. Disk file devices would have information on data transmission rates, rotational characteristics, and access (arm movement) characteristics.

A figure of merit calculation tries to take into account the variable characteristics of a component. Because the method of calculation quite often does not represent any physical attribute, the figure of merit is usually used as a method of classification. An example of such a calculation is given in the section on classification methods.

PROBLEMS

1. In the example given in 1.2.1, what is the reliability of the system if two of the three disk drives are required?

2. In the example given in 1.2.1, what is the reliability if one more tape unit is obtained for the configuration but is not required by the application?

3. In the example given in 1.2.1, what is the reliability of the system if the reliability of the disks and the tape units is 0.85?

4. In Problem 3, if the cost increase of the total system is 5% due to the improved reliability of the disks and tape units, how does this compare with the increase in reliability?

5. Consider the following two system diagrams with equal numbers of units (Fig. P1-5). In diagram (a), a complete system, which may be considered a parallel system, is on "standby." In diagram (b), each net is considered to be in parallel.
   (a) What is the reliability of each configuration?
   (b) If the cost of configuration (b) is 5% greater (because of the greater number of interconnections), how does this compare with the increase in reliability from configuration (a)?

6. Consider that a line printer (Unit 1) has a rated speed of 1000 lines per minute, independent of the mix of characters printed. Assume that a second printer (Unit 2) has a rated speed of 500 to 1500 lines per minute depending linearly on the proportion of numeric to non-numeric characters in each line (the less non-numeric, the higher speed.) Graph the speed of the two printers as a function of the proportion of non-numeric characters.

7. In the example given in Problem 6, which printer would you expect to have better performance in
   (a) scientific calculation?
   (b) commercial applications?
   (For classroom discussion, why the particular answers?)

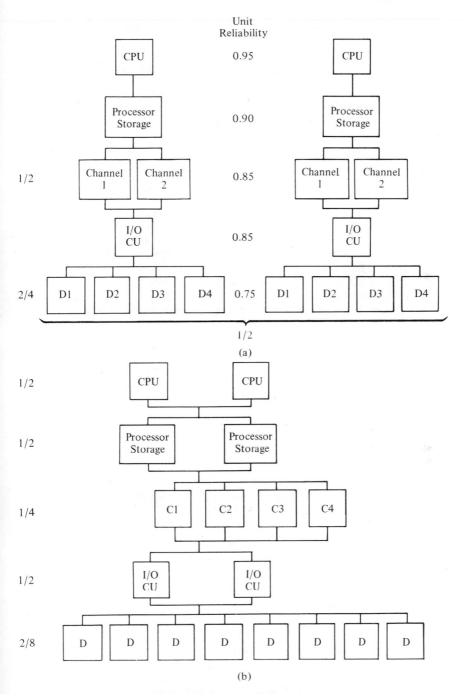

Fig. P1-5 Standby vs. interconnected systems.

8. Consider the unit characteristics of the following three tape units:

	1	2	3
Density (char/inch)	556	800	200
Linear speed (inches/second)	60	112	200
Gap distance (inches)	$\frac{1}{2}$	$\frac{3}{4}$	1

Rank these units by each characteristic.

9. Consider the unit characteristics of the following three disk units:

	1	2	3
Revolutions (RPM)	2400	3000	3600
Average access (msec)	100	150	200
Data rate (char/sec)	200,000	300,000	250,000
Volume (millions)	24	20	26

Rank these units by each characteristic.

2 HISTORICAL EVOLUTION

Although computers have been generally operational since the late 1940's, systems evaluation techniques have been lagging by at least a decade. In the early days, systems were designed with a fairly precise objective in mind. Designers and engineers had essentially one design criterion—make it as fast as possible with acceptable reliability. Sometimes, the reliability criterion was put by the wayside in the quest for faster and faster technology. Even when the computing systems became slightly more general in purpose, they still were optimized around relatively simple criteria. Three primary fields emerged: scientific, commercial and special purpose. Included in the special purpose category were such diverse applications as ballistic computation devices and real time data acquisition computers. Even though the latter category had extremes to it, individual systems tended to optimize around a particular application.

2.1. EARLY EVALUATION

Early methods of evaluating computers were well oriented to the intended use of the system. Calculators were judged by their ability to perform arithmetic. Commercial systems were judged by their ability to process records.

2.1.1. Evaluation of Calculators

Scientific computers were judged by the speed of certain discrete capabilities such as "add" time or "multiply" time. If the computer had a divide instruction, that time would also be taken into account. If not, quite often the prospective or potential user would ignore this capability. The principal use or application of these systems was to perform "calculations." They were used to replace the techniques of manual arithmetic and desk calculators, and, in some instances, the slide rule (although this is properly in the area of the analogue computer). It is not surprising, then, that the primary criterion of performance was the system's ability to perform arithmetic.

In many instances, the proposed use of the system was to perform a well defined application. The intended user had quite often reduced the physics of some particular problem through mathematics and numerical analysis to a succinct, almost traditional, computing approach. For each set of input data, this almost constant computing approach would be used time and time again to produce the desired results. This repetitive set of calculations would then be considered the main function or "main loop" of the calculation process. This knowledge of the application gave the potential user a slightly broader vehicle for his assessment of a computer's capability to perform his intended function. He could then "weight" the various arithmetic speeds of a system in relation to his calculation process.

To illustrate this approach, consider a simple example from the field of reduction of telemetry data. The physical problem is the conversion of data taken from an oscillograph trace into the actual values that the trace represents. The trace can be produced by a conversion process from the telemetered data. In the first stage, information is taken from the trace in manual or semi-manual techniques. Consider that the required information is on the trace in Figure 2.1.

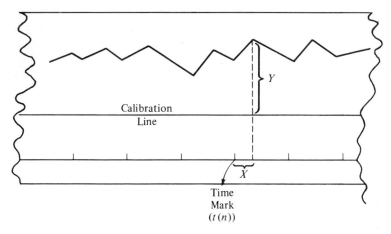

Fig. 2.1 Oscillograph trace.

Assume that a semi-manual technique is available so that the operator of the conversion equipment has to manually enter the value of $t(n)$, the nth time mark in the observation into a dial arrangement, but obtains the information for X and Y by means of two vernier dials controlling hair lines. Further assume that there is an automatic readout mechanism which will punch into a card the distance, X, from the time mark, and the distance, Y, from the calibration line. The net result of an individual reading is the punching into a card of the values $t(n)$, X, Y, and any other constant information which may be reproduced in each card of the observation. It should be noted that although this example assumes punched cards as the vehicle of information, there are techniques which allow the direct input of telemetering magnetic tapes directly into the computer.

Now the problem is to convert the time marks and oscillograph distances into the physical entities that they represent. Assume that the conversion is governed by the following formulae:

$$\text{Time of observation} = t(0) + t(n) + k1 \times X, \text{ and}$$
$$\text{Value} = v(0) + k2 \times Y,$$

where $t(0)$ and $v(0)$ are initial values of the observation.

A typical computing routine to convert this data would be as follows:

Read	Read a card with the information $t(n)$, X, and Y.
Load	Clear multiplier and load the constant $k1$.
Multiply	Multiply by X (assume result is in an accumulator).
Shift	This may be necessary to align the result.
Add	Add to previous result the value $t(n)$.
Add	Add to previous result the value $t(0)$, a constant.
Store	Store the result, the time of the observation.
Load	Clear multiplier and load the constant $k2$.
Multiply	Multiply by Y.
Shift	To align result.
Add	Add to previous result the value $v(0)$, a constant.
Store	Store the result, the value of the observation.
Punch	Punch the results.
Branch	Return to Read.

Adding up the various instruction types, we have the following as page 26:

Input/output	2
Load	2
Multiply	2
Shift	2
Add	3
Store	2
Branch	1
Total	14

In many computers, the acts of loading and storing are really variations of the ADD instruction. To summarize the instructions in that way would give the following:

"Add" type	7
Multiply	2
Shift	2
Branch	1
Input/output	2
Total	14

This simple example was chosen to demonstrate the method that was used to determine the main loop of an application. Do not consider it typical of the scientific computing community as originally defined because of the relatively high proportion of input/output instructions to the total number. A more typical distribution would be many thousands of instructions for each input/output operation. If this were the case, the instruction utilization for this example could be the following:

"Add" type	7,000
Multiply	2,000
Shift	2,000
Branch	1,000
Total	12,000

At this point we can perform an assessment of the work capability of a computer. Assume that we have a system whose characteristics for the problem above are as follows:

Add type time   4 microseconds (μsec)

Multiply   28 μsec

Shift   8 μsec

Branch   4 μsec

To perform the assessment, we may calculate the time of the main routine by multiplying the incidence of the instruction by the time of the instruction as follows:

Instruction Type	Incidence	Individual Time	Class Time
Add	7,000	4 μsec	28 msec
Multiply	2,000	28 μsec	56 msec
Shift	2,000	8 μsec	16 msec
Branch	1,000	4 μsec	4 msec
Total	12,000	– – – – –	104 msec

In this case, the total time through the conversion process is 104 msec.

Underlying the basic approaches of judging a computer's work capability by assessing its ability to do *arithmetic* is the tacit assumption that arithmetic processing is the principal activity of the system from a time point of view. Excluded from consideration is any amount of time that the system may spend in reading cards, tapes, or other media; writing output onto some media; and, in fact, time the central processing unit spends in formating, converting, and generally organizing or managing the data. This implied assumption, when even considered, was generally justified on the grounds that these "chores" occurred such a small amount of the time that they were not worth taking into consideration, and that furthermore, considering them would not influence the assessment of the computing system in the "scientific" environment. This was satisfactorily true during the days when the principal application of a computer was to replace a desk calculator, but cannot be a satisfactory assumption for computing environments today.

2.1.2. Evaluation of Record Processors

The scientific environment cannot take full blame for originating a method of assessment which simply doesn't apply to today's environments. The "commercial" data processing field originated assessment algorithms from the opposite end of the computing system's capabilities, namely its input/ output characterics. The overwhelming application of card processing equipment was in the commercial environment. Literally tons of data had to be passed through the processing equipment to produce payrolls, inventories, accounts, billings, and tons and tons of reports. In some cases, individual pieces or sets of data had to be repetitively passed through the equipment in order to produce the desired results.

Although the advent of the electronic computer is generally associated with scientific calculations, let us not forget that the first commercially available computing system was designed to process the large volumes of data found in the commercial environment. Since the data in the commercial environment was organized by "records," the main way of assessing a system's ability to perform was by determining its record reading and record writing rate. This rate was calculated for the applicable media for reading and writing in a system. In the case of card equipment on the system, the rate was expressed in "cards per minute," the familiar cpm. If there were line printers on the system, the output rate would be calculated in terms of "lines per minute," or lpm. In the case of magnetic tape, however, a different measure of rate evolved. This was caused by the advent of "variable record length" tape recording devices. Early tape units had "fixed block length" records on them. For these units, a "records per second" could be defined. Since the resultant rate of the variable record length tape units depended directly on the size of the record involved (even more than most people realized), it was desirable to have a rate independent of record length. The natural measure was the "character" rate of the magnetic tape drive. The "characters per second" or cps evolved to be the criterion for a magnetic tape drive's capability to perform a function. Unfortunately, record gap characteristics were often ignored.

This approach of considering a system's capabilities by looking specifically and, in fact, exclusively at its input/output capabilities tended to ignore any processing time whatsoever. Again, the justification of this assessment was based on the assumption that the ignored characteristics were infinitesimal as far as affecting the result of the evaluation. Rather than evolving the concept of kernels for commercial evaluation, there evolved a concept of "run" time, which was in reality a procedure based on data passing time. A fairly typical approach would be to time out a run by use of the diagram in Figure 2.2.

There was some justification in ignoring the process time, in that the numerical value of process time was some order of magnitude less than the corresponding values for reading and writing the data.

A more typical assessment problem is described in the following application. Here we have the classical case of "file update," in which a master file is modified by transaction cards and copied onto another unit. If there are any mismatches in either the transactions or master file or any discrepancies as a result of the processing routine, an exception is printed. The application organization is shown in Figure 2.3.

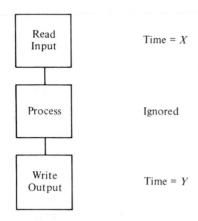

Total Time = $X + Y$
Repeat N Times = $N \times (X + Y)$ **Fig. 2.2** Run time calculation.

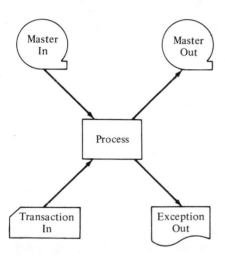

Fig. 2.3 File update organization.

Assume that we have record characteristics as follows:

File	Media	Volume	Record Length
Master-In	Tape	50,000	100 characters
Transactions	Card	1,000	80 characters
Master-Out	Tape	50,000	100 characters
Exception Report	Printer	100	75 characters

Furthermore, let us assume that there is no blocking or buffering and that all
activity in the system is completely sequential. The unit characteristics are

as follows:

Magnetic Tape   Start time of 10 msec and character time of 66.7 μsec.

Card Reader   100 cards per minute for 80 column card.

Line Printer   150 lines per minute for 100 character line.

In this case the card reader and the line printer are not sensitive to the number of characters in the record so long as the number is equal to or less than the capacity of the unit.

To form an estimate of the job time in the totally sequential environment, we simply calculate the file passing time for each of the files. To calculate the time of the transaction file on the card reader, we divide the volume by the rate, namely, 1000 cards divided by 100 cards per minute for a time of 10 minutes. Similarly, we apply the same type of calculation for the exception report on the line printer, namely, 100 lines divided by 150 lines per minute for a time of 0.67 minutes.

In the case of magnetic tape, however, we should obtain first the time for each record, because the performance of the unit is sensitive to both the number of records (volume) and record length. From the tape characteristics, we see that the record time is expressed by the formula:

$$T(r) = \text{start time} + (\text{record length}) \times (\text{character time}).$$

The Master File-In would result in the following calculation.

$$T(100) \quad = 10.0 + (100) \times (0.067) \text{ msec}$$
$$= 10.0 + 6.7 \text{ msec}$$
$$= 16.7 \text{ msec per record.}$$

For all records, the total time to read the Master File-In would be 835 seconds or 13.9 minutes. Since the Master File-Out has exactly the same characteristics, it would have the same time. At this point, we may obtain the total record passing time by merely summing the component times. This, of course, assumes error-free operation.

File	Time
Master-In	13.9 min
Transactions	10.0 min
Master-Out	13.9 min
Exception Report	0.7 min
Total	38.5 min

If the loading on the processor were on the order of 1 msec of calculation for each master file copied, plus 100 msec for each transaction, plus 100 msec for each exception report, the total process time would be 160 seconds, or less than 3 minutes. Including the process time in this example would have less than 10% effect on the estimated job time. In cases like this, ignoring the calculation time is justified.

2.1.3. Real Time System Considerations

The real time special purpose computers often required a much more sophisticated method of evaluation. Those systems which involved communications-oriented equipment did not have a simple operating environment. The input and output requirements were generally unpredictable except for an expected probability of activity. In a real time system where response time is critical in most cases, using averages for input/output and computing requirements would have provided insufficient information for an evaluation. Using only the maximum requirements would have provided an evaluation which, if used as the design criteria, would have produced an overdesigned system. To produce a more realistic evaluation, simulation was employed. This technique provided information based on the probability of input/output and compute activity requirements. However, the specialized evaluation problems that were encountered on the special purpose computers are the types of problems which we encounter today in the computing industry. Where once a special computer was designed for operations in a communications network, today we find that the general purpose computer is operating in that environment. To understand how we have arrived at this situation, there is a brief history of the evolution of uses of computers in Section 2.2.

Before leaving this section, we should note one attribute of these early activities. The individuals performing the assessments knew what to include in the evaluation because of their knowledge of the applications. Equally important was the fact that they knew what to eliminate from consideration. Although for general evaluations the techniques will not suffice, they applied in the era of the simple application performed on a particular system. It is possible to waste much time in trying to measure or evaluate attributes which have only a minor effect on the performance of the job. Consider the commercial file update application. We produced a time estimate of 38.5 minutes while ignoring process time. When that application is actually scheduled on a system, it may be scheduled for a time block of 40 minutes, 45 minutes, or even 60 minutes. So although it had about 7% error on our time estimate, the 2.7 minutes of process time would be completely lost in an operational environment.

2.2. PROGRESSIVE COMPLEXITIES

Today, the continued ignoring of certain items as was done in the early scientific or commercial environments can cause grossly erroneous results in the evaluation of computer systems. Several circumstances have combined over the years to produce this greater degree of error. Historically, there were first the technological changes to the computer systems, themselves. These were followed immediately by programming enhancements. The development of these two facilities has continued hand in hand.

2.2.1. Technology Improvements

One of the earliest concepts was the use of "buffered" devices. Briefly, these devices allowed the rather slow process of reading or writing of data to be overlapped with other activities, such as the reading or writing of other data, or the processing of the data by the central processing unit.

Let us consider the buffering of magnetic tape reading or writing as an example of a buffered device. To understand this concept, we shall first examine a timing diagram of the unbuffered activity using the device with the characteristics of 10.0 msec start time and 66.7 μsec character time. The timing diagram in Figure 2.4, starts at the time that the program calls for a Read of the information in the next record of the tape. (Assume 100 character records.)

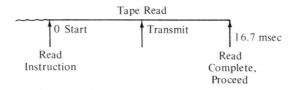

Fig. 2.4 Unbuffered magnetic tape Read.

First, there is the delay of 10 msec from the time of the Read to the time of the first character from tape. From that point on, there will be a character available for the processor's storage every 66.7 μsec. The reading of 100 characters takes approximately 6.7 msec. In a completely sequential environment, everything else is simply waiting on that one Read activity to complete. Following the completion of the reading of the record from tape, the tape device itself essentially coasts to a stop. It is then in a condition to respond to the next read request from the processor unit.

The intent of buffering such activity is to overcome the problem of having the whole system wait on this one activity. The structure of a buffering device usually takes the form of providing some volume, or capacity, of high speed storage whose access characteristics are more on the order of the speed of the main processor's storage. The designer of the buffer tries to allow for the record size of most of the records that are likely to be encountered. In some cases, this is very easy to do. For example, in structuring a buffer for a card reader which reads only 80 column cards, the buffer can be built to the maximum information size of such a card with perhaps a few extra columns of information which may be generated by the device itself. Similarly, designing a buffer for a printer which prints only a line of 120 characters can follow the same philosophy.

In designing a buffer for magnetic tape or other continuous media, the designer has to set a design point for the maximum amount of information which the buffer can hold. Traditionally, the design would be to a size which takes into account the common practice of the day plus some expansion factor to allow for improvements in the state-of-the-art. (Traditionally, this expansion factor has also been used up much faster than predicted.) In this example, assume that the designer has provided a buffer length of 500 characters from tape plus additional characters generated by the buffering device itself. If fewer than 500 characters are entered into the buffer, the remaining character positions are unused.

As far as the speed of the buffer is concerned, assume that a storage medium such as magnetic core which has a characteristic of 10 μsec per character transmission rate between itself and the processor's main storage is used. The time needed to fill or empty the buffer with the magnetic tape is governed by the speed of the tape drive.

For reading information from a magnetic tape, a simple buffer approach is used to cause the replenishment of the buffer from the magnetic tape as soon as the current information has been transferred to the main processor's storage. There can be some variance in how the first record is handled, but other than that the device will replenish automatically without the program having to instruct it to do so. The timing diagram in Figure 2.5 starts from the time of the Read in the program and assumes that the desired information is ready in the buffer.

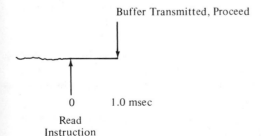

Buffer Transmitted, Proceed

0   1.0 msec

Read
Instruction

Fig. 2.5   Buffered magnetic tape Read.

In the case of reading a 100 character record, the transmission time is 1 msec. At that time, the main processor or any other device activity is free to proceed. This is in contrast to the unbuffered case of 16.7 msec of system delay.

Now consider the design of the automatic replenishment. Again, this is governed by the characteristics of the magnetic tape drive, itself. In this example, we have a 10 msec delay before the first character is available from the tape. So the question is: When should the tape drive be activated to start the next read activity? The designer can take advantage of the relative performance characteristics of the buffer and the tape drive in the following way. The longest time to transmit 500 characters from the buffer is 5 msec. This is one-half of the start time of the tape drive. Therefore, he can cause the initiation of the tape drive motion as soon as the Read instruction is executed by the program. In all cases the buffer will be clear and ready for replenishment as soon as the first character is available from the tape. This is shown in Figure 2.6.

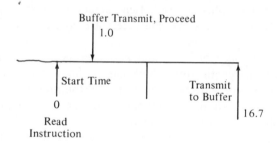

Fig. 2.6 Buffer replenishment.

At time 0, when the Read instruction is given, two things happen; the buffer starts transmitting its present contents into the main processor's storage, and the tape drive movement is initiated. At the time of 1 msec, the present contents have been transferred into storage (for the case of 100 character records), and the main processor is free to continue. At the time of 10 msec, the first character is available from magnetic tape for replenishing the buffer. Every 66.7 μsec, a character is read from the tape into the buffer. At the time 16.7 msec, the buffer has been replenished with the next 100 character record, and the tape drive coasts to a stop. It should be noted that for the case of 100 character records, the time 16.7 msec is the *earliest* time that the processor could cause the buffer to again read out its contents into the main processor's storage. Any request prior to this time would cause the processor simply to wait until the replenishment cycle is complete.

To illustrate the effect of buffering, let us return to the example of commercial data processing given in Section 2.1.2. In Figure 2.7 the file update organization is repeated with the volumes indicated.

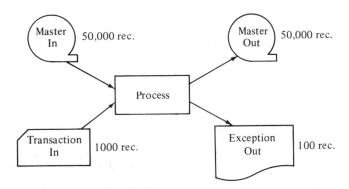

Fig. 2.7 File update organization and volume.

However, to evaluate the effect of buffered devices, we should consider the flow of the application. The flow chart of the application is given in Figure 2.8.

In the flow chart, there are two major branch points. The first is the comparison between the identification field of the Master File input record and the identification field of the transaction record. There are indicated in parentheses the expected number of times each one of the three exits will be utilized. (Perhaps it is optimistic to assume that no sequence error is encountered. This routine would also be utilized for the "no record found" condition.) Similarly, the second branch point of exception determination has the expected number of times through the two exits.

The exit to stop the operation at the Read Transaction block is not given an expected number of exits, because it is assumed to happen only once. In this case that would be one out of 1000 passes. (It is not one out of 1001, because the first Read of a Transaction card was made just after the Start block.) When this is encountered, the application program would cause the copying of any remaining Master File input records onto the Master File output tape.

In this illustration, we shall consider the effect on only the most frequent loop of the program. This is the loop consisting of the reading of a master record, the comparison to the transaction, and the writing of a master record. A complete job timing will be considered in a later section. For simplicity, any of the processing that would take place due to error or malfunction of equipment is omitted. The requirement for such activity will be discussed in later sections. Figure 2.9 gives a step sequence of the main loop.

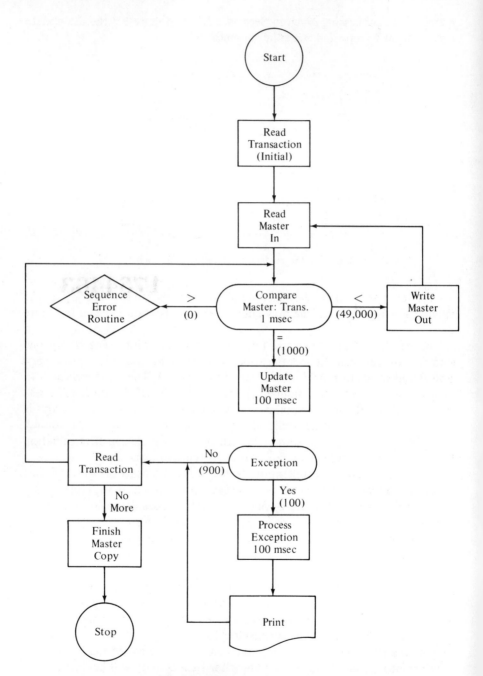

Fig. 2.8   File update flow chart.

Step	Time	Item	Process	Tape In/Buffer	Tape Out/Buffer	Time Increment
1	0	Read	T	16.7/1.0		1.0
2	1.0	Compare	1.0			1.0
3	2.0	Write	T		16.7/1.0	1.0
4	3.0	Read		must be delayed to 16.7		13.7
4.5	16.7	Transfer buffer		16.7/1.0		1.0
5	17.7	Compare	1.0			1.0
6	18.7	Write	T		16.7/1.0	1.0
7	19.7	– – –				

Fig. 2.9 Main loop step sequence (time in milliseconds).

The first column is a step number for reference purposes. The second column indicates the time that a particular step is initiated. "Process" is the time it takes for the CPU to perform a function. "Tape In" is the time that the tape drive takes to replenish its buffer for a 100 character record. "Buffer" is the time to transfer the present contents of the buffer to processor storage. "Tape Out" is the time to empty the output buffer onto a magnetic tape, and "Buffer" is the time to transfer the record from processor storage. "Time Increment" is the minimum time of the step. It is this time which is added to the time of initiation to determine the starting time of the next step in the sequence.

We shall start Step 1 at the point of reading a Master input record. This will be given the starting time of 0. On that step, the buffer starts transferring its contents into processor storage simultaneously with the starting of the tape drive. The replenishment of the buffer will take 16.7 msec. The transfer of buffer storage takes 1 msec. Since at the end of 1 msec the processor is free to proceed to the next step, the time increment is 1 msec. Step 2 initiation time is therefore 1 msec.

On Step 2, the processor performs the comparison between the key fields of the Master input record and the Transaction record. This step requires only the process time of 1 msec, therefore the time increment required is 1 msec. This will produce an initiation time of 2 msec for Step 3.

On Step 3, the writing of the Master record occurs. At this time the tape drive motion is initiated and the transfer to the buffer from processor storage is initiated. The tape drive will take 16.7 msec to complete its action, whereas the output buffer will require only 1 msec to complete the filling of the buffer. The time increment for this step is 1 msec. Step 4 can initiate at the time of 3 msec.

At this point we can see that we have made a traverse of the main loop. At the beginning of Step 4 we are at the same point as we were at the beginning of Step 1. This was obtained in a total elapsed time of 3 msec. However, at this time there are still in process tape drive activities that were initiated in previous steps. To determine the normal loop time, let us continue through a few more steps.

On Step 4, the reading of the next Master record is initiated. But this time, the buffer is still being replenished from the results of the previous read operation. It is not until the time of 0 + 16.7 msec that another read operation can be initiated. In this case, everything is essentially hung up until the buffer is ready to transmit its contents into processor storage. Step 4 increment is indicated as 13.7 msec which represents the delay until the buffer is ready. There is inserted a Step 4.5 to indicate the actual initiation of the contents of the read buffer into processor storage as well as the initiation of the tape drive motion to replenish the buffer as a result of this read operation. As a result of this action, the total increment of Step 4 is 13.7 msec of delay plus the 1 msec of buffer transfer time. Step 5 can start at the time of 17.7 msec.

Step 6 is the initiation of the Master record out to the buffer and subsequently to magnetic tape. The previous output tape operation was initiated at 2.0 msec. Based on the tape motion time, another such operation could not be initiated until the time of 2.0 msec plus 16.7 msec, the tape motion time, or 18.7 msec. In this case, the time of initiation of Step 6 is 18.7 msec. Therefore, the output to the buffer and the initiation of the tape drive can start immediately. The time increment of this step is 1 msec, which will allow Step 7 to initiate at a time of 19.7 msec.

Now let us consider this second pass of the main loop. Step 7 is at the same point in the flow chart as we were on Step 4; namely the reading of the master record. However, this time around the loop took a total time of 16.7 msec as opposed to 3 msec for the first time around. By inspection, we can see that if we were to continue this loop sequence, the loop time would remain at 16.7 msec.

This compares to the unbuffered case of a loop time of

(a) 16.7 msec for the reading of a master record,

(b) 1.0 msec for the processor to compare the key fields,

(c) 16.7 msec for the writing of the master record.

The unbuffered case would therefore have a loop time of 34.4 msec for the same operation. In this illustration of buffering, the process time and the reading and writing of the master records were all overlapped within the time it takes to read or write a single record.

The next technological improvement which had an effect on system performance was an early application of the concept of "cycle stealing." The basic concept of cycle stealing is to utilize some equipment for more than one purpose in such a way as to minimize interference on its primary purpose. In this simple example, we shall illustrate the early concept of "stealing" cycles from the processor's storage for the purpose of improving the performance effects of input/output devices. Naturally, the primary purpose of processor storage is to supply the central processing unit with the instructions and data to allow it to do its job. The configuration which will allow the "borrowing" of space or capacity and the "stealing" of cycles is shown in Figure 2.10. The principal element which allows this facility is the data synchronizer. Its purpose is to control the flow of data to and from the input/output units (and their associated control units) and processor storage. The data synchronizer may be implemented as a separate piece of equipment or incorporated into the function of the control unit itself. It is shown here as a separate unit to explain its function. To understand its intent, let us first

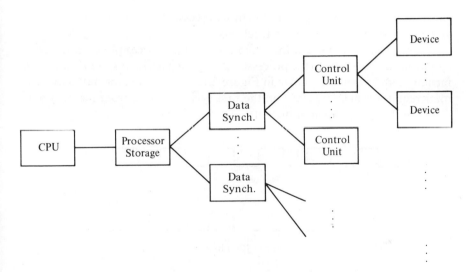

Fig. 2.10   Configuration of data synchronizer.

consider the relationship of a processor storage unit and its central processing unit (CPU). As is well known, the CPU fetches its instructions and fetches, or stores, the associated data to process the job at hand. In Figure 2.11, there are shown the cycles of information available from the processor storage and the requirements of the CPU.

The diagram is expressed in terms of the regularly recurring memory cycle. In this example, the CPU requires a memory fetch for its next instruction on Cycle 1, and a data fetch on Cycle 2. At this point, the CPU is assumed to have sufficient information for it to complete its operation until the next instruction fetch. Cycles 3 and 4 are not required by the CPU. On Cycle 5 the CPU again required an instruction fetch, and on Cycle 6 it again requires a data store or fetch. Overall, the requirement that the CPU places on proces-

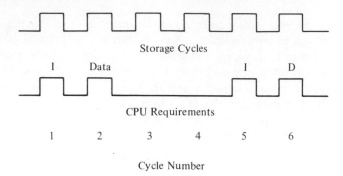

Fig. 2.11   CPU/processor storage.

sor storage may be referred to as "memory accesses" whether the accesses are stores or fetches for data or instructions.

To meet the requirement that the input/output devices place on the data synchronizer for access to the processor storage, a particular system may have memory requirements as shown in Figure 2.12. In this case, the data synchronizer requires a memory cycle on the first cycle available from memory and again on the fourth cycle of memory.

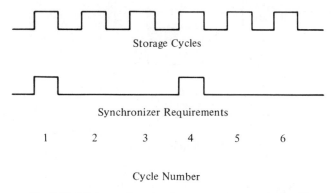

Fig. 2.12   Data synchronizer/processor storage relationship.

The intervening cycles are not required for the input/output operations. If the processor storage were doing nothing more than satisfying the requirements of the input/output devices' demands through the data synchronizer, in this case it would be utilized only 33% of available time.

In Figure 2.13 there is indicated the total requirement of both the CPU and the data synchronizer. Again, the diagram is expressed in terms of the regularly recurring memory cycle. On Cycle 1, both the data synchronizer and the CPU require access to memory. The question is, which one shall receive priority? Since the characteristic of an input/output device is electro-

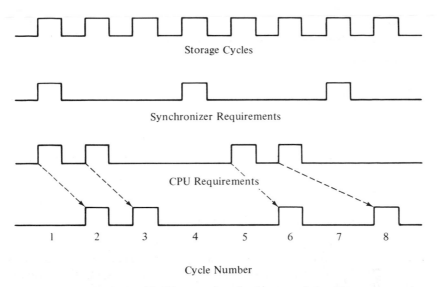

Storage Cycles

Synchronizer Requirements

CPU Requirements

1   2   3   4   5   6   7   8

Cycle Number

Fig. 2.13   CPU/data synchronizer/storage relationship.

mechanical, it is assumed that a delay in its requirements could cause a failure in the transfer of data. Therefore, a cycle is "stolen" from the CPU in order to satisfy the demand of the device. The CPU is delayed one cycle in its process, so that it makes its memory access on Cycle 2. The data fetch then occurs on Cycle 3. Cycle 4 is used by the data synchronizer. In this case there is no request from the CPU for a memory access, so there is no contention for the memory cycle. Memory cycle 5 is not required by either unit, so it is a free cycle. It should be noted that in Figure 2.11 the CPU did require Cycle 5. Here we assume that Cycle 5 is not now required because of the one-cycle delay encountered on Cycle 1. Memory cycle 6 is required by the CPU and, since there is no contention from the data synchronizer, the CPU proceeds without delay. On Cycle 7, the data synchronizer again takes priority, so that the second data fetch of the CPU is delayed to Cycle 8.

In keeping with the basic examples of this section, we shall defer until later the evaluation of contention problems. Let us rather examine the gross characteristics of the effect of a data synchronizer utilizing part of the processor's storage as a buffer. Retaining the example of the main loop of the file update application, we must first examine what programming changes are required. First consider that there is no automatic delay function available from the equipment as there was in the case of the externally buffered devices. Therefore any required delay for the replenishment of buffers must be determined by programming and implemented by programming. Figure 2.14 indicates the additional programming necessary.

The purpose of the Wait block is to delay further processing until the

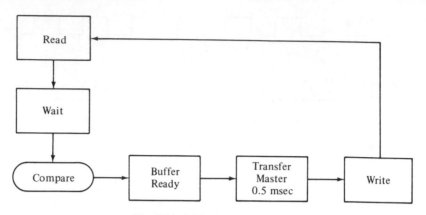

Fig. 2.14 Main loop flow chart.

information from the tape is totally contained in processor storage. It is assumed that the determination of the need to wait is by the CPU's interrogation of the data synchronizer. If a delay is required for the record to finish reading in, a suitable wait loop is established within the block. Similarly, the Buffer Ready block preceding the Write is to determine that the previous contents have been totally written onto tape and that the memory space is available to take more data. Its characteristics are the same as the Wait block.

There is another new block in this loop, the Buffer Transfer block. The purpose of this block is to transfer the information that was located in the input area of storage to the output area of storage. It is assumed that if updating did occur, that information would have been incorporated in the input area.

In Figure 2.15, the step sequence for storage buffering is given. Since the

Step	Time	Item	Process	Tape In	Tape Out	Time Increment
1	0	Read	T	16.7		T
2	0	Wait	16.7			16.7
3	16.7	Compare	1.0			1.0
4	17.7	CK Buff	T			T
5	17.7	Transfer	0.5			0.5
6	18.2	Write	T		16.7	T
7	18.2	Read	T	16.7		T
8	18.2	Wait	16.7			16.7
9	34.9	– – –				

Fig. 2.15 Step sequence—storage buffering.

processor is actually involved in each of the operations, there will be an entry for process time in all cases. In some cases, there will be an indication, "T," to indicate that the time the processor takes is trivial compared to the time base that we are keeping. In this case, the implication is that the time is much less than 0.1 msec.

On Step 1, which is at time 0, the read of the Master record input is initiated. After a very small amount of process time, the system is free to continue. Therefore, Step 2 is also indicated as being initiated at time 0. (If we were carrying a greater precision, the time would be indicated as something like 0.010 msec.) On Step 2, the CPU determines whether the input from the master tape is yet contained in storage. Until the read operation is complete, the CPU will remain in that block. In this case, it must remain in Wait for the full 16.7 msec. Step 3 can then initiate at the time of 16.7 msec. On Step 3 the comparison occurs, requiring 1 msec of CPU time. Step 4 initiates at the time of 17.7 msec. Since there has not been any prior activity for the output buffer, the answer is "yes" and we immediately go to Step 5.

On Step 5, the CPU must transfer the contents of the input area of storage to the output area of storage. This is accomplished in 0.5 msec of processing. Step 6, the writing of the Master record output, initiates at the time, 18.2 msec. After that, we again return to the reading of the next Master input record.

The timing for this loop is 18.2 msec, which represents the time it takes to read a master record, do the comparison, and transfer buffer areas. We can consider that the writing of the output record is completely overlapped with this amount of activity. However, since the entire operation of this system is under program control, including the allocation of processor storage for the purpose of buffering, we can better utilize the characteristics of the equipment by assigning four buffer areas for the purpose of improving overall loop time. The intention is to overlap the process time of major blocks with the overlap of reading and writing. The allocation of processor storage is shown in Figure 2.16. In this example, we shall allocate two buffer areas for input and two for output.

As before, we shall transfer input areas to output areas as part of the tran-

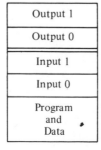

Fig. 2.16 Processor storage allocation.

scription process. The flow chart of the main loop is given in Figure 2.17. Notice that there is an Initial Read block which is not part of the main loop.

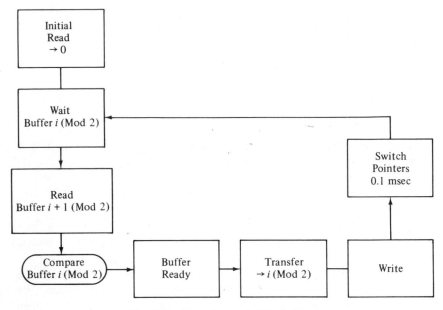

Fig. 2.17   Flow chart—double buffering.

In practice, this block would contain all initializing activities, such as making sure that all pointers in the program point to the correct buffer to begin with. There is also another functional block between the initialization of the writing of the Master output record and the Wait block for the next input. The purpose of this block is to modify all instructions which point to the various buffer areas.

We must also keep track of which buffers are active for which purposes, so there is indicated the checking or processing of buffer (i(mod2)). All other notations are the same as for previous examples. The step sequence for this case is given in Figure 2.18.

Notice that if we were to attempt to establish a loop time by taking the difference in initiation times of Step 2 and Step 9, we would have a time of 18.3 msec. However, if we calculate the difference between Steps 3 and 10, the loop time is only 16.7 msec. Taking differences between successively greater steps at the same point in the flow chart remains at 16.7 msec. This, of course, is the main loop time. It is typical in evaluation techniques to have initial results that differ considerably from results taken at a later

Step	Time	Item	Process	Tape In (Buffer i)	Tape Out (Buffer i)	Time Increment
1	0	Read	T	16.7 (0)		T
2	0	Wait (0)	16.7			16.7
3	16.7	Read	T	16.7 (1)		T
4	16.7	Compare	1.0			1.0
5	17.7	CK Buff (0)	T			T
6	17.7	Transfer	0.5			0.5
7	18.2	Write			16.7 (0)	T
8	18.2	Switch	0.1			0.1
9	18.3	Wait (1)	15.1			15.1
10	33.4	Read (0)	T	16.7 (0)		T
11	33.4	Compare	1.0			1.0
12	34.4	CK Buff (1)	T			T
13	34.4	Transfer	0.5			0.5
14	34.9	Write	T		16.7	T
15	34.9	Switch	0.1			0.1
16	35.0	Wait (0)	15.1			15.1
17	50.1	– – –				

Fig. 2.18   Step sequence—double buffering.

point in the timing routine. This is because the process has not yet had a chance to achieve a "steady state" in its operation.

As the system under study becomes more complex, it is often better to examine its timing characteristics by the use of a timing diagram rather than through the use of a step sequence chart. In Figure 2.19, there is given a timing diagram of the double-buffered case.

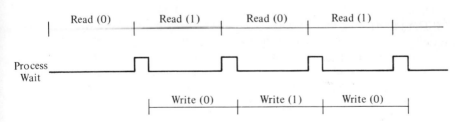

Fig. 2.19   Timing diagram—double buffering.

In this diagram, the three process blocks of Compare, Buffer Transfer, and Switch are all lumped into the same process line. If, however, it were important to distinguish these various items, they could be identified on the timing diagram. There is also indicated for reference the relationship between the timing diagram and the step sequence chart. The CPU is indicated as being active (upstate) or waiting (downstate). Depending on the architecture of the system, it may or may not actually be processing instructions.

Considering only the effect of technological improvement to enable the overlapping of computing, reading, and writing records, we see the following main loop times for our particular example:

Sequential operation:	34.4 msec
External buffering:	16.7 msec
Single storage buffers:	18.2 msec
Double storage buffers:	16.7 msec.

It is assumed that the completely sequential equipment is less costly than the external buffered system, and that the system with the data synchronizer is also less costly than the external buffered system. In the two cases of storage buffering, the same equipment configuration was present. The primary difference in approach was the way in which the application program was designed to utilize processor storage.

For evaluation purposes, the analyst has to consider the system's ability to overlap in his assessment procedures. The problem in applying this concept is perhaps best demonstrated by the following example.

Consider an application that has equal units of time for reading of all input data, processing the data, and writing out all output data. Consider further that this application is performed on a system that has the capability to overlap reading, processing and writing, fully. If each of these equal units of time were expressed as a time T, and the computing procedure accomplished full overlap, then the total time of the application would also be the time T. On the other hand, if the computing process called for all data to be first read, then for all processing to be done, and then for all writing to occur, the application time would be not T, but three times T!

The point being made here is that, given the capabilities of a computing system, the assessment of its attaining any particular goal depends on the programmed use of its capabilities. In this example, had the analyst known the particular procedural characteristics of the application as was the case in previous examples, he could have applied selective overlap factors to assess the particular computing system's ability to perform that application.

The examples given above are a very small part of the technological innovations which have been incorporated into computer design. Notable innovations are the concept of parallelism in its various forms, communications devices, and, perhaps the most dramatic innovation, the large capacity random access device. Technological changes are continually being made available to potential users for the improvement of their operations. Some of these will be discussed in light of the evaluation problems which they present. A complete survey of innovations in system design and technology is outside the scope of this book. But in addition to technological changes, there have been changes in the intended use of computer systems that have had perhaps an even more dramatic effect in the evaluation of computer systems. As mentioned earlier, the intended use of a scientific computer was to perform arithmetic and the intended use of a commercial computer was to perform data processing. In the 1960's, however, the intended use of a computer became the automation of application requirements of government, business, and industry ("automation" in the sense of Diebold's definition, rather than Harder's earlier definition).

Facilities which have been added to computing systems to achieve this type of automation have been primarily in programming packages, although technological facilities have also been supplied.

2.2.2. Programming Improvements

The earliest and simplest programming improvement was the "loader." This basic program was used to load other programs through some input media into the processor storage of the central processing unit. The format of the programs being loaded was in the peculiar format which the central processing unit expected in order to access information from its storage unit. If the computer expected "binary" information, that is just what the loader provided. If the computer expected to find "alphanumeric" information, the loader supplied that. Although each program which was written had some provision to load itself into storage, the packaged loader was designed to load *any* program into storage. This was one of the first programs to set standard procedures or "protocols" for other programming activities. In order to use it, each programmer had to conform to the particular way in which the packaged loader expected to find the programs for loading.

In the case of the binary machines, an improvement over the binary loader was the facility of an "octal" loader. In this case, the loader had imbedded in it a procedure for converting from octal representation on the media to binary representation in the storage unit. This octal loader was a natural extension to the octal conversion routines that were typically used with binary processing.

Along with the age of the simple loaders, there were the simple yet basic utility routines to aid the programmer in the development of his program. The earliest types were the "dump" routines. These routines either punched onto some media, printed on some media, or in some cases read out onto magnetic tape for later printing, the contents of the computer's storage. A modicum of formatting was supplied in these dump routines to facilitate reading the information. A good working knowledge of octal/decimal conversion was a desirable, and in fact, almost mandatory requirement for the programmers of binary machines. Whether the dump was in octal or alphanumeric representation, the programmer also needed to know what type of code structure was used in the processing of the instructions used in his particular system.

For the binary user, there were also decimal conversion routines as part of packages for input and output of data. No longer was it necessary to stand by the printer, mentally converting one's output from octal to decimal. The computing system would now provide this added service to the user. In addition to these data manipulation routines, mathematical packages were provided. These consisted of routines such SINE(X), LOG(X), and even double or multiple variable functions. These standard packages eliminated the need for an individual programmer to write out the full routine as long as he adhered to the conventions and limitations set by the routines.

For the alphanumerically oriented system, there were also packaged routines. Typical among these were such functions as program dump, tape print, sort, and other routines which were normally required in business applications.

To use these routines, the programmer would usually get a copy of the package in card deck form, and have it read into the system along with the rest of his program. If it were a utility routine such as tape print, he would load the system with a copy of the routine and then process his information against it.

Around the same time that these packages occurred, a new aid came into being: the "assembly" program. Variously applied to all types of systems, this new type of processing program allowed a programmer to write his programs in a stylized format that was more to his way of thinking. Instead of using a conglomeration of numbers to represent, for example, an Add instruction, the programmer could write the word "ADD" or in some cases the letter "A" to represent the desired instruction. The assembly program would convert the "mnemonic" into the representation expected by the system, i.e., "CPU readable." Another innovation occurred in the assembly process (in two half-steps): the "symbolic" address. Instead of referring to data by an absolute storage location, one could refer to it symbolically. The first half-step was the "regional" addressing, in that the data were given an ordinal address relative to some regional starting point. (This is analogous to a vector of numbers, $n1$, $n2$, $n3, \ldots$) The second half-step was the truly symbolic address such as MASTERIN, NEWX, START, and other cryptic words that had more meaning to the programmer.

Another feature which became included in symbolic assembly programs was a provision for "subroutines." These were pre-packaged routines of generally used functions which were structured so that many different programs or parts of a program could use them. But since the various programs wanted to use these subroutines (often collected together in a "library") in different storage locations depending on the unique requirements of the particular program, there was a desire to "relocate" these routines to any arbitrary portion of main storage. Not only did this have an effect in the assembly program, but there also was created the "relocatable loader". This type of loader accepted coding which was ostensibly ready to be loaded into the computer storage for execution, but reassigned the relevant addresses so that the coding would fit with its host program.

To illustrate the effect of the assembler, let us consider the following example. The problem is to evaluate a polynomial expression given by the formula

$$y = k_0 + k_1 x + k_2 x^2 + k_3 x^3 + k_4 x^4.$$

Simple numerical analysis indicates that the way to evaluate the expression is in the form

$$y = (((k_4 x + k_3)x + k_2)x + k_1)x + k_0.$$

Let us assume that an IBM 7094 architecture is utilized in the system which is processing the problem. Assume the following storage contents for this problem:

The program itself starts in location 100 (all of these entries are in octal).

The variable X in 1000.

The solution Y will be stored in 1001.

The constants K4, K3, K2, K1, K0 are in 1002–1006.

The straight line computing procedure to evaluate the expression would be as shown in Figure 2.20.

Step	Instruction	Result
1	Load K4 to MQ	Place K4 in MQ
2	Flt Mult by X	K4(X) in AC
3	Flt Add K3	K4(X) + K3 in AC
4	Long Rt Shift to MQ	PREV in MQ
5	Flt Mult by X	(K4(X) + K3)X in AC
6	Flt Add K2	(K4(X) + K3)X + K2 in AC
7	Long Rt Shift to MQ	PREV in MQ
8	Flt Mult by X	((K4(X) + K3)X + K2)X in AC
9	Flt Add K1	((K4(X) + K3)X + K2)X + K1 in AC
10	Long Rt Shift to MQ	PREV in MQ
11	Flt Mult by X	(((K4(X) + K3)X + K2)X + K1)X in AC
12	Flt Add K0	Y in AC
13	Store Y	Store Result (Still in AC)

Fig. 2.20   Polynomial evaluation straight line code.

If one were coding the computing procedure in binary, the following program would be developed as shown in Figure 2.21.

Location	Instruction
001 000 000	000 101 110 000 00 0000 000 000 001 000 000 010
001 000 001	000 010 110 000 00 0000 000 000 001 000 000 000
001 000 010	000 011 000 000 00 0000 000 000 001 000 000 011
001 000 011	000 111 110 101 00 0000 000 000 000 000 100 100
001 000 100	000 010 110 000 00 0000 000 000 001 000 000 000
001 000 101	000 011 000 000 00 0000 000 000 001 000 000 100
001 000 110	000 111 110 101 00 0000 000 000 000 000 100 100
001 000 111	000 010 110 000 00 0000 000 000 001 000 000 000
001 001 000	000 011 000 000 00 0000 000 000 001 000 000 101
001 001 001	000 111 110 101 00 0000 000 000 000 000 100 100
001 001 010	000 010 110 000 00 0000 000 000 001 000 000 000
001 001 011	000 011 000 000 00 0000 000 000 001 000 000 110
001 001 100	000 110 000 001 00 0000 000 000 001 000 000 001

Fig. 2.21   Binary coding.

Although programming in this representation is extremely rare today, you can see the possibilities of making an error in even this simple example. However, this is the type of representation that is usually displayed on the console of a computer. Let us examine exactly the same program expressed in octal representation. It would have the form shown in Figure 2.22.

A bit better in readability for those who are familiar with the particular data structure of the system. But for those who are not familiar with the particular system it may not provide any information. The assembly lan-

Location	Instruction
100	0560 000 01002
101	0260 000 01000
102	0300 000 01003
103	0765 000 00044
104	0260 000 01000
105	0300 000 01004
106	0765 000 00044
107	0260 000 01000
110	0300 000 01005
111	0765 000 00044
112	0260 000 01000
113	0300 000 01006
114	0601 000 01001

Fig. 2.22   Octal coding.

guage, on the other hand, is intended to provide ease of use and readability. The same program expressed in assembly language would appear as shown in Figure 2.23. For one who knew the problem and the numerical analysis, the assembly language coding would indicate the computing procedure that was used with little difficulty in interpretation.

Location	Instruction	
1	LDQ	K4
2	FMP	X
3	FAD	K3
4	LRS	36
5	FMP	X
6	FAD	K2
7	LRS	36
8	FMP	X
9	FAD	K1
10	LRS	36
11	FMP	X
12	FAD	K0
13	STO	Y

Fig. 2.23 Symbolic coding.

The above example was given in regard to a 7090 architecture. To show how an assembly language program is even more time saving, consider a System/370 architecture.

The 370 is essentially a byte addressable computer with capabilities to handle multiple bytes as units of work. They may be in the form of half-words (2 bytes), full words (4 bytes), and double words (8 bytes). (Internal characteristics of the 370 allow operations on up to 256 bytes as a unit.) Instructions are arranged in "syllables" of two bytes each. The instruction mnemonics and general system characteristics can be found in IBM publications on the System/370.

In this example, we have storage arranged as follows:

The program starts in 12000.

The variable X in 1000.

The result Y in 1004.

The constants K4 through K0 in locations 1008 to 1014.

The base register pointer is in INDEX.

Notice that locations are expressed in hexadecimal notation.

The assembly language coding for the 370 would be as follows:

Location			Instruction
12000	L	14, INDEX	Load INDEX to GP14
12004	LE	4, X	Load X into FP4
12008	LE	0, K4	Load K4 into FP0
1200C	MER	0, 4	Multiply FP0 by X
1200E	AE	0, K3	Add K3 to FP0
12012	MER	0, 4	Multiply FP0 by X
12014	AE	0, K2	Add K2 to FP0
12018	MER	0, 4	Multiply FP0 by X
1201A	AE	0, K1	Add K1 to FP0
1201E	MER	0, 4	Multiply FP0 by X
12020	AE	0, K0	Add K0 to FP0
12022	STE	0, Y	Store result

The location is given for reference only. When one is writing the code, location is not required. Furthermore, the various data definitions are not shown.

The result of the coding is shown in the following storage map. Again, all entries are in hexadecimal notation.

	0	1	2	3	4	5	6	7	8	9	A	B	C	D	E	F
1200X	58	E0	xx	xx	78	40	E0	00	78	00	E0	08	3C	04	7A	00
1201X	E0	0B	3C	04	7A	00	E0	0F	3C	04	7A	00	E0	10	3C	04
1202X	7A	00	E0	14	70	00	E0	04	---							

Notice that one would have to know the starting point of some instruction as well as the lengths of all instructions involved if it were required to work from a storage listing as shown above. Fortunately, formatted storage dumps are provided to aid the readability of the information.

In Figure 2.24, there is indicated the ordinal ratio between the time of an individual preparing code in either absolute or hexadecimal representation and the time that a computer would take to process the result of his work.

It is typical to see the coding time expressed in days or hours of preparation. This is the time spent after the problem has been defined, the numerical analysis or application design has been performed, and the computing pro-

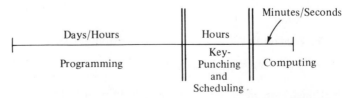

Fig. 2.24   Programmer/computer ratio—absolute coding.

cedure has been established. The access time to the computing system can vary considerably, depending on the programmer's proximity to the installation, the priority which his particular work has in relation to all other work to be performed, and the handling time required by personnel in the center. Let us assume that it is at least measured in only two digits of hours. The time the computer takes to load and execute his program is generally measured in terms of minutes or seconds. This, of course, is a proper relationship, since a single computing system may cost over one hundred times the cost of a single individual. (This, of course, is a variable in itself.) The intent of the assembly language is to reduce coding time greatly at the expense of adding computing time. The mapping of this effect is shown in Figure 2.25.

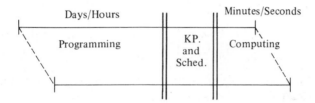

Fig. 2.25 Effect of assembly language.

The coding time, measured in days or hours, is reduced by increasing the computing time measured in minutes or seconds. There is now the added presence of the assembly process which was not even in the previous system workload.

Since there were in existance libraries of subroutines, it was a natural step to create libraries of complete processing programs or subroutines. As an adjunct to the program libraries, "Autolocator" and "Autoloader" utility programs were introduced. The purpose of these utilities was to obtain a program from some "auxiliary storage" and relocatably load it into the computer's main storage under direction of some requested ordering sequence (long ago called load control).

The next perturbation on the use of a computing system was perhaps one of the most important contributions to the field of computer science, the "compiler." The purpose of the compiler was to allow a program to be written in a "source language" which was as close to the natural vernacular of the users as possible. The classical example of the higher level language is "FORTRAN" (FORmula TRANslation). (There are of course many compilers today, well described in the literature.) The function of the compiler was to reduce higher level source language to a form that an assembly program could reduce for loading into the computer storage for execution. Although this implies a two step process, compilers can reduce source code directly to a form for loading into a system without invoking a separate assembly program.

Using the same example of polynomial evaluation to illustrate the power of a higher level language, the source statement for the problem is simply

$$Y = (((K4*X + K3)*X + K2)*X + K1)*X + K0.$$

The compiler and its associated processing programs reduce this one line statement into a machine readable form similar to the original coding as shown in the binary code for this example. There is usually provision for some output from the compilation process which gives the programmer a "listing" of the coding in an assembly language format. This is the link between the content of the original source statements and the coding that will eventually be processed in the computer. Various other options are usually available to give the programmer more information on what has happened to his program in the computing system. Typical of this output is a "symbol table," showing where each symbolic expression or name is used.

The performance effects of the higher level language and its compiler are similar to the effect of the assembly program. The intention is to reduce the hours and days of programmer preparation time by using additional minutes and seconds of the computing system time. Hopefully, the effect is even more favorable than in the case of using assembly language.

An even greater effect on performance comes from the following. Not only was the compiler's source language designed to reduce programming time and provide more readability, but it was to provide these facilities in such a way as to reduce the number of coding errors. One might well say that the primary intent of the higher level language is to reduce source errors, i.e., errors which the programmer has made in the creation of his program. In the earlier examples of preparing a program using either an absolute representation or an assembly language representation, there were many possibilities of error. Although the possibility is slight with such a short example, the possibility grows considerably when creating large programs that may contain thousands of instructions.

Compounding the problem of the simple incidence of errors is the problem that some errors may not be discovered because of the presence of other errors. This is called the "masking" effect. Multiple runs are usually required to discover errors which were masked. Discovering and eliminating these errors is the process called "debugging."

In previous examples, the process of writing the program was shown as a simple block of time, and the process of compiling and executing was also shown as a simple block of time. In reality, the picture is more complex. Indicated below is a more typical sequence of activity for the preparation, debugging, and execution of a program utilizing a "local batch oriented" system, i.e., the system is not terminal oriented. It is shown in step form rather than graphic form because of large differences in time between the processor's activity and the time to complete the work. Briefly, the programmer sees the following:

1. Preparation of coding 5 days.
   Computer time $= 0$

2. Submit for processing and get results 2 days. (error found)
   Keypunch time $= 1\frac{1}{2}$ days
   Computer time $= 1$ minute

3. Make corrections and resubmit 1 day.

4. Wait for results 1 day. (error found)
   Computer time $= 2$ minutes

5. Make corrections and resubmit $\frac{1}{2}$ day.

6. Wait for results 1 day. (error found)
   Computer time $= 2$ minutes

7. Make corrections and resubmit $\frac{1}{2}$ day.

8. Wait for results 1 day. (no error found)
   Computer time $= 3$ minutes

In Steps 2, 4, 6, and 8, we see that the computing system has been utilized. However, the time of computation is far different from the delay in getting results that the programmer sees. This large amount of time is the "turn-around" time or "response" time of the computing center. This time includes any transportation of material as well as handling of material within the center. Later, we shall examine in more detail the elements that make up turnaround or response time of the operation.

To demonstrate the effect of a higher level language, let us assume that the use of it doubles the computer time used, but decreases the preparation time by a factor of five with a decrease in the incidence of error by a factor of two. Also assume that there is a decrease in keypunch time by a factor of four. In this example, the programmer might see the following:

1. Preparation of coding 1 day.

2. Submit for processing
   and get results 1 day. (error found)
   Key punch time less than $\frac{1}{2}$ day
   Computer time $= 2$ minutes

3. Make corrections and resubmit $\frac{1}{5}$ day.

4. Wait for results 1 day. (error found)
   Computer time $= 4$ minutes.

5. Make corrections and resubmit   1 day.
6. Wait for results   1 day. (no error found)
   Computer time = 6 minutes

Several points are assumed in this demonstration. The first is that because the keypunching took less than one-half day, a run on the computer could also be made within the same cycle. If this were not the case, then step two would probably remain a two day cycle. Step three represents the reduction in time to make corrections proportional to the time reduction of original programming. Again, this is most certainly not always the case. There are cases when the error correction time for a higher level language is longer than the time to correct in a lower level language. This is because the identification of the error may be relative to the coding after it has been processed by the compiler. The programmer may have difficulty relating the identification back to his original source code. This is one of the reasons that we see sections of lower level language imbedded in higher level coding. (It should be noted that there are more cogent reasons for imbedding lower level languages than merely error correction. Particularly there is the need to overcome a deficiency or inefficiency in the higher level language.) To demonstrate this, I have indicated step five as an increase from one-half day to one full day.

Finally, we assume that one complete cycle of error discovery and correction has been eliminated. This saves one and one-half to two days on the project schecule.

In the first example, the project time was on the order of 11–13 days and the total computing time was 8 minutes. With all of the assumptions on the use of the higher level language, the project time was reduced to 5–6 days and the computing time was increased to 12 minutes. It is difficult to cost out the worth of a schedule decrease on a project in the abstract, because there are so many possible elements. For example, what was the programmer doing while waiting on the results of his machine runs? Was he simply doing nothing, or was he in fact pursuing other work? Were there in turn others who could not proceed with their work until the successful run of the program or were they also performing other work? For a given set of conditions about the time worth of a project, a costing can be performed to determine the financial worth of cutting a schedule in half.

The cost of achieving the schedule improvement may be examined in terms of additional cost of computing time. In this case, the computing time rose from 8 minutes to 12 minutes. One may view the increase as a 50% increase in computer cost, or one may view a four minute difference as insignificant and ignorable, depending on one's point of view. This will be discussed in later sections.

2.3. OPERATIONAL ASSISTANCE

The various acts of compiling, assembling, loading, executing, etc., although sometimes combined in a procedural routine, were usually considered to be separate steps in the sequencing or "job control" of the problem to be computed. An important innovation of job control was the facility to automatically link the various steps of a job throughout its progression. The various components (compilers, loaders, etc.) were joined together in a programming system package. This allowed the user to specify, by a set of job control cards, the steps that he wanted performed for his job. No longer would an operator have to intervene manually between the various steps, once all necessary control, source language, and data for a job had been supplied.

Given this type of control facility, it was a natural step to provide a cohesive control over sets of jobs, usually grouped together in batches. This job control facility was to set the pattern for most operating systems in use today. The reason for this is that the job-to-job control provided a facility to assist operations personnel rather than just the programmers. A primary intent was to make computing systems easier and therefore more efficient to operate. Early in the concept of an integrated job control system was the ability to provide more of the commonly used routines to all users of the system on a centralized basis rather than merely having a subroutine library where each programmer includes copies of routines in his program. The primary example of this ability is the common "input/output control system" (IOCS). In earlier days, the input/output routines had to be integrated (assembled, compiled, etc.) into each program which wanted to make use of it. Given the IOCS under a job control monitor, each programmer could merely assume that the facility would be in the right place at the right time. To utilize the services of the IOCS, each program could merely transfer control to the routine, supplying suitable direction, and expect to have control transferred back at the proper time.

Summarizing the previous components, we have the primary elements of an operating system, namely:

(a) the job control monitor (or supervisor)

(b) the language translators (compilers, assemblers, etc.)

(c) the loaders (from very simple to very sophisticated)

(d) common service routines (e.g., IOCS)

(e) the application programs.

Systems have varying degrees of sophistication for each of these elements.

Job control can be from the simplest job transition (job-to-job) routines to extremely complex priority type job queue schedulers. The loader function can be from the simple "load this deck" type to those which link together entire procedures under the control of an "editor." The service routines such as IOCS can range from the very simple act of reading data from a device specified by the application program to the locating of a uniquely identified piece of data found somewhere in a complex of various devices. Even the language translators have various degrees of sophistication, ranging from the simple batch compilers long used in computing systems to highly optimized, interactive compilers used in terminal or communication-oriented systems.

To understand the effect of including routines and programs into an operating system to improve operational efficiency, we should examine the activities that they are trying to improve. In Chapter 1, system turnaround was defined. The diagram is repeated here in Figure 2.26.

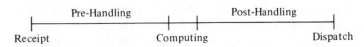

Fig. 2.26   System turnaround.

Studies of earlier systems indicated the proportion of time from the arrival of a job at the center until entry into the computer was on the order of 44 percent. These studies also indicated that from the time all output had been taken from the computer until it was dispatched was on the order of 55 percent. In other words, the job was under the direct influence of the computer only 1 percent of the time in a classic batch-oriented system. Usually, today, the picture is not as grim on even the classic batch processing in spite of the fact that we still find typical operations with an average turnaround time of two to four hours, processing jobs that have an average process time of only six minutes.

When a job arrives at the computing center, there are many manual or semimanual activities to perform. Almost all are candidates for replacement by programmed routines. Typical functions that are performed are as follows:

(a) Checking to see that the account number assigned to this project is valid and that this programmer has the right to use the account.

(b) Checking to see that the proper job identification and job control cards are present.

(c) Classification of priority to determine when the job should be placed on the system. Should it be run immediately or should it be deferred to second or third shift.

(d) Classification of the job by type of compiler that is to be used. This could be caused by the combination of machine room practices and capabilities of the programming system on the computer.

(e) Assignment to a batch of jobs. This could be on a time of day basis or as a result of the compiler requirement, or both.

(f) Possible transcription to some other media for insertion into the computer system itself. This could be performed on some auxiliary system.

Every time one of these functions is performed by operating personnel, there will probably be a backlog of work built up.

There are similar functions which must be performed following the processing of the job prior to its availability for dispatching. Among these are the possible removal of data for the off-line printing of results, the bursting of paper, accounting control (simply to insure that the job was processed), determination of routing information, etc. Again, many, if not all, of the functions are candidates for replacement by programmed routines utilizing facilities of the computer system. The principal direction of operating systems is to eliminate manual action in the processing of the work to be done.

The purpose of providing this brief history of computing is to identify and highlight elements which the analyst must take into consideration when performing either an absolute evaluation to project work load or a comparative evaluation to assess the capabilities of various systems. Much of the foregoing activity is usually called systems "overhead." If one is in a negative mood, it may be called systems "degradation." This terminology has developed because the performance of these functions takes time on a computing system which could have otherwise been spent in performing either arithmetic work or data processing. This is understandable, because that was probably the reason for acquiring the system in the first place. Each of the basic elements of an operating system has evolved to produce efficiencies or economy for the using installation. The tradeoff will always be computing system capability against manual or semimanual procedures.

PROBLEMS

1. If the data reduction program for the oscillograph problem described in Section 2.1.1 had performed 10 conversions (both X and Y) for each read and write, what would be the instruction mix of the problem?

2. For the simple file maintenance routine described in Section 2.1.2
    (a) What would be the job time if Master In and Master Out used a blocking factor of 5 (i.e., process 10,000, 500-character records)?
    (b) What is the percentage of error in this case if a nonoverlapped process time of 2.7 minutes is ignored?

3. In the example of external buffering in Section 2.2.1, what would be the main
    loop time if the buffer had a readout time of
    (a) 5 microseconds?
    (b) 20 microseconds?

4. In the single buffered example of cycle stealing described in Section 2.2.1,
    what would be the main loop time if Master In and Master Out used a block-
    ing factor of 5? (Assume no appreciable process time increase is required.)
    What modifications to the program flow chart in Figure 2.14 are needed?

5. If a computer system costs $180/hour and a programmer costs $120/8-hour
    day (including overhead costs), what is one minute of computer time expressed
    in minutes of programmer time?

6. Assuming the rates given in Problem 5, and assuming that all information
    given is a direct cost, i.e., the programmer is not working on any other problem,
    (a) What is the cost of 11 days of programmer time plus 8 minutes of com-
         puter time?
    (b) What is the cost of 6 days of programmer time and 12 minutes of com-
         puter time?
    (c) Express as a percentage of the answer to part (a) the cost of the additional
         four minutes of computer time.

7. Assume that five people are spending full time in performing the functions
    outlined in Section 2.3 at a cost of $300/week each (again, this includes over-
    head). On a break-even basis, how much time per week could a computer
    spend on performing that function, assuming $180/hour?

3 ESTIMATING CPU PERFORMANCE

Before examining techniques, we should consider the end use of any calculation. There are two primary areas for which information is derived:

(a) comparative evaluation

(b) timing estimates.

A comparative evaluation is the production of a *relative* estimate of capability between two or more systems in such a way as to closely represent the expected performance of the systems when installed in an operating environment. The closeness of representation distinguishes this type of assessment from ordinal classification. One system is usually chosen as the "base" system to which all other relative estimates are compared. In the production of a relative estimate, there is an underlying assumption that the answers produced are truly indicative of the relative performance of the systems being compared. This may or may not be the case. Sometimes, attributes which contribute to system performance are not taken into account. For example, the early scientific community evolved an assessment of a complete system's potential by merely using the weighted comparison of arithmetic attributes.

Within CPU considerations, two approaches to assessing a system's ability to perform calculations have evolved: the "instruction mix" method and the "kernel" method. Their primary difference is more in the interpretation and subsequent use of the results rather than in their representation of any calculating or processing phenomena. A mix generally purports to represent a broader range of use than a kernel does. This is because a kernel purports to represent some simple calculating procedure acting on some well-known inputs and producing well-known results. The use of the word "simple" is justified in this context, although it should definitely be pointed out that some kernels are enormous in size, complexity, and analysis time. A kernel is structured after the scope of interest is determined. Quite often, and in fact usually, a complex problem is broken down into a series of simple kernels for evaluation. After all kernels have been evaluated, they are recombined according to some weighting function, just as instruction times are combined in a mix process.

A timing estimate can serve two purposes. First of all, it is an end product in itself, and, secondly, it is usually a necessary step in the calculation of comparative performance. The techniques of producing the absolute evaluation can vary depending on the end use because of accuracy requirements. If, for example, a technique is known to contain a consistent error which produces some bias in the result, it may still be satisfactory for the intermediate calculations of a comparison because there is an underlying assumption that the error will wash out in the final calculation. Another reason for using a procedure that has a known inaccuracy is that the scope of the evaluation may be such that the data are not known for any refinement of the process. On the other hand, if a job time is the end result of the calculation, then the tolerance for error may be very small.

3.1. CLASSIFICATION

Classification is probably the most popular form of analysis. Its purpose is to *rank* the various systems in light of some criterion. Classification is seen in much of the literature on computing systems and is also generally found in publications of companies which provide consultation on computing. There are many different schemes which form a basis of classification. A trivial but valid method of classification is the listing of all product types ranked by "average" (often assumed) purchase or rental price. We may ask whether this is in fact a serious evaluation technique at all. The answer to such a query would be that if such a classification imparts meaning to the recipient, then it is definitely a valid evaluation technique.

The next level of classification is one which is based on some particular attribute of the computing system, such as capacity of processor storage, memory cycle time, add time, etc. This is similar to the classification of devices that was described earlier. In classifying systems by a single attribute, we quite often find the systems grouped in the generic terms of "small," "intermediate," and "large" systems. Defining the boundaries of this type of classification is much akin to defining the boundaries of the socio-economic levels in that we get into such classifications as "small intermediate," "large intermediate," "very large," etc.

Classification by a single attribute, such as memory cycle time, can sometimes provide erroneous information. Consider an "intermediate" computing system which has processor storage with a memory cycle time of two microseconds (2 μsec), which is being classified with a "small" computing system that has a processor storage with a memory cycle time of 1.5 μsec. A classification scheme based on memory cycle time alone would rank the small processor ordinally above the intermediate processor. This would imply that the small processor is faster than the intermediate one.

To overcome deficiencies such as the above example, techniques to provide "figures of merit" have been derived. A figure of merit is generally a type of calculation which tries to take into account *principal* attributes of a product in some weighted fashion in order to provide an ordinal classification of the capability of that product in relation to other products. As an example of such a calculation, in 1965, the author proposed to a government agency a method of classification which would overcome the anomalies of classifying by memory cycle time, alone. The proposal was a classification based on "maximum memory bus rate." (Before describing this method, it should be noted that more precise calculations of memory bandwidth as an approach to comparative evaluation of central processing unit/processor storage capabilities are in use.)

Maximum memory bus rate ($MMBR$) is defined by the following formula:

$$MMBR = \frac{\text{Data Length}}{\text{Memory Cycle Time}} \times (\text{Degree of Interleave}),$$

where Data Length is the total number of bits of information (including parity and control bits) which is accessed in one memory cycle,

Memory Cycle Time is the time for a physically identifiable package of memory to readout one data length of information and be ready to repeat the operation,

Degree of Interleave is a numerical value assigned to the ability of the system to have one or more physical packages of memory operating concurrently.

The purpose of the classification scheme was to provide a guideline to the capability of the technology of the system as opposed to a determination of its capability to perform any particular application. For this reason, total number of bits available on a readout cycle was chosen as an attribute rather than number of data bits only. The fact that some of the total bits available are used for parity and control is a decision of the designer of the system. If someone else had the memory available, they could use the total number of bits in any way they desired.

The most imprecise element of the formula is the degree of interleave.

Although it does represent the maximum bus rate, it tends to exaggerate a system's capability over what we should expect from the system. Experience has shown that using the square root of the degree of interleave is a better approximation to reality. Although the square root would improve the "tracking" of the classification scheme, it has little effect on the ranking of the systems. Using degree of interleave as expressed in the formula avoids the assessment of the effects of various memory bus schemes such as time-shared bus, distributed bus, or multiple bussing.

We now reconsider the previous example of classification, but with added information. The small processor reads out nine bits of information in one memory cycle, and the intermediate processor reads out 36 bits of information in one memory cycle. Both systems have a degree of interleave of one. We can now construct the following classification.

For the small system:

$$MMBR = \frac{9 \text{ (bits per memory cycle)}}{1.5 \text{ (memory cycle time in microseconds)}} \times 1$$

$$= 6 \text{ megabits/second.}$$

For the intermediate system:

$$MMBR = \frac{36 \text{ bits}}{2 \text{ microseconds}} \times 1$$

$$= 18 \text{ megabits/second.}$$

Using this classification scheme, the intermediate system is *ranked* higher than the small system.

3.2. INSTRUCTION MIXES

The instruction mix method is a technique to produce a number which has a broad representation of use. Given an instruction repertoire of a computer, the incidence of use of the various instructions is obtained. Applying the individual instruction times, the incidence will provide, when normalized, an "average instruction time." This average instruction time can then form a basis of comparison between CPU's.

The basis of the method is essentially the approach shown in Chapter 2, describing the data reduction program. To illustrate the application of the instruction mix, let us repeat the data reduction program in Figure 3.1.

To complete the program, we add a read instruction at the beginning to read the variables into the system, a write (or punch) instruction to record the values, and a branch instruction at the end of the program so that the program will keep looping until all cards are processed. Input/output instruc-

Load   Clear the multiplier and load K1
Multiply   Multiply by the variable X
Shift   Shift the accumulator into the correct alignment
Add   Add T(N)
Add   Add T(0)
Store   Store the value T
Load   Clear the multiplier and load K2
Multiply   Multiply by the variable Y
Shift   Shift the accumulator into the correct alignment
Add   Add V(0)
Store   Store the value V

Fig. 3.1   Data reduction program.

tions are generally omitted from an instruction mix on the basis that if the CPU is tied up for the entire duration of the read or write operation, there will be an unusually long time for those operations. A second reason for omission is the attitude that those instructions are really indicative of the input/output capability of the system rather than merely the CPU. Arguments on whether this type of instruction should or should not be included can probably go on forever. The important point to note is *whether* a particular instruction mix contains these instructions or not. To understand the influence of these instructions, we will keep them in the mix.

The instruction mix for this program is in Figure 3.2.

Type	Incidence
Add	3
Branch	1
I/O	2
Load	2
Multiply	2
Shift	2
Store	2
Total	14

Fig. 3.2   Data reduction instruction mix.

Assume that we have two CPU's with instruction characteristics as shown in Figure 3.3.

To obtain an average instruction time for CPU A, we multiply the individual instruction times by the incidence of the instruction in the mix as shown in Figure 3.4.

Dividing total time by total number of instructions we have an average instruction time of 30.4 msec. We see that the two I/O instructions have had the predominant effect on the calculation. To understand the performance of the CPU without the I/O operations, we simply remove the incidence and total

Instruction	CPU A	CPU B
	(timing in milliseconds)	
Add/Branch	1	1
I/O	200	200
Load	1	1
Multiply	7	5
Shift	2	1
Store	1	1

Fig. 3.3 CPU's for data reduction.

Instruction	Time	Incidence	Total (msec)
Add	1	3	3
Branch	1	1	1
I/O	200	2	400
Load	1	2	2
Multiply	7	2	14
Shift	2	2	4
Store	1	2	2
Total		14	426 msec

Fig. 3.4 Instruction timing table.

time of those instructions. This gives us twelve instructions with a total time of 26 msec, producing an average instruction time of 2.17 msec.

Applying the same approach to CPU B we obtain for the fourteen instruction case an average instruction time of 30.0 msec. Looking at the non-I/O instructions only, we have an average instruction time of 1.67 msec. The average instruction times which we have from the mixes of this particular problem appears as follows:

Mix	CPU A	CPU B
with I/O	30.4 msec	30.0 msec
without I/O	2.17 msec	1.67 msec

Many times, the comparison of the average instruction times for various CPU's are expressed as relative performance factors compared to a base system. If we let A be the base computer in this case, we see that comparing B using the mix with I/O produces a relative performance of 1.013. This means that CPU B should process those instructions 1.3% faster. Comparing B on the basis of the mix without I/O instructions produces a relative performance of 1.30! Again, the point is not whether we should or should not include I/O instructions in the mix, but whether they were or were not included. In using a mix approach, we should consider not only the representation of the mix, but also the criteria for inclusion in establishing the mix.

In the previous example, the number of written instructions was the same as the number of executed instructions. This is because we considered only one pass through the routine. However, if we made 100 passes through the routine, the number of executed instructions would be 100 times the number of written instructions. In this case, the relative proportion of the instructions did not change because each instruction written is involved in the loop. In general, however, the proportion does not remain constant, so we must distinguish between a mix based on written instructions and one based on executed instructions.

The word "static" is used to identify mixes or other attributes based on the incidence of the instructions as written. The word "dynamic" is used to identify properties based on the incidence of the instructions as executed. A purely static instruction mix may be obtained from a listing of the program. No effort is made to assess multiple passes through any particular section of the coding. A dynamic instruction mix can be obtained utilizing measurement techniques to obtain the information about the instructions as they are being processed.

We can always improve over the pure static approach by trying to assess the number of passes through various sections of written code so that those sections can be weighted in relation to other sections. Our work here will be concerned with dynamic conditions unless otherwise noted.

A simple instruction mix might have the characteristics shown in Figure 3.5.

Instruction	Incidence
Load/Store	22
Add/Subtract	20
Multiply/Divide	6
Branch	34
Logical operations	10
Shifting	6
Miscellaneous	2
Total	100

Fig. 3.5 Typical instruction mix.

It appears that we can follow the same procedure as in the previous example in applying instruction times to this mix. But, first of all, several unanswered questions come to mind for today's central processor units. We find that CPU's have many different instructions within the general categories listed above. For example, we can have a floating point add, a fixed binary add, and a decimal field add, all with several variations with regard to processor storage and CPU register operands. So the question is: which add time should be used for the instruction mix? There are similar variations to the other categories as well. If no further information about this particular mix is available, the answers to these questions might well be to take the fastest instruction of the computer for each class listed above. (After all, at least, that approach has the attribute that it is as good as any, and certainly better than most.) With no further information about the mix, there is really no justification for any other approach.

At this point, let us assume that we have two computers with the attributes shown in Figure 3.6.

Instruction	CPU A	CPU B
(Fastest of class above)		
Load/Store	4	2 μsec
Add/Subtract	4	4
Multiply/Divide	10	6
Branch	2	1
Logical	4	4
Shifting	6	4
Miscellaneous	4	2

Fig. 3.6   CPU instruction times.

Calculating the average instruction time for each CPU based on the mix in Figure 3.5, we have the following:

$$CPU\ A = 3.80\ \mu sec,$$
$$CPU\ B = 2.62\ \mu sec.$$

The relative performance factor of CPU B, based on A, is 1.45.

Now, let us consider an augmented instruction mix with further information about each class as shown in Figure 3.7.

The relevant instruction times of the two CPU's are shown in Figure 3.8. Calculating the average instruction time for each CPU, we have

$$CPU\ A = 4.70\ \mu sec,$$
$$CPU\ B = 3.58\ \mu sec.$$

The relative performance factor of CPU B, based on CPU A, is 1.31. Using this mix, CPU B has dropped from 45% faster than CPU A to 31% faster.

Let us now add another complexity. Consider the effect on relative per-

Instruction	Incidence
Load/Store	
Index	12
Arthmetic	10
Add/Subtract	
Index	6
Fixed Point	10
Floating Point	4
Multiply/Divide	
Fixed Point	3
Floating Point	3
Branch	
Index	20
Arithmetic	14
Logical	
Register type	5
Memory type	5
Shifting	
Less than 6	4
Greater than 6	2
Miscellaneous	2
Total	100

Fig. 3.7 Augmented instruction mix·

formance if the 10 fixed point instructions were not binary (as assumed), but decimal instructions operating on a six digit field. Furthermore, let us assume that CPU A has the capability to deal with decimals directly with a 12 microsecond instruction, but that CPU B has to perform decimal operations with a subroutine because it does not have direct decimal capability. Let us further assume that CPU B's subroutine takes 120 microseconds to operate. In this event, the average instruction time for CPU A is 5.50 μsec, and the average instruction time for CPU B is 15.18 μsec. Under these circumstances, the relative performance of CPU B, based on CPU A is 0.36. In other words, it now operates about one-third as fast as System A.

One may question whether CPU B, perhaps a "scientific" computer, would be operating in an environment utilizing the obviously commercial attribute of a decimal instruction. The answer is certainly "Yes." We find that many applications are performed on individual computers. Even the small scientific computer operating in a university's basic research laboratory may have commercial applications on it some times, especially if the researcher finds that he has to produce various accounts of his activity under some con tract or grant.

In progressing through the previous examples, each stage included more information in an attempt to overcome one of the deficiencies of the instruc-

Instruction	CPU A	CPU B
Load/Store	(time in microseconds)	
Index	4	4
Arithmetic	4	2
Add/Subtract		
Index	4	4
Fixed point arithmetic	4	4
Floating point	16	12
Multiply/Divide		
Fixed point	10	8
Floating point	12	10
Branch		
Index	2	1
Arithmetic	4	2
Logical		
Register type	4	4
Memory type	4	4
Shifting		
Less than six places	6	4
Greater than six	10	6
Miscellaneous	4	4

Fig. 3.8 CPU instruction times.

tion mix approach. When presented as above, the mix loses the contextual purpose for performing the instruction in the first place. This loss of information occurs at two distinct levels of operation.

First we consider the major level. At this level, we find sets of instructions performing major tasks or applications such as an IOCS routine or a language compilation. The problem program has its own instruction set, but is dependent on both the method in which the code was produced as well as the basic services available to its under an operating system or control program.

When considering various systems, we can reasonably expect the control program services and the compilers themselves to be completely different in their internal structures and instruction sets. This would cause the instruction mix of these functions to be highly volatile. Obtaining a mix of one system and then applying it to another for these functions can probably produce the greatest degree of error in a mix comparison. Because of the dependency of the problem program on these services, the instruction mix of the problem program can also vary, but would probably not produce as great a degree of error.

A simple example of differences of instructions sets in control program functions can be found in methods of handling interrupts in various systems. A CPU which has quite a bit of the interrupt decode mechanism built into the hardware may require only a few instructions to identify the interrupt and transfer to the routine for processing the interrupt. On the other hand, a CPU which does not have interrupt definition built into the hardware may require many instructions just for the purpose of interrupt identification. The number of instructions involved in these two approaches can vary on a ratio of four or five to one. In other words, if the first CPU required ten or twenty instructions to identify the action required for an interrupt, the second CPU could require 40 to 100 instructions to achieve the same function.

In the case of language compilation, we find differences not only across the various languages such as APL, ALGOL, FORTRAN, COBOL, PL/1, JOSS, BASIC, etc., but major variances within a language. We normally expect this to be the case when comparing two or more systems, but we also find this between various compiler options of a single language on a single system. The options generally depend on the "design level" of the compiler and on the degree of optimization which the compiler performs. The design level of a program is the specification of what facilities are available to the program to perform its intended function. The critical facilities are the amount of processor storage and the number and type of input/output units. If only a small amount of storage is available, then the compiler would have to be structured in several "phases" or passes of data. If only a serial medium such as magnetic tape is available for intermediate storage of results, the compiler would tend to be structured in a serial processing fashion. Furthermore, if the tape could be read in a forward direction only, then the compiler would plan on having to rewind the tape between passes of data. On the other hand, if these restrictions were removed, then the compiler could assume a much more efficient form. The effect on the instruction mix is largely unpredictable but, of course, is measurable. The obvious change in the instruction mix would be to decrease the ratio of input/output oriented instructions to the other process instructions. If, however, the compiler changes from a serial structure to a "tree" structure, the instruction set utilized would be vastly different.

The degree of optimization in a compiler has a direct effect on the number and mix of instructions utilized in the process of compilation and also on the number and mix of instructions executed in the problem program.

Let us consider a test program (Figure 3.9) under a variety of compiler and system options. (When using a particular language, there are many items which would not be required in practice, such as the word CALCULATE, or the line numbers.) The intention of this simple routine is to perform the calculation from THERE to HERE 1000 times with a new variable W, each time. To do this, we will index on the value I to both control the number of times through the routine as well as identify the various values of W and

Z. (All values are in processor storage, and the arithmetic mode is floating point.)

(1)   DO THERE TO HERE 1000 TIMES, INDEXING ON I
(2) THERE   CALCULATE X = A + B∗Y
(3)   CALCULATE Z(I) = X + C + D∗W(I)
(4) HERE   BRANCH BACK TO THERE ON I
(5)   CONTINUE WITH SOMETHING ELSE

Fig. 3.9   A test program.

A straightforward compiler which does not make any attempt at optimization might produce the code shown in Figure 3.10.

	Location	Instruction
	100	Load Index Reg. to initial value I
(THERE)	101	Load Y into an arithmetic register
	102	Multiply by B
	103	Add A to previous result
	104	Store X in memory
	105	Load W(I)
	106	Multiply by D
	107	Add C to previous result
	108	Add X to previous result
	109	Store Z(I)
(HERE)	110	Change Index (Add/Sub index reg.)
	111	Branch on index to THERE (based on value and limit)
	112	Go to Something Else

Fig. 3.10   Non-optimizing compiler code.

Instructions 105 and 109 are index controlled to keep the various values of W and Z straight. With the exception of instruction 100, which is used to initialize the value of the index register, and instruction 112 which points to something else to do after this routine has been completed, all instructions are executed 1000 times. This instruction mix for this code is given in Figure 3.11. Clearly, we can ignore the effects of instructions 100 and 112.

Now consider that the compiler is operating in a system with multiple arithmetic registers *and* that it tries to take advantage of them. (It should be noted that a compiler operating with multiple registers which does not try to optimize would produce essentially the same code as the previous example.)

A typical algorithm in an optimizing compiler would be to assign the various registers to the most used variables and constants. For this routine, the compiler would scan the various operands and discover that the variable X is used twice as often as the others. The rest of the operands are used

Instruction	Incidence
Load/Store	
Index	1
Arithmetic	4000
Add/Subtract	
Index	1000
Arithmetic	3000
Multiply/Divide	2000
Branch	1001
Total	11002

Fig. 3.11 Non-optimized instruction mix.

equally with the obvious exceptions of W(I) and Z(I). The operands A, B, Y, C, and D are then assigned on a first come, first serve, basis. The results of the algorithm would produce the following register assignments for a four register CPU:

Floating Point (0):   General arithmetic purposes (Multiplication must be here)

Floating Point (2):   Reserved for X

Floating Point (4):   Reserved for A

Floating Point (6):   Reserved for B.

The code produced under these assumptions would appear as shown in Figure 3.12.

	Location	Instruction
	100	Load Index Reg. to initial value
	101	Load A to FP(4)
	102	Load B to FP (6)
(THERE)	103	Load Y to FP(0)
	104	Multiply FP(6) by FP(0), Result in (0)
	105	Add FP(4) to FP(0), Result in (0)
	106	Store X in memory
	107	Move FP(0) to FP(2), save X in register
	108	Load W(I) to FP(0)
	109	Multiply by D
	110	Add C
	111	Add FP(2) to FP(0)
	112	Store Z(I) in memory
(HERE)	113	Add/Sub Index
	114	Branch on index to THERE
	115	Go to Something Else

Fig. 3.12 Multiple register compiler code.

We see that we have increased the static number of instructions from 13 to 16. However, it is assumed that the instructions which involve register to register operations are very much faster than those which involve memory to register type operations. Instruction 106 is inserted because X is a calculated variable which could be invoked at any time by any other routine. Although this routine can use X from a register, it is also saved in memory for any possible future use. The instruction mix for this appears as shown in Figure 3.13.

Instruction	Incidence
Load/Store Move	
Index	1
Arithmetic-memory	4002
Arithmetic-register	1000
Add/Subtract	
Index	1000
Arithmetic-memory	1000
Arithmetic-register	2000
Multiply/Divide	
Memory	1000
Register	1000
Branch	1001
Total	12004

Fig. 3.13   Multiple register instruction mix.

We see that the dynamic instruction count has risen from about 11,000 instructions to about 12,000. Again, the justification for the increase would be that some 4000 of the instructions would be very much faster than those requiring all operations from memory.

Finally, let us consider that we have a compiler which performs the functions of the previous example and also performs an important additional function. Let us assume that it has the ability to determine "extraneous" coding within a loop. In the original example, we can see that the calculation of X is merely repeated 1000 times with no new information produced after the first time through the loop. The same old value of X is produced every time. Some compilers have the ability to detect such coding practices. Assuming this to be the case, that section of code is taken out of the loop and added to the initialization routine. Within the loop, an incidence analysis is again performed to determine register assignments, but this time the constants A and B are not even part of the analysis. The register assignment under these conditions would be as follows.

Floating Point (0):   General arithmetic purposes

Floating Point (2):   Reserved for X

Floating Point (4):   Reserved for C

Floating Point (6):   Reserved for D.

The code produced under these assumptions would be as shown in Figure 3.14.

	Location	Instruction
	100	Load Index Reg. to initial value
	101	Load Y to FP(0)
	102	Multiply by B
	103	Add A
	104	Store X in memory
	105	Move FP(0) to FP(2)
	106	Load C to FP (4)
	107	Load D to FP(6)
(THERE)	108	Load W(I) to FP(0)
	109	Multiply FP(0) by FP(6), result in (0)
	110	Add FP(4) to FP(0), result in (0)
	111	Add FP(2) to FP(0), result in (0)
	112	Store Z(I) in memory
(HERE)	113	Add/Sub Index
	114	Branch on Index to THERE
	115	Go to Something Else

Fig. 3.14   Optimizing compiler.

Again, the static number of instructions is 16, but this time the dynamic count changes dramatically. The instruction mix is as shown in Figure 3.15.

If we now compare the three mixes obtained from performing the same problem as a result of the different compilations, we have the table shown in Figure 3.16. Case I is the simple compiler with no optimization, Case II is the compiler that tries to effectively assign multiple registers, and Case III is the compiler that tries to eliminate extraneous code as well as optimize register assignments.

Because we have retained the total instruction count in establishing this mix, we can see the relative value of Case III over Case I or Case II. To determine the value of Case II in regard to Case I, we would have to time out the routine with actual instruction times.

An additional complication which also causes loss of contextual information is the practice that many mixes are expressed in terms of a percentage incidence or in terms of an incidence per hundred, thousand, or million

Instruction	Incidence
Load/Store/Move	
Index	1
Arithmetic-memory	2004
Arithmetic-register	1
Add/Subtract	
Index	1000
Arithmetic-memory	1
Arithmetic-register	2000
Multiply/Divide	
Memory	1
Register	1000
Branch	1001
Total	7009

Fig. 3.15 Optimized instruction mix.

Instruction	Case I	Case II	Case III
Load/Store			
Index	1	1	1
Arith.-memory	4000	4002	2004
Arith.-reg.	–	1000	1
Add/Subtract			
Index	1000	1000	1000
Arith.-memory	3000	1000	1
Arith.-reg.	–	2000	2000
Multiply/Divide			
Memory	2000	1000	1
Register	–	1000	1000
Branch	1001	1001	1001
Totals	11002	12004	7009

Fig. 3.16 Summary of instruction counts.

instructions, total. When this occurs, even the little information that the total line gave us in the previous table is lost. Consider the information on the three previous cases of compilation expressed as an incidence of instructions, based on one hundred instructions as shown in Figure 3.17.

In this example, it is hard to determine that the three instruction mixes in fact represent the same problem being executed under three different compiler options.

Instruction	Case I	Case II	Case III
Load/Store			
Index	t	t	t (t = trace; further entries will be left blank)
Arith.-memory	36	33	29
Arith.-reg.		8	
Add/Subtract			
Index	9	8	14
Arith.-memory	27	8	
Arith.-reg.		17	29
Multiply/Divide			
Memory	18	8	
Register		8	14
Branch	9	8	14
Rounding error	1	2	
Totals	100	100	100

Fig. 3.17 Instruction mix percentages.

Returning now to levels of information loss in mixes, the second level of loss of contextual information occurs at the instruction level itself. It is useful to consider this level of loss in yet two further stages, the intra-instruction stage and the inter-instruction stage.

At the intra-instruction level there is, of course, the variation due to data. A floating point multiply instruction time generally depends on the data content of the operands. The timing generally depends on such items as the number of zeros in the operands and the number of carries in the production of the result. There are many other instructions which have "data dependent" timing. When applying instruction times to mixes in this category some average or, again, the fastest possible time is used. The variation contained within the instruction itself is also found at the intra-instruction level. An example of this is the number of positions to be shifted in a register. That number is generally contained in the instruction rather than being identified by the data. Similarly, the length of a decimal field operand is generally contained in the instruction. As one might expect, even at this level we are not in a pure world. In some systems, the information in the instruction does not completely identify the time variable because of over-riding influences in the data itself. For example, even though we may specify the number of positions to shift a register, a particular CPU may have the ability to detect a series of zeros and speed up the operation.

In providing instruction time estimates for an instruction mix application, this type of variation is provided for by using some average of all possible times for the instruction, or the fastest time within the definition. Again, the question of whether one should or should not use an average or fastest time is not as improtant as knowing which time is used.

The inter-instruction level is concerned with peculiar groupings of two or more instructions to perform a particular operation. An example of this would be the operation involved in maintaining a count or a tally of some event in a memory location. Given the occurence of the event, we want to add a one to the memory location containing the tally. A natural instruction for this would be simply "add one to memory." Such an instruction may or may not be present in any particular CPU. If one is not present, then the CPU may have to perform a triplet of instructions such as:

Load memory into a register

Add one to the register (the constant one may be in memory)

Store result back to memory.

If this particular triplet of instructions was maintained as a separate entry in an instruction mix, the analyst could then take advantage of any "add to memory" instructions which were implemented in the CPU's under study. If, however, the individual instructions of the triplet were distributed to their usual classes, the opportunity to assess the add to memory capability could well be lost.

Another point is raised in the example of the triplet. This is the general loss of *sequence* information. In considering the performance of high-speed processors which utilize parallelism, pipe-lining, ultra-high speed backing storage, or other such design approaches, the sequence of instruction execution is of paramount importance. In fact, the sequence of instructions can be more important than the number of instructions. (In some situations, five to ten additional instructions can be concurrently executed within the time it takes to perform, say, a floating point divide.)

At this point, we have examined the principal disadvantages of utilizing instruction mixes for the determination of performance of various CPU's. On a positive note, the advantage of using an instruction mix lies in its ease of application. Once we have a mix, it is relatively simple to apply instruction times of various CPU's to the mix and get answers. Of course, the analyst will have to use judgment in applying CPU's with different architectures to a particular mix. However, if the mix is well defined, this effort will be minimized.

Let us consider some of the attributes of a well-defined instruction mix in light of the disadvantages that have been noted. First, we would like to separate the instructions performed on behalf of the compiler (and other such functions) from those executed on behalf of the problem program. We would also want to separate the instructions involved in any control program service from those executed within the application code. Finally, within the application code, we would like to have functional identification of important groupings of instructions rather than the dispersal of those instructions into their normal categories. As for overcoming the loss of sequence information, that is where we must turn from the mix approach to some other technique (e.g., kernel).

In establishing an instruction mix of the application code, the sample size must be taken into consideration. Ideally, it would be large enough to have some stability to overcome (or average out) variations due to such items as compiler options. In setting up the mix, we would also want to consider whether we should divide the applications into two or more categories. The classical subdivisions are commercial and scientific. These categories may or may not be used, depending on the activity under investigation. If there is a major application which accounts for a large portion of the system's time, we might structure an instruction mix of that application alone.

In summary, one should decide the intended representation of the mix before launching an effort to obtain the mix.

3.3. KERNEL EVALUATION

Kernel analysis differs from job analysis in that a kernel analysis is based on only the "essential" part of the job. The essential part is determined by finding that part of the application which takes the greatest time or forms the critical path of the job. Within a particular application, there can be more than one kernel. Consider the flow of an application as given in Figure 3.18.

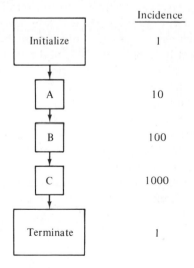

Fig. 3.18 Application flow.

The initialization and termination phase are executed once, while Section A is executed 10 times, Section B 100 times, and Section C 1000 times. This relationship would indicate that Section C would be the prime candidate as the kernel. But the choice of kernels should be based on the most time consuming portion of the application.

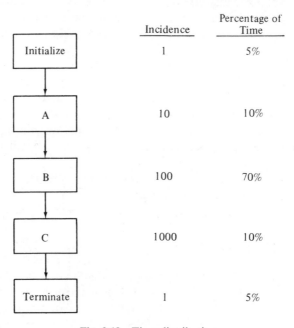

	Incidence	Percentage of Time
Initialize	1	5%
A	10	10%
B	100	70%
C	1000	10%
Terminate	1	5%

Fig. 3.19   Time distribution.

Consider the same application in terms of contribution to overall application time. It could appear as shown in Figure 3.19. In this case, we see that initiation and termination phase each account for 5% of the time; Sections A and C account for 10%; and Section B accounts for 70% of the application time. Under these circumstances, Section B would be the prime candidate for kernel analysis. Therefore, if we examined only Section B, we would be accounting for 70% of the application time. Adding Section A or Section C would account for 80%. Adding both Section A and Section C would account for 90% of the time. Adding to this the initiation phase and the termination phase would be a 100% analysis and therefore a complete job analysis.

To understand the advantage of a kernel analysis over a complete job analysis, assume that each of the five sections of the program contain equal amounts of coding. Therefore, in examining Section B, only, we can account for 70% of the application time by doing a kernel analysis on only 20% of the code.

In plain language, a kernel analysis involves actually writing and timing the instructions necessary to perform a particular function. This type of analysis overcomes some of the deficiencies of an instruction mix analysis. It does identify the major loss of contextual information in that it identifies the use of control program services as well as any required compilations, etc. It also identifies the inter-instruction relationships including the very important concept of sequence information. It also identifies the instruction dependent portion of the intra-instruction information. Depending on what type of data is available for the kernel analysis, it may identify a portion of the data dependent attributes of the instructions.

A kernel analysis is especially useful when comparing systems of different architecture. It provides the opportunity for the full instruction repertoire of each system to be applied to a particular problem. In assessing various CPU's by the instruction mix method, there is a large probability that the full instruction set of a CPU will not apply to the individual classes in the mix. Even though the full set may not be used in any particular kernel, those which are applicable will be taken into consideration. Consider the example of the evaluation of the polynomial expression

$$Y = (((K4*X + K3)X + K2)X + K1)X + K0.$$

If the system from which we took the mix information had an architecture that involved always loading a multiplier register to perform a multiplication from memory, its code would appear as shown in Figure 3.20.

```
Load K4 to multiplier
Multiply by X, result in accumulator
Add K3 to accumulator
Move accumulator to multiplier
Multiply by X
Add K2
Move accumulator to multiplier
Multiply by X
Add K1
Move accumulator to multiplier
Multiply by X
Add K0
Store Y
```

Fig. 3.20   Polynomial evaluation.

The mix obtained from this code is in Figure 3.21.

Consider that we now have a second system, which we wish to evaluate, that has special registers and instructions to perform in a single instruction the multiplication between a special multiplier register and the accumulator, leaving the result in the accumulator, followed by an add from memory into the accumulator. Further assume that the special multiply register is not

Instruction	Incidence
Add	4
Load	1
Move	3
Multiply	4
Store	1
Total	13

Fig. 3.21 Instruction mix of polynomial evaluation.

disturbed by the operation. If this system were evaluated by the above mix, this special instruction would not be taken into consideration. Of course, if the mix had a classification of "polynomial evaluation," it could have been taken into account by a knowledge of the application.

Taking advantage of the architecture of the second system to perform the polynomial evaluation would result in the coding shown in Figure 3.22.

```
Load X to multiplier (special register)
Load K4 to accumulator
Multiply/add K4*X + K3
Multiply add Previous *X + K2
Multiply/add Previous *X + K1
Multiply/add Previous *X + K0
Store Y
```

Fig. 3.22 Polynomial evaluation with multiply/add.

We could reasonably assume that performing the polynomial evaluation in this way would be very much faster than performing the set of instructions given by the mix. It may not be on the order of two to one as indicated by the total number of instructions (seven to thirteen). However, given actual instruction times, we could determine the improvement.

The kernel can take into effect the influence of input/output in the performance of the problem. In many cases, however, this is not taken into account. The omission lies with the analyst rather than the technique. Although not pertinent to CPU evaluation, one may assess the time of a job which is known to be, say, print bound by simply considering the number of lines of print and the speed of a printer in lines per minute. If there were an application of this nature with 100,000 lines of output, a system with a 1000 line per minute printer would take about 100 minutes to execute. Ignoring such items as skip time may or may not influence this time estimate, depending on the incidence and length of skips. Knowing what to ignore can be as important as the evaluation itself.

An important consideration for the analyst is the influence of the programmer actually performing the coding for any problem. There is some personal bias involved in writing code. It may not be intentional on the part of the programmer, and, in fact, he may not be conscious of any bias. (It is rare to find malice involved.) The bias is more concerned with the individual's knowledge of the application and, the system on which he is coding as well as his own creative ability. Let us remember that programming is in a sense a creative art the same as painting. Just as the field of jurisprudence has the "prudent man" philosophy which pertains to the administration of estates and other fiscal affairs, we seem to need the concept of the "prudent programmer" in the field of computer science. We have seen many cases of a program being produced by an "average" programmer which upon a brief inspection by an expert in the application or the system has been modified to run many times faster than the original. We have also seen situations where a neophyte programmer can change a problem to achieve the same effect, because he saw something that the experts had overlooked. The prudent man philosophy is based on the assumption of reasonableness. Given a set of circumstances, did the person perform his duties as well as anyone could have expected? We should expect the same from the prudent programmer—did he write the code as we should reasonably expect?

To indicate the variation due to programmer bias, consider the following example. As part of an evaluation of various systems and language facilities, we also wanted to find out the variation due to programmer bias. Initially, we gave a mathematical problem with its computing requirements to three different programmers whom we considered to meet the prudent programmer attributes. The problem was similar to the following:

$$X = \frac{N}{\sum_{J=0}^{N} \frac{N!K^J}{(N-J)!}}$$

$$\text{for } N = 10, 20, \ldots, 100$$

$$K = 0, 0.1, 0.2, \ldots, 2.5$$

We also had an artifically short time period for them to program the problem and provide the answer back to us.

In each case, because of the lack of any time to investigate the nature of the problem, the coding was performed in a classical three-level nested DO loop such as is typically found in FORTRAN coding. The timing results on the three systems appeared as follows (the numbers are not actual but represent the order of magnitude):

System A	System B	System C
1000 units	600 units	800 units

We then allowed each of the programmers time to study the problem and asked them to provide their best programming effort to produce the shortest running time. The result of that round of programming resulted in the following timings.

System A	System B	System C
500 units	400 units	300 units

We also asked that three additional people assist on the coding of the problem after this round. Each was considered an expert on a particular system. The result of that coding was as follows:

System A	System B	System C
400 units	300 units	10 units!

In this case, the programmer on System C saw the problem in a whole new light. Furthermore, he used a programming technique which was not available for the other systems. So we see that the performance of System C compared with System A has progressed from an improvement factor of 1.25 to an improvement factor of 40.0. Summarizing the improvement factors for each round, we have the following results as shown in Figure 3.23. System A is the base in each round.

Round	System A	System B	System C
1	1.00	1.67	1.25
2	1.00	1.25	1.67
3	1.00	1.33	40.00

Fig. 3.23   Comparison within each round.

If we express all improvement factors in relation to the first round of System A, we have the results in Figure 3.24.

Round	System A	System B	System C
1	1.00	1.67	1.25
2	2.00	2.50	3.33
3	2.50	3.33	100.00

Fig. 3.24   Comparison to common base.

If we consider the variation within System C alone, using the first round as a base, we have the results shown in Figure 3.25.

Round	Time	Factor
1	800	1.00
2	300	2.67
3	10	80.00

Fig. 3.25 Comparison of System C.

The variation due to programming approach alone in this case is a factor of 80.

Naturally, at this point we wonder which would be the correct comparison to use. If we use round one, System B is the best. Using round two, we see that System C is best. Using round three, System C is fantastically best. The only way to eliminate programmer bias is to have a problem performed by some rigid computing procedure or have a large number of problems with a large number of programmers. Having a rigid computing procedure can dampen creative programming. Having a large number of problems and program-mers can be quite expensive. The alternative is to use the prudent programmer philosophy.

It should be noted that using an overestimation can be as misleading as an underestimation. Because an expert in a particular application or system can produce excellent job times on a particular system is no indication that the prudent programmer in any particular installation can produce the same results.

As mentioned earlier, the objective of the kernel evaluation is to find the portion of coding which takes the greatest or principal amount of time. Also recall that there may be more than one kernel in an application. To determine the kernel of an application requires a knowledge of the application. We should determine first whether the application is bound by its input/output requirements or by its computing requirements. In the area of CPU evaluation, we should be concerned with those applications which are bound by the computing requirements. If the input/output and the CPU are evenly matched, we should approach the problem from a systems point of view, which will be discussed in the next chapter. If the application is bound by the CPU activity, we should consider what portions of the coding are governing the application. Examining a static description of the program may provide the information that we need. If there are sections of code which represent a major portion of the time whenever they are invoked (which we will call the duration) and are invoked most of the time (which we shall call the incidence), then we can determine the kernels from the static code. On the other hand, if the kernel is not obvious from an examination of the static description, we must resort to dynamic techniques.

The structure of a kernel can depend on its data organization. For example, the solution of certain partial differential equations with a limited amount of processor storage calls for a particular technique. However, with sufficient processor storage (either the problem small enough to fit into normally expected sizes or high-speed directly-accessible auxiliary storage in very large capacities to hold the problem) we can resort to totally different methods. Given an amount of storage and a problem size to fit into the storage, a solution by the method of alternating directions is very much faster than a solution utilizing a method of repeated serial passes of data. However, the method of alternating directions depends on all data being available in directly addressable storage.

Just as we saw in the instruction mix method, the analyst must determine what conditions apply to the evaluation. He should determine what was and was not included in the definition of the evaluation. He should determine whether approaches applicable to one system can be applied to other systems. He should understand any data dependencies that influence the coding of the kernel. In short, he should understand the application and all of its attributes.

3.4. FUNCTIONAL MIXES

The functional mix is something of a cross between the instruction mix approach and the kernel approach. It is based on an examination of the skeleton of the application. Again, this method allows input/output to be taken into consideration, but many times it is not done. We start with the flow chart of an application as given in Figure 3.26.

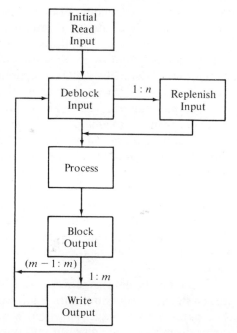

Fig. 3.26 Application flow chart.

Here we see the major flow of the problem. The ratio of entries into the particular section of code is indicated at the input replenishment block and the output writing block. A $1:n$ ratio means that the section will be entered once for each n entries of the preceding section. In this case, the sections represent buffer replenishment and buffer emptying of input/output based on the blocking and buffering scheme used in the system. In this example, we have processing at every pass, so the next step is to break down the portions of the process section as shown in Figure 3.27.

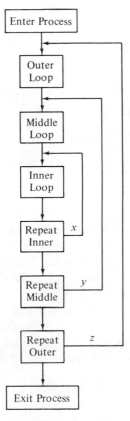

Fig. 3.27 Process flow chart.

Here we see a rather classical three-level loop problem. For each entry into the process step, the outer loop is performed z times, the middle loop, $y \times z$ times, and the inner loop, $x \times y \times z$ times. Each of these sections of code would be broken down to determine their function. The functional coding in the inner loop could appear as shown in Figure 3.28.

In this case, we see that Sections A, B, and E are executed each time we go through the inner loop. Section F is entered only once for x times through the routine. (This is typical of a termination phase.) Sections C and D are

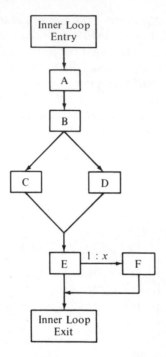

Fig. 3.28   Inner loop flow chart.

assumed to be data dependent. At this point, we may not be able to predict the number of times through Section C as opposed to Section D. Before trying to establish the nature of the data which would determine the alternate entries, we should first examine C and D to answer an initial question. Which is easier, performing the kernel analysis of C and D or determining the incidence of the data characteristics which would cause the entry? If the kernel analysis of C and/or D would be very time consuming, we would want to launch a study of the data. On the other hand, if we cannot determine the characteristics of the data, we must perform a kernel analysis on each section.

Having performed a kernel analysis on both Sections C and D, we should examine the relative times of the two sections. If it takes very nearly the same time to perform either C or D, we can ignore the data attributes which would cause an entry into one or the other. If the time of one section is very much larger than the time of the other, we should attempt to determine from a study of the data the incidence of choosing between the two sections. We have at least four alternatives in timing out the inner loop if that information is not available. We could take the larger time for each pass through the inner loop. This would be the most conservative approach, but obviously penalizes the time of the routine. We could take the average of the two times, but we have no more justification for a one-to-one average than any other average. We could take the shorter time for each pass of the loop. This is of course, optimistic, and could be as misleading as the first alternative. Finally, we could express the time as an option formula. Let us consider that for the passes through the routine, all other sections require 500 units of time. Assume that Section C takes 100 units and Section D takes 500 units. We can add C to the base 500 and leave the time that D exceeds C as an option. This can be expressed as

Inner Loop Time = 600 units (add 400 for each time the data meets the criteria of XXX).

In this case we have not solved the problem; we have merely passed on to someone else the problem of determining the number of times the nature of the data will cause an entry into Section D rather than Section E. Hopefully, they will be acquainted with the data and can determine the relative incidence of entries.

The functional mix tends to use items which reflect the execution of a set of code rather than execution of an instruction. Therefore, we see items such as those following:

Initiate a Read operation
Check End of Block
Change Pointers
Post result
Allocate Buffer
Update Table
Field Scan
Table Look Up
Evaluate Polynomial
Calculate $F(x)$ (given some formula)
Calculate Square Root
Extend Item Cost
Distribute Cost
Tally an Item
Convert Data Formats
Edit for Print Line

In Figure 3.29, the flow chart of the application is shown with an assumed volume. We will process 1000 records into the system blocked five at a time. Similarly, 1000 records will be blocked, also written five at a time. For each record, we will make five passes of the outer loop. For each pass through the outer loop, we will make ten passes of the middle loop, and for each pass of the middle loop, we will make five passes of the inner loop. Therefore, there

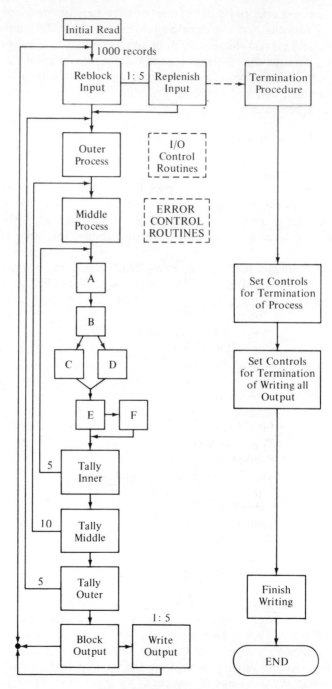

Fig. 3.29   Detailed flow chart.

will be 5 times 10 times 5 times 1000 passes of the inner loop or an incidence of 250,000 times. Tabulating the functional mix of the problem, we have the following:

Item	Incidence
Input Deblock	1000
Input Read	200
Outer Process	5000
Middle Process	50000
Inner Block A	250000
Inner Block B	250000
Inner Block C or D	250000 (data dependent)
Inner Block E	250000
Block F (Inner Exit)	50000
Middle Tally Block	50000
Outer Tally Block	5000
Output Blocking	1000
Output Writing	200

In addition to the major portion of the program which produced the numbers above, there are three additional sections. The first is the termination routine which closes off all of the processing on an orderly basis when there are no more records to process. Its general characteristic is to make sure that all records are processed correctly and written out correctly. It does this by forcing entries in the main program. For example, the final block of information read in may have less than five records in a block. If the output writing block is invoked only when a buffer has five records, it will never write out the last one to four records. If, for example, there were only three records in the final block, the termination routine will cause the output blocking routine to transfer to the output writing routine at the end of three records rather than the normal five.

There is also another set of routines in the system, either in processor storage or auxiliary storage: the error control routines. These routines provide the correction facilities whenever an error is detected which is not automatically corrected by the hardware. A typical routine would be to handle errors detected while reading data in from auxiliary storage such as a tape unit. The first thing that the error routine would do is to interrogate various sections of the programming system and hardware indicators to identify the files involved. Typically, the routine would then backspace the tape and try to read the record again. The re-read philosophy is based on the assumption that most of the read failures are transient in nature. This may be caused by such things as dust or other foreign material deposited on tape, a weak recording signal, flaking of the magnetic oxide, slight skewing of the tape along its guides, or some other item. The number of times that the error routine attempts to re-read the record can vary from installation to installation. It is not unusual to see up to one hundred re-reads before the error routine gives up. Failing to successfully read the information, the routine then turns control over to a secondary routine oriented to the particular application program. This secondary routine determines whether it can reconstruct the lost data by any means, or skip that particular record and continue processing the others, or in fact has to give up the ghost and abort the run.

There are similar routines for handling other detected errors in the system. The reason for identifying these routines as part of functional mixes is that they can become quite lengthy and time consuming. If in this example we had only three errors while reading the input, the error routine could cause up to three hundred additional reads of the input tape—fifty percent more reads for the purpose of error correction than we had expected in normal reads alone. If the application were bound by the input tape, our time would be $2\frac{1}{2}$ times longer than projected. This increase in time is based on an error rate of only 1.5 percent: 3 records out of 200.

Finally, there is also shown the set of routines for the input/output control section. These routines, in Figure 3.30, provide input and output to operate in parallel with the processing of the data. We have indicated in the main flow chart the initiation of the read operation. That block usually transfers control to the I/O control section to actually set up the right buffers and to initiate the auxiliary devices activity. When this is accomplished, control is passed back to the read block so that the program can continue. If there are no data available in memory for the program to continue, the read routine will cause the program to wait until data are available.

Assuming that data are in memory and the program is proceeding, the next entry into the I/O control section will be caused when the device completes the transfer of new data as requested. At that point, whatever program section in process is interrupted and control is passed to the I/O control section. The routine does all of the housekeeping to let the deblocking routines and other sections of the program know that more data are available. At that point, the I/O routines may or may not initiate another read from the device. If the programmer who set up the application provided the "go-ahead" to the I/O control system, then it will automatically initiate the reading of the next sequential record. This is done in coordination with the read block on the main flow chart. On the other hand, if the I/O routine cannot provide this function, the next initiation of I/O must come from the application program, itself. After the I/O control section has performed its function, control is passed back to the particular program section that was in process when the I/O interruption occurred (unless a higher priority program gained control). Similar functions are provided for the writing of output.

In this particular application, we can assume that the input will be re-

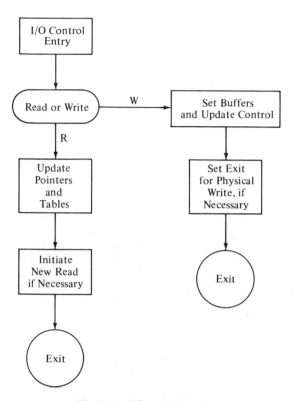

Fig. 3.30 I/O control section.

initiated automatically by the I/O control section, but that the writing of output will be initiated by the main program each time. In this case, we will have 601 entries into the I/O control entry block. 200 are from the initiation of writing, 200 from the termination of writing, 1 from the initiation of the first read, and 200 from the termination of a previous read. The 199 additional reads are initiated within the same pass of the section as the termination of the previous read.

This example is oversimplified, but demonstrates the type of activity which should be taken into account when structuring a functional mix.

Given the table of functional items and their incidences, the next step is to perform the equivalent of a kernel analysis for each item. Assuming that we have done this, let us examine the inner loop to complete the exercise.

Assume that we have calculated the following times for the inner loop sections as shown in Figure 3.31.

Sections C and D were the data dependent alternatives. If we simply average the two times and use 325 units, the inner loop time of blocks A

Section	Time
A	100 units
B	200
C	350
D	300
E	200
F	150 (1:5 only)

Fig. 3.31   Inner loop function times.

through E is 825 units. Our error in using a simple average is on the order of 3%. A timing table for the inner loop appears as shown in Figure 3.32.

Section	Time	Incidence	Total Time
A	100	250000	25,000,000
B	200	250000	50,000,000
C, D	325	250000	81,250,000
E	200	250000	50,000,000
F	150	50000	7,500,000
Total			213,750,000

Fig. 3.32   Inner loop timing table.

A similar calculation can be performed for all items of the functional mix.

The disadvantage of the functional mix is essentially the same as for the kernel analysis. Each item must be programmed in each system under consideration. In addition to the advantage of more accuracy in estimating, there is another advantage. A functional mix of a single application was demonstrated. We can in fact establish a functional mix of many applications, especially where common routines are being used by the applications. For such routines as the I/O control section, deblock routines, error control routines, and many other service functions, we can establish functional mixes across the entire load on a computing system. Today, we find most of these functions established in the operating systems as control program services. This even extends into the main flow of the application program as "macro-instructions." For example, the tallies on the three loops of the above example could well be structured with the same coding, but using different index registers and other pointers. Given a high incidence of such a function, a macro-instruction may be constructed so that the application programmer need write only a single instruction. After that, the translator program (compiler, assembler, etc.) can provide the complete machine level coding to perform the function. Determining the time of a functional item once will suffice for all of the applications in the functional mix. The unique portions of each application must be addressed for a separate analysis.

3.5. OTHER CONSIDERATIONS

In Section 3.1, we considered another class of indicators of CPU performance, an example of *rate*. Rate is normally used in the design cycle of a CPU, especially where we are implementing a new computer in an established architecture. The simplest characteristic is the basic cycle of the CPU. Within a basic cycle, we normally see such items as inter-register transfers or cycles through an adder. In the middle 1960's, we saw computers with cycle times from 500 nanoseconds to 50 nanoseconds. We can reasonably expect to see even faster cycle times. The cycle in itself does not provide much information to anyone not intimately familiar with the design. In some CPU's, an instruction can be decoded within a single cycle. On others, it may require two or three cycles. This is just for the *decode* of the instruction. Additional cycles are required to obtain information from memory and to execute the instruction.

The next higher level of information is the instruction rate. This information is generally expressed as some number of instructions per second. We usually see the rate expressed in thousands of instructions per second, called "KIPS", millions of instructions per second, called "MIPS", or billions of instructions per second, "BIPS". When we see the expression trillions of instructions per second, I suppose it will be referred to as "TIPS". The student can proceed through the next few magnitudes at his convenience.

The instruction rate is variable within a CPU, depending on what types of instructions are considered in the rate. Typically, a few basic instructions that we see rated are the fastest instruction or set of instructions in the system, e.g., an add instruction. We also see instruction rate information based on a mix of instructions or on a kernel. When an instruction rate is based on a combination of instructions, the analyst needs to know the basis of the combination. Other than that, taking the rate of the fastest instruction will probably provide the greatest amount of information to the analyst.

Occasionally, using instruction rates for the comparison of CPU's of different architecture can be misleading. Consider the case of two different CPU's performing the function X. It was desired to compare the instruction rates (not the rate of performing the function). The first CPU had a rate of 5, while the second CPU had a rate of 15. (Again, these numbers are ficticious, but are indicative of the magnitude.) It appears that the second CPU is much faster than the first. However, the first CPU was using an instruction set which allowed much more function to be performed in one instruction. This expanded instruction was slower than the types equivalent to the second system. When function times were compared, the first CPU performed it about twice as fast as the second. The second CPU had to perform many more very high speed instructions to perform the same function. It is dangerous to use instruction rate information to compare CPU's of different architectures unless the analyst fully understands the complete nature of the comparison.

Variations of memory bandwidth or memory bus rate are also used to express CPU performance. Again, this is normally used in the design phase of the system. The designer uses this information to achieve a balanced design so that the memory bus can handle not only the CPU's requirement for data and instructions but also peak data rates to and from auxiliary storage.

3.6. A NOTE ON CPU PERFORMANCE

This chapter has been devoted to estimating CPU performance. In many cases, the performance of the CPU is the governing factor in a system's performance of an application or set of applications. However, too many times, the CPU has been used as the guide to system's performance erroneously. This is due particularly to ignoring input/output requirements. The techniques of instruction mixes, kernel analysis, or functional mixes allow for I/O activity to be taken into consideration; the omission lies with the analyst.

Historically, the CPU was the most expensive element of the whole computing installation. In the early 1960's, we saw that not only was the CPU a minor part, but that the entire computing system accounted for less than half the cost of an installation. Within the computing system, the CPU was becoming the minor cost element, especially where large banks of data or communications networks are involved. We still find estimates of CPU performance as useful end products when used in the right environment. And, of course, it is a necessary ingredient in assessing system's performance.

PROBLEMS

1. Given the following processor storage characteristics:

CPU	Cycle Time	Bits/access	Interleave
A	1.00 μsec	32	8
B	0.75 μsec	128	2
C	0.50 μsec	64	2

(a) Calculate MMBR using the formula in 3.1. Rank the CPU's.

(b) Calculate MMBR using the square root of the degree of interleave. Rank the CPU's.

2. Assume that CPU A in Figure 3.8 has available to it a high speed floating point arithmetic unit at an additional cost of 25 percent of the CPU cost. The unit provides the following instruction times.

Floating point Add   8 μsec
Floating point Mult/div   6 μsec

Using the instruction mix of Figure 3.7,

(a) What is new average instruction time?

(b) What is the relative performance of the CPU with the new feature compared to the unmodified CPU?

(c) On the basis of CPU performance only, is the cost increase worthwhile?

3. In the case of the decimal instruction requirement in Section 3.2 is it worthwhile on the mix in Figure 3.7 for the manufacturer of CPU B to add a hardware decimal feature which performs its function at the following cost?

(a) Operates at a speed of 10 μsec at 30 percent increase in CPU cost.

(b) Operates at a a speed of 20 μsec at a 15 percent increase in CPU cost.

(c) Still using the same mix, what is the relative cost/performance between these two options?

4. We have three CPU's and their associated instruction times in microseconds.

Instruction	CPU A	CPU B	CPU C
Load Index	0.75	1.50	4.0
Load Arith-mem	0.75	1.50	4.0
Load Arith-register	---	0.75	2.5
Add Index	0.75	1.50	4.0
Add Arith-mem	0.85	2.50	7.0
Add Arith-register	---	1.75	6.0
Multiply-mem	2.00	7.50	20.0
Multiply-register	---	6.75	19.0
Branch	1.00	1.50	4.0

Assume that CPU A operates only with compiler output as shown in Figure 3.10, CPU B operates only with output as shown in Figure 3.12, and CPU C operates with that shown in Figure 3.14. Omitting the time of the compilation itself,

(a) Which CPU can perform its *own* case fastest?

(b) What is the relative performance of the three using A as a base?

(c) What is the average instruction time for each CPU in its own case?

(d) Using the instruction mix percentage summary in Figure 3.17, calculate the average instruction times for the three CPU's for each case.

5. We have two CPU's and their associated instruction times in microseconds.

Instruction	CPU A	CPU B
Add	0.75	1.00
Load	0.75	0.75
Move	0.50	0.75
Multiply	1.50	2.00
Store	0.75	0.75
Multiply/Add	---	2.50

(a) Given the coding in Figure 3.20, what is the relative performance of B compared to A?

(b) Now use the coding in Figure 3.22 to produce the time for CPU B. What is its relative performance compared to CPU A, using the original code?

(c) What is the average instruction time for CPU B in each of the two cases?

6. Assume that a CPU has the following instruction times when the instructions are considered individually. (These are the same times as CPU B in Problem 5.)

Instruction	Time
Add	1.00
Load	0.75
Move	0.75
Multiply	2.00
Store	0.75

(a) Use these times to calculate the time of the polynomial evaluation as given by the mix in Figure 3.21.

Now assume that whenever an add instruction is immediately preceded by a multiply instruction 0.25 μsec. can be deducted from the add time.

(b) Use this assumption to calculate the time of the polynomial evaluation as given by the code in Figure 3.20.

(c) What is the average instruction time in each case?

(d) What is the relative performance of the kernel to the mix?

7. If in the case of averaging the block times of C and D as shown in Figure 3.31, the transit time of C was 100 units and the transit time of D was 550 units,

(a) What is the percentage error in calculating the time of the inner loop from A through E?

(b) If it turned out that 90 percent of the entries were through D, what is the percentage error in both the original case and this case?

4 SYSTEMS ANALYSIS TECHNIQUES

In the preceding chapters, there has been a concentration on estimating the performance of units, whether of auxiliary units or the central processor unit itself. As stated before, when the performance of a job is governed by the performance of an individual unit, such as the CPU, then a unit assessment will provide a usable assessment of the system.

We will now be concerned with the evaluation of a system performing work where its assessment is not satisfactorily covered by the assessment of a unit. This situation is common because of the interdependency between the CPU and its associated input/output operations.

Presented in this chapter are some of the simpler techniques to project system performance. We will be concerned with the determination of throughput and/or response time attributes. There is a gray area between a synthetic technique and a simulative technique. (The general area of simulation will be discussed in the next chapter.) The principal distinction here will be in the detail level of the technique.

4.1. RELATIVE SYSTEMS THROUGHPUT

For some time now, the concept of throughput for computing systems has been accepted. Unfortunately, there have been many definitions of this popular word. Basically, throughput is an expression of work capability per unit time. If the application being performed were limited by the ability to read or print lines, the throughput would be discussed in cards per minute or lines per minute. If the application were more complex, the throughput of the system could be considered in terms of its end product, e.g., invoices per hour. In the case of a compiler, the throughput could be described in terms of (input) statements processed per minute.

In the case of a system installed in a "job shop" environment, the throughput of the system would be discussed in terms of jobs per hour, day, or shift. In the case of a message switching system, throughput could be peak message capability per minute. The peak rate would probably be chosen since there could be a wide variation of actual message rates, depending on the operators' inputs.

When we consider interactive systems such as those found in the concept of time sharing, response time for a given load is generally used as the expression for the system's performance. However, a throughput rate of transactions per minute could be established for such a system.

Because of the diverse usage of the term throughput, we need a more succinct definition when using the term as a basis of comparison between two or more systems. "Relative systems throughput" may be defined as follows:

Relative systems throughput is a relative estimate of the performance of a computing system when compared to some base computing system. It is the ratio of the time of computation *of a given load* on the base system to the time of computation of *that same given load* on the comparing system. It may be expressed by the formula:

$$RST = \frac{Tb}{Tn},$$

where *RST* is relative system throughput
Tb is the time of computation of the base system
Tn is the time of computation on the comparing system.

Notice that the RST definition does not explicitly take into account the other attributes of a computing system, response time (or turnaround time), and availability. Relative system throughput is therefore an assessment of a system's processing capability during that time that the work is under the influence and control of the system and the system is operating in an error free mode. The reason for choosing this ratio rather than the inverse is essentially esthetic. If a system is bigger or better, we like to see a higher rating number associated with it. This is in line with figures of merit computation.

The definition of the base system is as follows:

The base computing system is an operational entity consisting of interconnected components and devices of an electronic computer, *and* a set of programs which allow work to be performed (control program, compilers, etc.), *and* a set of procedures or application programs, *and* the data which are processed by those programs.

In the definition of the base system, the elements of the interconnected computer are collectively known as "the configuration." The set of programs which allow work to be performed are generally known as "the programming support." These two elements taken together are generally referred to as "the system's options." The procedures and the application programs along with their data are referred to as "environmental options" or usually "environments." Within the environments, we also include information about the use of the system's options, especially the use of the compilers and other major features. Even though the number of system options is very large (almost astronomical when taking into account the number of combinations available), it is still quite small when compared to the number of environmental options. To aid in the interpretation of results and to allow timely computational processes, there is a tendency to establish "average" environments. In the early days, the two natural environments were our old friends, scientific and commercial. If any particular system were to be projected for use in both of the environments, then two evaluations were made.

As computers became more "general purpose" in their application, getting away from the traditional roles of scientific or commercial, and as users also started putting more diverse applications on their systems, the need for a re-orientation of environments became more demanding. The primary re-orientation was in the form of expanding the number of "average" environments along some line of interest, such as the end use of the product. Another way of establishing environments would be by basic industry orientation. This would be especially useful to manufacturers and consultants who are concerned with a wide application of the systems. Yet another way of establishing environments would be by patterns of use along the lines of "small," "intermediate," and "large" users. Naturally, a combination of these criteria along with any other criteria of interest to the recipient of the evaluation can be constructed.

The re-orientation has had a subtle effect on techniques of comparative evaluation. Where once a technique was sensitive to particular attributes found, for example, in scientific computation, the techniques for multiple environments must be sensitive to *any* attribute of the system which may be called upon by any of the environments.

4.2. FORMULA TIMING

The intention of formula timing is to provide timing estimates to perform certain applications. To cover a broad range of input data, ideally we would want a formula which is in itself relatively independent of the data content. At the subroutine level, we may consider the simple example of performing a square root of some variable. The routine may normally take 100 μsec to perform, except when the input variable is zero or negative. Then it may take only 10 μsec to exit the routine to either the normal exit (with a zero function) or an error exit (with no function computed). The time of that routine is data dependent. We can assume that the negative argument is an error and does not happen often in practice. We may or may not assume that the zero entry is normally expected. If it is not, then we can use the normal time of 100 μsec whenever we need to estimate the time of the square root routine.

Sometimes the formula is a little more complex. Consider a formula for the time to calculate an area by Simpson's rule. A typical formula would appear as follows:

$$T = A + R(B + C*N + D*M + E*(M**2)) + F*N$$

where T is time of computation
A, . . . , F are constants for the problem
R is the number of points supplied as part of the original curve
M is the degree of the interpolation polynomial
N is the number of equidistant pairs

Even though the formula is complex, the input information is generally known to the user. The constants are produced by the originator of the program.

In some cases, it is easier and more useful to provide timing tables rather than just the formulae. An example of this approach would be the provision of timing estimates for a sorting routine. Such a table is shown in Figure 4.1.

System: X
Main Storage Available: Y
Media: Z
Record Size: 200 char.

Units	Channels	Switched?	Time in Minutes for Volumes in Thousands				
			5	10	20	50	100
5	1	No	2.7	5.1	10.0	27	58
5	2	No	2.3	4.0	7.9	21	43
5	2	Yes	2.1	3.6	7.0	18	37

Fig. 4.1 Sort timing table—extract.

There are many variables in using such a table. Depending on the control program used in a system, an entire volume of sort tables may be selected.

Next in consideration is the particular machine or system type. The next criterion is the main storage available to perform the sort. The media used (number and type of I/O devices) is, of course, very important to the timing.

In Figure 4.1, there is chosen an extract of a sort timing table for system X with main storage Y and media type Z available. The three particular lines show the effects of having 5 I/O units available across a variety of channel arrangements. In the first line, all five units are on one channel. In the second line, the units are distributed across two channels. In the third line, the units are "switchable" across either channel as determined by the program. So given, say, 50,000 records of 200 characters, we see that with a configuration of 5 units on 1 channel, the sort routine will take 27 minutes. On the other hand, if the configuration has 5 units on 2 channels with switching, the time is 18 minutes.

To consider another approach, let us choose the act of timing compilations. For projecting compile time, one may do a calculation involving amount of CPU time required, amount of I/O time required, dependencies of data sets and other attributes; or we can consider the act of compiling to be just another application and the compiler to be a known application program. It is possible to express a timing formula for this application just as one can express a timing formula for a known sort program or a known matrix inversion program. Even though a complete timing expression would have a large number of terms (twenty or so), in many cases we can calculate to satisfactory accuracy using a three term equation. Therefore the job time of compiling is expressed by the formula:

$$T_c = K + n*R + p*S,$$

where T_c is time of compilation

K is a constant factor in the process of compiling
R is the time per source card of input
S is the time per additional subprogram after the first

In evaluating the equation, n is the number of source cards in a program and p is the number of additional subprograms after the first.

Assume that we had a formula for timing compilations as follows:

$$T_c = 1.0 + 0.012n + 0.24p \quad \text{(time in seconds)}$$

Further, assume that we wished to time out 100 compilations, distributed as shown in Figure 4.2.

To make the estimate calls for the repetitive application of the formula. A timing table can be constructed to aid in the application.

In Figure 4.3, we see that each class of compile activity is arranged with the input data to the formula. We have the number of jobs in each class, the

Number	Source Statements	Subroutines (after first)
50	200	0
20	500	3
20	1000	5
10	2000	10

Fig. 4.2   Distribution of compilations.

number of source cards in each job, and the number of subroutines in each job. Next, we calculate the time for each job in the class, and then multiply that time by the number of jobs in the class. Summing the class time over the whole set of jobs, we have a grand total of 882 sec, or about fifteen minutes to schedule for the act of compilation.

Number of Jobs	Source	Subprograms (after first)	Time/Job	Time/Class
50	200	0	3.4 sec	170.0 sec
20	500	3	7.7	154.0
20	1000	5	14.2	284.0
10	2000	10	27.4	274.0
			Total:	882.0 sec

Fig. 4.3   Compile timing tables.

This estimate is for the act of compilation only, and does not include any other application activity. Furthermore, it does not take into account any effects of multiprogramming. (This will be considered later.) It does represent the amount of time that should be scheduled on a computing system in a complete serial processing fashion.

In defining a time of compilation, we should consider just what went into the time. In many systems, the act of compilation is broken down into many separate pieces. For example, we have systems which first read all required data into a temporary auxiliary storage and then call for the compilation. The compiler itself may not produce machine readable code, but may rely on yet another program to organize the coding for execution. In some cases, there is yet another program to load this code into storage for the program to actually start. When discussing timing formulae, the analyst must determine what is or is not included. Was it the entire process from the reading of the first bit of input until the program is ready to begin execution, or was it for a smaller portion which covers only the act of compilation itself.

4.3. PROFILE CONVERSION

As a means of introduction, consider that each job on a system has a "basic system profile" as shown in Figure 4.4. A basic system profile is merely a method of graphically representing the summary of activities in a system.

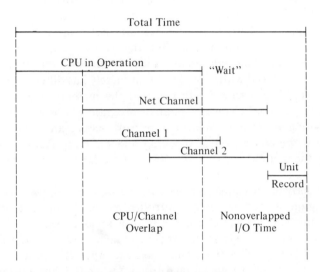

Fig. 4.4 Basic system profile.

This figure indicates a breakdown of the activity within a job execution. The bar graph is, of course, an averaging or summary process in that input-output occurs throughout a program and does not all occur at the end of execution as the graph might imply. The characteristics to be noted are:

(a) CPU in Operation. This is defined as the amount of time the CPU is doing some computing as opposed to merely branching in a wait loop or holding in wait state.

(b) Net Channel. The amount of time that one or more channels are in operation, reading or writing records. This time includes the delay time of the units and their actual data transmission time.

(c) Channel 1, Channel 2. These are the representations of individual channels in operation. It is also from this data that we obtain channel-to-channel overlap.

(d) Unit Record. The amount of time that the system is engaged in unit record operation.

(e) CPU and Channel Overlap. A measure of the time that the CPU is doing useful computing while one or more channels are in operation.

(f) Nonoverlapped I/O Time. The amount of time that the CPU is in a "wait condition," unable to proceed with computation until an input or output operation is completed.

The method of calculation is to apply unit improvement factors to the section of the job profile which is under the influence of the unit. (Contrary to public opinion, a CPU speed increase will not cause a system to "wait" any faster. It may cause more of it, but that doesn't help much.)

The method of profile conversion is ideally suited to the situations where a unit is to be replaced with a like kind that merely has different performance characteristics. The reason for this is that the method does not take into account any potential change of control program philosophy or change in the computing procedure. Within a narrow scope, an exception to this restriction is the conversion of blocking and buffering factors. Within this restriction the method has the advantage that a large number of configuration options can be examined using very simple and high speed algorithms.

The underlying principle to profile conversion is that any block of time, called a region, is predominately controlled by some unit's activity. If more than one unit is operating concurrantly in a region, then the effect on the region is governed by the lessor improvement factor involved. If, for example, a region has both CPU activity and magnetic tape activity, and if the projected CPU has an improvement factor of 1.5 while the tape has an improvement factor of 2.0, the region is affected by only the improvement factor of 1.5.

In the profile in Figure 4.5, there are indicated two points of invariance,

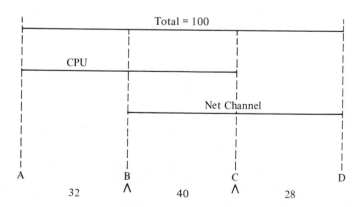

Fig. 4.5 Points of invariance.

points B and C. When projecting improvements in performance due to CPU improvement, point B is chosen as the point of invariance. This is because all other activity from B to D is dominated by some other element. (From C to D, the CPU is not active at all.) On the other hand, when projecting improvements in performance due to I/O improvement, point C is chosen as the point of invariance. Similarly, this is because the region A to C is dominated by CPU activity. (The region A to B does not have any I/O component to affect its performance.)

When projections are made which involve both CPU and I/O improvements, the region B to C is compressed by the least improvement factor of any activity in the region, and then the other areas are recalculated to their new profile.

Consider the following numeric example:

Total Job Time	=	100 (units of time)
CPU Only	=	32 (A to B)
Overlapped I/O	=	40 (B to C)
Nonoverlapped I/O	=	28 (C to D)
CPU Improvement	=	4 times faster

Since the input/output is not effected, the *time* of that activity will remain the same. The relationship between overlapped and nonoverlapped time will change, but the sum is invariant.

Applying the CPU performance factor to the CPU only portion of the profile, one obtains the following:

CPU Only = 32/4	= 8 (New A to B)
Sum of Other Activity	= 68 (B to D)
Total Job Time	= 76

Relative system throughput for that profile would be:

$$RST = \tfrac{100}{76} = 1.3.$$

To demonstrate the effect of input/output improvement, let us assume that the profile in Figure 4.5 consists solely of CPU and magnetic tape activity. Further assume that the magnetic tape improvement factor is 2.0. The calculation is as follows:

Sum of other activity	72 (A to C)
Tape Only = $\frac{28}{2}$	14 (new C to D)
Total	86

Relative system throughput for the profile would be:

$$\text{RST} = \tfrac{100}{86} = 1.16.$$

Before proceeding to the next example, we may wonder just where did we get the CPU improvement factor of 4.0 and the magnetic tape improvement factor of 2.0. These unit improvement factors must be obtained just as described in previous chapters. In the case of the CPU, if the circuitry does not provide for a uniform increase of each instruction, then the improvement factor must be determined by either an instruction mix calculation, a kernel evaluation, or a functional mix calculation.

Similarly, the improvement factor of magnetic tape is governed not only by its motion and transmission characteristics, but by the length of the physical records that are used. Again, unless each of its characteristics is uniformly increased, the average physical record length of the profile must be established.

Up to this point, we have made simple single variable projections with the basic system profile. Before proceeding to the two variable case, we should discuss the attributes of the resulting profile in each example.

When we projected system's improvement due to an improvement in the CPU component as shown in Figure 4.6, the region A to B was identified as the new CPU only area.

Although the region B to D was identified, the new point C was not. Even though the region B to D remains constant, the point C collapses towards B because of the CPU improvement. The complete projection would be as follows:

Region	Old	New
A to B	32	8
B to D	68	68 (invariant)
B to C	40	10
C to D	28	58 (obtained by (B–D) minus new (B–C))

The new profile in this case is shown in Figure 4.7.

We have a similar case in the projection of a new system's profile by the improvement of magnetic tape only. In this case, the point B collapses towards the point C. The new profile is shown in Figure 4.8.

Region	Old	New
A to C	72	72 (invariant)
A to B	32	52 (obtained by subtraction)
B to C	40	20 (new B to C)
C to D	28	14

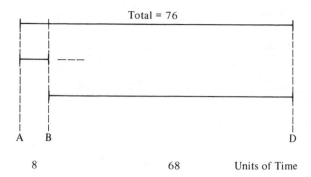

Fig. 4.6 Intermediate profile.

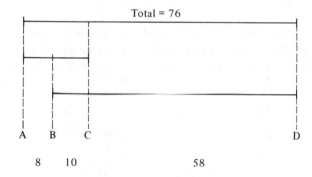

Fig. 4.7 Result of CPU improvement.

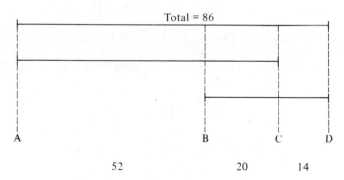

Fig. 4.8 Result of tape improvement.

Now let us consider making both improvements at the same time. In Figure 4.9, the region A to B is governed by the CPU improvement because that is the only activity in the region.

Similarly, the region C to D is governed by the speed of magnetic tape.

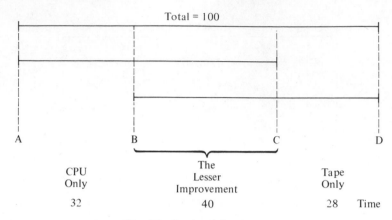

Fig. 4.9   Regional dominance.

In the region B to C, both the CPU and the magnetic tape are active. The length of time of the region is governed by the lesser improvement factor, in this case that of magnetic tape. Therefore the region B to D will be affected by the magnetic tape improvement factor. The initial calculation is as follows:

$$\text{CPU activity} = \tfrac{32}{4} \quad = \; 8 \; (\text{new A to B})$$
$$\text{Magnetic tape} = \tfrac{68}{2} \quad = 34 \; (\text{new B to D})$$
$$\text{Total} \qquad\qquad\quad = 42$$

Relative system throughput for the result of these changes is

$$\text{RST} = \tfrac{100}{42} = 2.38.$$

Again, we can place the point C to establish the new region of overlap B to C. This is obtained by dividing the original region by the greater improvement factor, in this case, the CPU. The complete projection is as follows:

Region	Old	New
A to B	32	8
B to C	40	10
C to D	28	24

The new region C to D is obtained by subtracting the new region B to C from the new region B to D. The resulting profile of this case is shown in Figure 4.10.

Using a basic system profile, simple approximations may be made to

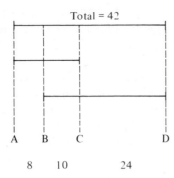

Fig. 4.10   Result of CPU and tape improvement.

determine the effects of blocking and buffering on magnetic tape. This of course assumes that there is processor storage available to handle the increased space requirements. The method of calculation is to determine a tape improvement factor from each of the assumed record lengths and then apply that factor as shown above.

It is possible to use profile conversion to project system performance due to a change in CPUs with different architectures if the assumption that the problem procedure did not change is reasonably valid. In this case, we can obtain through kernel analysis or functional mix analysis the relative performance factors of the CPU's. This factor can then be used in a profile conversion.

The profile conversion works least well when direct access devices are concerned. This is because two of the three attributes of speed of a direct access device are random, but bounded, in nature. In the general case, a direct access device has a physical arm motion to position read/write heads over the track or tracks which contain the data, a rotational delay while waiting for the data to pass under the read/write heads, and the transmission rate. In order to utilize profile conversion, we should distinguish at least between the time spent in moving the arm and the time spent in rotational delay and data transmission. Such a profile is shown in Figure 4.11.

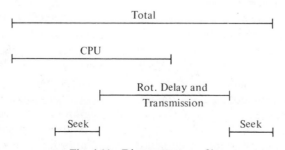

Fig. 4.11   Direct access profile.

In the case of a drum type device which does not have a movable arm, there are the attributes of rotational delay and data transmission rate. For a drum type device, there is, of course, no requirement to determine arm movement activity.

Considering first the portion of time spent in rotational delay and data transmission, we need to have additional information concerning the average record length just as in the case of magnetic tape. However, we also need to know the number of records transmitted. This portion of the calculation is applicable to both direct access devices with movable arms as well as drum type devices. The first element of calculation is to determine whether we can approximate from the given data, the average rotational delay of the direct access device from which the system profile was obtained. This information is used as a check to determine the validity of using a profile conversion technique.

Assume that we are taking a basic system profile from a system which has input/output on a direct access device with the characteristics of a 40 msec rotational period and a transmission rate of 200 kb/sec. Further assume that the information from the profile indicates that we have spent a total of 48 seconds reading or writing records regarding a direct access device. Further assume that we have obtained the information that the activity represents the transmission of 2000 records having an average record length of 1000 characters. Using average record length, we can calculate the average time that it takes to fetch a record using average rotational delay plus transmission time. In this case, we have an average rotational delay of 20 msec ($\frac{1}{2}$ of 40 msec rotational period) plus 5 msec of transmission time (1000 characters times 0.005 msec per character). For 2000 such records, we have a theoretical time of 50 seconds of record fetch time. This is sufficiently close to the observed time of 48 seconds to justify using average rotational delay on some projected device.

If we had observed only 20 seconds of record fetch activity on the basic system profile, we can calculate that there is on the average only 5 milliseconds of rotational delay in fetching each record. This is the area in which the analyst must be wary of using profile conversion to project the effects of converting to a faster device. With that magnitude of rotational delay, we can assume that the program in the system has been "tuned" to the rotational speed of the device and is trying to minimize rotational delay as such. Sometimes, this is referred to as having the program "in synch" (synchronization) with the device. The danger in using profile conversion is in the fact that a projection may be made to a device with a sufficiently fast rotational period so that the CPU cannot perform the necessary instructions to ask for another operation from the device in time to catch the beginning of the record on that rotation of the device. The net result is that the device would have to make a complete rotation (or almost complete rotation) in order to position the data under the read/write heads for record transmission. If we were projecting the effect of replacing the 40 msec rotational device with a 30 msec device, it could well turn out in actual practice that rather than having an average rotational delay of 5 msec, we may find an average of 29 msec just because the CPU could not do the processing in time to request another record.

The second portion of time to consider is the time spent in arm movement for the direct access device. In this case, in addition to the amount of time spent in moving the arm, we need to know the number of times the arm moved. We should distinguish the number of arm movements from the number of requests for position (seeks), because not all seeks result in an actual arm movement. If we divide the total arm movement time by the number of times the arm had to move, we can calculate the average distance and time of each movement. For example, if we have 40 seconds of arm movement time and 1000 times that the arm had to move, we can calculate an average motion time of 40 msec per move. Given the physical characteristics of the device, we can then calculate the number of tracks or cylinders traversed on the average. If we also account for the total number of seeks, we can then determine the number of seek requests that did not result in an arm movement.

In using profile conversion to calculate a new arm motion time, we must assume that the data on the device maintain the same spatial relationship. If the data are rearranged on the device then profile conversion of an arm movement may provide misleading results.

Let us consider the following profile as shown in Figure 4.12. Here we have the profile broken into five regions.

A to B is CPU only. B to C is disk arm movement overlapped with CPU in operation. C to D is record fetch (rotational delay plus data transmission time) overlapped with CPU operation. D to E is record fetch, nonoverlapped,

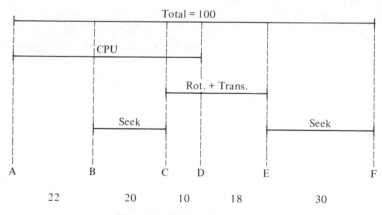

Fig. 4.12 Disk profile example.

and E to F is arm movement, nonoverlapped. Assume that we have the following times in each region as follows:

CPU only	22 sec
Arm Move/CPU	20
Record Fetch/CPU	10
Record Fetch only	18
Arm Movement only	30
Total	100 sec

Let us also assume that the system which produced the profile had a device which had the following characteristics:

Arm movement (Minimum)	20 msec
(Average)	75 msec
(Maximum)	150 msec
Rotation Period	40 msec
Transmission Rate	200 kb/sec

The additional information about file structure is that we transmitted 1000 records with an average record length of 1000 characters each, and that we performed 1000 arm movements during the arm motion time. First checking the record fetch time to see if the rotational delay approaches the average, we have a theoretical average record fetch time of 25 msec (20 msec average rotational delay plus 5 msec of transmission time). The profile indicates that we have an average of 28 msec for each record fetch (28 sec divided by 1000 fetches). There is a 12% difference between the observed fetch time and the theoretical fetch time. We will probably be safe is using an average fetch time for the projected device.

We now check the observed average arm movement time against the theoretical arm movement time. The observed average is 50 msec (50 seconds divided by 1000 arm moves). This is somewhat less than the rated average for the device. At this point, we can use one of two approaches. We can either linearly interpolate between the average and the minimum to establish a proportion for the projected device, or we can recognize the fact that many devices have a non-linear relationship between distance traveled and arm movement time. The former is certainly the easier approach and may suffice for the evaluation. However, if the degree of error in doing so is intolerable, then we can utilize the precise specifications of the observed unit to determine the average distance traveled (track to track distance) and then apply the distance formula on the projected device to determine its particular arm movement time for the number of records involved.

In this example, let us merely interpolate linearly between the minimum and average arm movement times to establish a proportion for the projected device. Assume that the new device has characteristics as follows:

Arm Movement (Minimum)	15 msec	
(Average)	45 msec	
(Maximum)	100 msec	
Rotation Period	40 msec	
Transmission Rate	300 kb/sec	

First, we will calculate the improvement in record fetch time by calculating a theoretical average fetch time for the new device and establishing a fetch improvement time for that portion of the profile. Then we will establish an arm movement improvement time by taking the same proportion between minimum and average arm movement time on the new device that was established for the observed device. An arm movement improvement factor will then be established for that activity.

The average fetch time of the new device for a 1000 character record is 23.3 msec. (Average rotational delay of 20 msec plus a transmission time of 3.3 msec.) The improvement factor due to record fetch is therefore 1.07 (25 msec divided by 23.3 msec).

Taking the linear proportion of minimum to average access time of the projected device, we have an average arm movement time of 31.4 msec. The improvement factor for arm movement is therefore 1.59. (An observed average of 50 msec divided by a new theoretical average of 31.4 msec.)

Utilizing the same rules of conversion as before, since there is no change in CPU characteristics, we see that the region A through D is dominated by the CPU, and therefore remains the same. At this point, however, we can at best bound the effects of the direct access device improvement. The regions B to C and E to F are portrayed as two separate regions, but are in fact two portions of a continuum of activity. The question then becomes, should we use only the region E to F in reducing job time, or should we use the sum of the regions B to C and E to F to calculate an improvement. The conservative approach would be to use only the region E to F. Using the conservative approach, we see the following calculation. Nonoverlapped arm motion time is 30 sec. The improvement factor for this region is 1.59; therefore the new region time is 18.9 sec.

The optimistic approach would be to consider that the total amount of arm motion time is 50 sec, the sum of regions B to C and E to F. Using the improvement factor of 1.59, the total reduction in time is 18.6 sec, the difference between the observed time of 50 sec less the new time of 31.4 sec. Using this philosophy, we would start reducing first of all the unoverlapped arm movement region as much as possible, and then reduce the overlapped region by any amount not accounted for. Reducing the nonoverlapped region of

30 sec by the amount of 18.6 sec leaves a new nonoverlapped region of 11.4 sec in the new profile.

When using profile conversion to project effects due to arm movement time, the best thing to do is a double calculation, one conservative and one optimistic. The range between the two results will indicate a confidence range for the conversion technique. The reason that there is no firm point of invariance is that the profile is an averaging or summary process. The region B to C represents the total amount of time that the CPU was able to proceed with some amount of computation after initiating an arm movement. The region C to D indicates that the CPU is able to carry on with computation through the issuing of a positioning command and into part of the fetch of the record itself before it has to wait on the complete transmission. However, the region C to D may be present because of the fact that although the CPU issued a seek, no arm movement in fact took place. It could also happen when there is a transmission without any associated positioning command. This could well be the case when processing a set of sequential records from a direct access device. There may be only one positioning requirement for many records transmitted.

In the case of converting the record transmission portion, empirical studies indicate that we can still use the point D as a point of invariance. Although it may appear that point C is the time at which any arm movement is terminated, thus allowing a record transmission to initiate, this is not the case. Again, we should keep in mind the fact that the profile is a summary of activity and does not contain *ordinal* information about the sequence of events. To maintain ordinal information of the sequence of events, we should turn to a simulative approach.

In view of the restrictions above, we should use profile conversion techniques in the case of direct assess devices to determine the *boundaries* of system performance. With this in mind, let us calculate the boundaries of performance on the example given in Figure 4.12. The conservative approach results in the following calculation:

$$
\begin{array}{lll}
\text{Region A to D} & & = 52.0 \text{ sec (dominated by CPU)} \\
\text{Region D to E} = \tfrac{18}{1.07} & & = 16.8 \text{ (record fetch improvement)} \\
\text{Region E to F} = \tfrac{30}{1.59} & & = 18.9 \text{ (arm movement improvement)} \\
\text{Total} & & = 87.7 \text{ sec.}
\end{array}
$$

The relative system throughput for this calculation is

$$ \text{RST} = \tfrac{100}{87.7} = 1.14. $$

The optimistic approach would be the following.

Region A to D   52.0 sec

Region D to E   16.8

Region E to F   11.4

Total   80.2 sec

The relative system throughput in this case would be

$$RST = \frac{100}{80.2} = 1.25.$$

Although we have indicated the simple interrelation between only the CPU and a single input/output device, the technique can apply to a profile in which several devices are operating concurrently. In the case of sequential devices such as magnetic tape, punched card equipment and printers, the technique is applied to each block of time just as we did in the case of magnetic tape alone. In the case of multiple direct access devices, we can have an overlap between the arm movement of one device with the record transmission of another. In this case, we should break the profile into many more portions as shown in Figure 4.13.

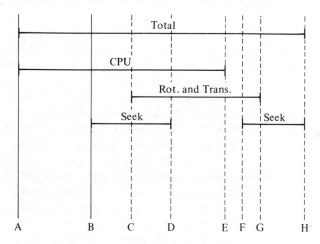

Fig. 4.13   Detailed profile of arm movement overlaps.

In this case, the regions are as follows:

A to B   CPU only in operation

B to C   CPU and arm movement

C to D   CPU and arm movement and data fetch

D to E   CPU and data fetch

E to F   Data fetch only

F to G   Arm movement and data fetch

G to H   Arm movement only

For those regions which have multiple activities, the least improvement factor governs the decrease in time for the region. In calculating an optimistic approach, we can take the sum of regions B to D and F to H in calculating arm movement time affected.

As the number of different types of activity are in concurrent operation, the complexity of the system profile becomes greater. We soon reach a point where the complexity taken into account with the enlarging confidence range of the results again indicates the need to resort to some other technique rather than continuing with profile conversion. When used in the correct circumstances, profile conversion offers a way to quickly calculate the boundaries of expected system performance for a wide range of configuration options.

4.4. SYNTHETIC MODELS

Synthesis is the determination of the whole from the combination of the parts. In computer system evaluation, a synthetic model builds up the total picture of the computing process by combining the parts, in this case, the subsystem activity. The synthetic model constructs the system activity from subsystem parts such as CPU activity, unit record activity, direct access activity, magnetic tape activity, and communications activity. These subsystem components are in turn structured from individual device activity. The device activity is determined from the incidence and volume of activity. The synthetic model combines the characteristics of the application program, the control program services and philosophy, and the configuration.

Many times, we are concerned with the performance of a system across a set of programs. In this case, we can exercise one of two options in setting up the evaluation technique. First, we can keep the characteristics of each individual application discrete, so that we can determine the effects of various system options for each program; or we can pre-average the entire set of applications so that we can determine the effect of the various system options for the *fixed set* of programs. When we pre-average the applications, we loose the individuality of the programs. The advantage to pre-averaging the characteristics is that this act can provide a relatively high speed algorithm to use in the analysis process. The basis of the synthetic technique will allow either option. The structure is a matter of convenience to the analyst.

4.4.1. Primitive Model

The applications are first analyzed for their subsystem activity. These subsystem activities are expressed in such forms as number of cards read,

number of lines printed, number of magnetic tape reads and writes distributed by record lengths, number of direct access device reads and writes
distributed by record lengths and location of files, and the amount of computing required in the CPU. The amount of CPU activity required may be
expressed as an amount of computing for each record read or written, or it
may be expressed as a total amount of computing time required for the complete application. This information forms the set of input to the model
which is generally known as the "application characteristics." In Figure 4.14,

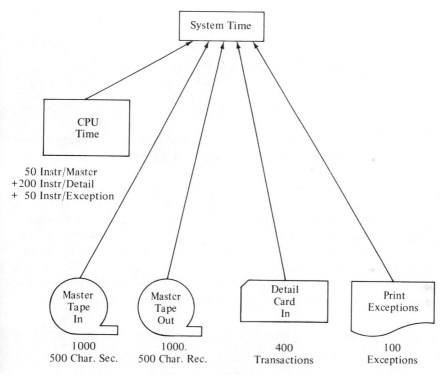

Fig. 4.14 Application characteristics.

we have the characteristics of a straightforward sequential processing
program. Here we see the CPU requirements expressed in terms of a particular type of product with number of instructions for each master record
processed, each transaction record processed, each detail record processed,
and each exception record printed. The other volumes for the class of device
are shown.

To synthesize this application on a particular configuration, we start with
the activity of individual devices. Let us assume that we have a configuration
which includes a 500 card per minute reader, a 1000 line per minute printer,

and magnetic tapes which have the characteristics of a 5 millisecond start/ stop time and a 90 kb per second transmission rate. From the volumes given above, we can construct the time of the device activity as shown in Figure 4.15.

Activity	Device	Rate	Volume	Time
Master In	Tape	5.0 + .011/char. msec	1000/500 char.	10.5 sec
Master Out	Tape	5.0 + .011/char. msec	1000/500 char.	10.5 sec
Detail In	Card reader	500 cpm	400 cards	48 sec
Exception Out	Printer	1000 lpm	100 lines	6 sec

Fig. 4.15   Device requirements.

The input magnetic tape requires 10.5 seconds of activity as does the output tape. The card reader requires 48 seconds, and the printer, 6 seconds.

In determining the time that the CPU requires, we are faced with several alternatives, depending on the amount of information that we are given or can assume about the CPU. Basically, all we know about the CPU activity is the type of CPU and the number of instructions that type of CPU requires to fulfill the application needs. If that is truly the limit of our knowledge, we can use an instruction execution rate of our configuration's CPU to estimate the amount of CPU time required. If we assume that we have a CPU capable of executing a maximum of 10,000 instructions per second, we can then translate the CPU requirements into a time as shown in Figure 4.16.

Instructions/activity	Time/activity	Activity	Time
50/master read	5.0 msec	1000	5.0 sec
200/detail	20.0 msec	400	8.0 sec
50/exception	5.0 msec	100	0.5 sec
Total			13.5 sec

Fig. 4.16   CPU time based on instruction rate.

The analyst may have further knowledge of the nature of the application and can therefore apply a more refined estimate of the CPU time. If, for example, he knows that the application is a commercial application such as an inventory update, he may be able to use the results of an average instruction time calculation from an instruction mix of a similar application. Given this knowledge, the average instruction time of that type of mix may be on the order of 200 microseconds per instruction rather than the 100 microseconds per instruction that is obtained from the maximum instruction rate. In this case, the CPU time requirement would be on the order of 27 seconds rather than the 13.5 seconds obtained from maximum instruction rate.

If in addition to the type of CPU and number of instructions required for the application the analyst had the mix of the particular instructions, he could then form a better approximation from an average instruction time calculation.

If we had the actual nature of the computation in its functional form rather than simply a number of instructions with or without the mix of instructions, we could then perform a kernel evaluation of the computing process to obtain an even more refined estimate of the CPU requirements of the application. Again, the amount of refinement depends on the amount of information which is supplied as input. To continue with the problem, let us assume that the only information that we have is that given by the instruction rate calculation.

The next step in a synthetic model is to determine the amount of time required by the other subsystems. In this case, we have three subsystems, the CPU, the magnetic tape subsystem, and the unit record subsystem. (The term unit record usually applies to the class of devices containing card read/ punch units and printers.) In considering the relation of the devices within a class, the focal point of consideration is the control unit philosophy associated with the device. Here, we consider the control unit to be the mechanism which provides a data path for the transmission of data and control information to and from the CPU. Since there is a very wide range of data channel or data synchronizer designs as well as a variety of control unit designs, the complete path will be taken as a single mechanism.

The first class that we will consider is that of the unit record equipment. We have two devices operating in this class, the card reader and the printer. We must consider whether the control unit philosophy allows overlap between the two units. If the control units do not allow any overlap of operation between the two units, then the times of each device are additive. We would then have a subsystem time of 54 seconds. If, on the other hand, the control units allowed overlap of the two operations, the analyst must determine the extent of overlap. There may be some amount of activity which is mutually exclusive within the operation. In buffered unit record equipment, the transmission of data may take place for only one device at a time. This time, of course, is very small compared to the total cycle of the device itself. Another overlap consideration is whether there is more than one control path for the class. We may have independent controls for each device, or there may be a common control for all devices. Independent control will allow more simultaneous operation than a single path for all devices.

Finally, consideration must be given to how well applications achieve potential overlap. In this simple case, let us assume that we have a control path which allows complete overlap between the card reader and the printer. The printer time of 6 seconds can be completely contained within the card reader time of 48 seconds. The class time would therefore be 48 seconds.

In constructing a synthetic model, we should provide for a variable overlap factor, k, which ranges in value from zero to one. This factor is used to calculate the amount of device time which will be overlapped in the model. In the model, it will be used to obtain the proportion of the lesser device time that will be considered as overlapped. If we had an overlap factor of .5, for this example, we would consider one-half of the printer's time to be overlapped because its time is less than the card reader's time. Under these circumstances, we would have a class time of 51 seconds.

If we had more than two devices in a class, we would have additional overlap factors to determine the relationships. The usual computing method is to establish overlap factors for n devices in diminishing order of time of device activity. Given three devices, in reality, we would be concerned with the overlap of A to B, B to C, C to A, and the common overlap of all three. However, the synthetic model can approximate reality by considering overlap on a cascade method only. If the times of the individual devices are in the order, A, B, C, then the model needs only two overlap factors; a factor for the amount of time B is overlapped and a factor for the amount of time C is overlapped. If two or more devices have the same time associated with their activity, the model can arbitrarily choose the first encountered device as the basis of calculation. Assume that we have three device times as follows:

Card reader   100 sec

Card punch   50 sec

Printer   60 sec

The model would first order the devices in order of decreasing time of the device. The result of this would be to establish the card reader as device A, the printer as device B, and the card punch as device C. The next step would be to apply the overlap factors to the times for devices B and C to determine the amount of time which would be overlapped. In the computing procedure, we would actually determine the amount of time which is *not* overlapped since it is the residual time which will be added together to obtain the class time. In Figure 4.17, we have a timing table to establish the class time for this example.

Notice that device A has an "implied" overlap factor of zero. If the computing procedure uses a method which actually processes the base device

Device	Time	k	$1 - k$	Residual
A	100	0	1.0	100 sec
B	60	0.5	0.5	30 sec
C	50	0.8	0.2	10 sec
Total class time				140 sec

Fig. 4.17   Unit record class timing table.

through the overlap equations, a zero factor will force the use of the full time for device A. If the procedure does not process device A in that manner, then the zero overlap factor is superfluous.

In the case of the unit record class, a different approach is usually taken as opposed to the general approach given above. The basis of the following approach is that although lumped together in a general class, the characteristics of the card reader, the punch, and the printer may be maintained. In other words, the analyst usually has better knowledge of their capabilities. The approach simply skips over any ordering of devices based on time of activity and applied overlap factors to the individual units. So instead of having an overlap factor for some device, B, we have an overlap factor for the printer, as such. However, alternative computing routines must be utilized, depending still on which particular unit has the longest computing time. Without this dependency, we can find ourselves in something of a strange situation. To illustrate, assume that we have device times and overlap factors as shown in Figure 4.18.

Device	Time	k	$1 - k$	Residual
Reader	100	0.8	0.2	20 sec
Punch	50	0.8	0.2	10 scc
Printer	60	0.8	0.2	12 sec
Total class time				42 sec

Fig. 4.18   Unit record class—erroneous algorithm.

If a computing procedure blindly applied overlap factors without regard to some basic device, we could obtain an answer which not only is less than what we would expect if there were complete overlap between all three units, but does not even match the shortest device time. The solution is for the computing procedure to scan the times of activity for each device and determine the longest time in the set. For that device, its overlap factor is forced to zero. This, then, provides a base for determining the time of the class.

Repeating the above table with this replacement algorithm, we have the result as shown in Figure 4.19. Here, the computing procedure produces an answer which is more realistic.

Device	Time	k	$1 - k$	Residual
Reader	100	0	1.0	100 sec
Punch	50	0.8	0.2	10 sec
Printer	60	0.8	0.2	12 sec
Total class time				122 sec

Fig. 4.19   Modified unit record class time.

Before proceeding to the other algorithms of a synthetic model, we should address the determination of the overlap factors. For operations which are forced to be mutually exclusive such as a card read/punch unit which on a single cycle can either read a card or punch a card but not both, the analyst can easily establish an overlap factor of zero. The principal concern is determining an overlap factor to use in the model for devices which are capable of complete overlap. In this case, the analyst has three paths open to him. He can use a factor of one in all cases, but this will probably be more optimistic than is actually found in nature. Secondly, he can manually create an estimate of overlap factors by analyzing the particular applications that will be processed in the model. This can be quite time consuming even for a single application of any complexity whatsoever. If we use this approach over a large number of applications, the manpower requirements may be prohibitive.

The third approach would be to use measurement techniques to obtain the relevant overlap factors for types of applications currently being processed. In later chapters we will discuss methods of establishing overlap factors from measurement techniques.

Returning now to the synthetic model itself, let us examine the structure of the magnetic tape class. Here we have the simple operation of an equal number of similar records read in on one tape and written out on another. Magnetic tape input required 10.5 seconds, and magnetic tape output also required 10.5 seconds. With only two units in this class, we simply apply an overlap factor to one of them. For simplicity, let us assume that we have an overlap factor of 0.5 within the magnetic tape class. This produces a class time of 15.75 seconds (10.5 + 5.25) for magnetic tape activity.

Let us review our assumptions and class times for the original problem.

In Figure 4.20 we have the three classes of activity, the CPU, the magnetic tape subsystem, and the unit record subsystem. We obtained the CPU time

Class	Time
CPU	13.50 sec
Magnetic tape	15.75 sec
Unit record	48.00 sec

Fig. 4.20　Class summary.

by considering the number of instructions required for each activity and then applied an instruction rate calculation to obtain the total CPU requirement for the problem. In the magnetic tape subsystem, we calculated the reading and writing times and then combined them using an overlap factor of 0.5. In the unit record class, we again calculated the amount of time on each device, and then assumed that the printer had an overlap factor of 1.0.

At this stage, we are ready to combine the classes together to provide an estimate of system time. Again, the basis of calculation is the use of overlap factors. And again, the synthetic model procedure should examine the various classes to determine the longest time involved to force a zero overlap to determine the longest time involved to force a zero overlap for that class and therefore establish a base for the summation of times. In a simple model, the combining algorithm will operate in essentially the same manner as shown in the timing table in Figure 4.21.

Class	Time	k	$1 - k$	Residual
Unit record	48.00	0	1.0	48.0 sec
Magnetic tape	15.75	0.8	0.2	3.2 sec
CPU	13.50	0.8	0.2	2.7 sec
Total system time				53.9 sec

Fig. 4.21　System timing table.

In this case, the overlap factor for unit record activity was forced to zero because it was the largest time.

This rather primitive synthetic model requires very little computation for the performance of the exercise itself. The first set of inputs are the summarization of the various volumes of activity, including the CPU requirements, of the application or applications under study. The second set of inputs are the configuration parameters. In this set we have the device and CPU performance characteristics and the methods of interconnection called the control paths. Even though we have treated a control path as the entire path from the CPU to the device, it is possible to break these paths into a tree structure which would depend on the number and type of channels as well as the number and type of physical control units.

4.4.2. Overlap Factors

The primary parameters within a synthetic model are the various overlap factors. The analyst, in structuring his model, has a large degree of freedom in the method by which he handles the entire set of overlap factors. He can treat them as a set of constants which are imbedded in the computing procedure itself. In this case, a particular constant will be applied to the evaluation of all configurations and all applications. This is, of course, the most restrictive method of handling the factors. Unless the analyst has an easy method of changing the constants once the procedure is programmed, they will tend to remain at their initial value irrespective of the need to change them.

The analyst may elect to include the overlap constants with the application input. Here, he would have a great deal of flexibility, but would require more input data along with the volume data. Furthermore, including the overlap constants with the application data may take into account overlap actually achieved with an observed application, but not take into account the capability to overlap in some new configuration. For example, we may observe applications actually running where the unit record subsystem had no overlap whatsoever with any of the other subsystems. Here, the probable overlap factor for this class, which would be supplied as input with the application volumes, would be zero. If we had as input for the configuration a unit record subsystem which allowed complete overlap of activity, the overlap constant would not recognize any of that capability.

The analyst also has the option of including overlap factors with the configuration input data. Here, he can take into account the capability of the various subsystems and devices, but does not take into account any peculiarities of any particular application. Even though, for example, the unit record subsystem is capable of complete overlap with all other activities, there may be an application processed which does all of its printing at the end of a run.

Still another choice would be to read in the set of overlap factors as a completely independent set of inputs. In this case, the analyst could examine the relationship of the applications to the configurations and thus establish the overlap factors for that case. This would be ideal if the number of combinations of applications and configurations is very small. Consider, however, that if we were examining 10 applications across 20 different configurations, we would have to construct 200 sets of overlap factors. Again, the manpower requirements may be prohibitive.

A compromise approach would be to try to take into account the nature of the application and separate the capability of the configuration. An approach would be to structure a set of factors which would consist of binary factors on the part of the configuration, zero and one, and proportional factors on the part of the application. To produce an overlap factor used within the computing procedure, we simply multiply the application factor and the configuration factor. So if an application allowed the card reader and the card punch to operate with some concurrency, the application overlap factor could be a number like 0.8. If the configuration allowed overlap between card reading and card punching, its factor would be 1.0. Multiplying the two would produce an overlap factor of 0.8. If, on the other hand, the configuration did not allow any overlap between reading and punching, the configuration factor would be zero. Multiplying in this case would produce an overlap factor of zero, as expected. The advantage to this scheme is to balance in some way the capability of the application and the capability of the configuration.

4.4.3. Improving Sensitivity

Since the calculation requirements for a synthetic model are quite modest, programming the method on a computer we would find that we are limited to the input/output rate of the host processor for even a low speed computer. The calculation process is relatively independent of the size or actual running time of any application characteristics which are processed by the model. This is because the application characteristics are inserted in terms of summaries of activity for the individual units. The running time of the model is more dependent on the number of devices and the tree structure of the configuration.

If we had a configuration structure as shown in Figure 4.22, we would require more computation than for the simple example that we used earlier. Although we have been referring to the "unit record" subsystem or the "tape" subsystem, on a complex configuration, each branch of the tree would be another subsystem. So in the figure, we would have disk file subsystem "A," subsystem "B," and so forth. Then within each subsystem we would have the various device activities.

Even with the advantage of having very modest computing requirements for a system time projection, the main disadvantage of a synthetic model is insensitivity to some attributes of the application and/or configuration. For this reason, the analyst can quickly determine the fact that he does not really need to maintain the individual characteristics of a set of applications under study. He can pre-average all of the volume requirements into one super-application characteristic. The desire to do this would be important when addressing the problem of configuration options across a given set of applications. Let us assume the size of a more practical problem in the application of a synthetic model. We may wish to examine 2000 different configurations across a set of 300 applications. In the design of a system across a set of 300 applications, we can quickly grow to 2000 configurations by simply consider-

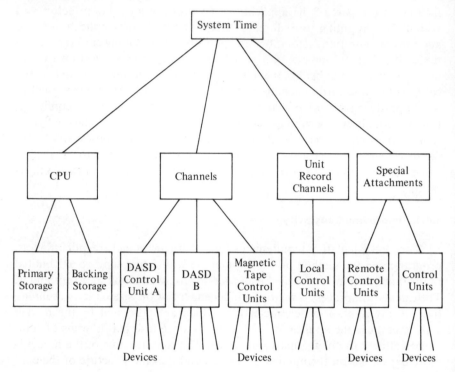

Fig. 4.22   Configuration tree.

ing 10 different CPUs, 20 combinations of magnetic tape subsystems, and 10 combinations of unit record subsystems. Although the total system time required for the synthetic model may not be dramatically affected because of input-output requirements, we can reduce the calculation requirement by pre-averaging the 300 applications into a smaller number of representations. In the pre-averaging activity, we would want to keep homogeneous sets of applications together, although there would be nothing to preclude averaging the set into one entry. If we were to do this, we would reduce the calculation requirement by a factor on the order of 300. Depending upon the organization of the implementation of the model, we could also reduce the input/output requirements of the model. Again, the decision to do this would depend upon the use of the answers obtained from the model. Going in the opposite direction, we can also take some steps to improve the sensitivity and therefore the effectiveness of a synthetic model. We mentioned earlier the ability to have the overlap factors themselves more sensitive to the applications and configurations.

We can also have various options available for generating the time of the CPU for the applications. In the original example, we were simply given a number of instructions performed on some observed type of CPU. Although the analyst may have had additional knowledge of the application in determining average instruction time, we still had only the option of applying that time to the instruction requirements of the application. Within the synthetic model, we can structure CPU requirements in a way which provides more sensitivity. A way of doing this would be to break down the requirements not by number of instructions required, but as a functional mix. Furthermore, this mix can be distributed across various sections of the application. If we have such a structure, there is more work for the analyst in that he has to prepare many estimates of CPU performance rather than just one for any single application. However, if greater sensitivity is required, this is one way to achieve it.

There is a compromise point on structuring various CPU performance indicators. This would be in conjunction with the pre-averaging of applications. If we were to average the 300 applications down to, say, 30 applications, then we may be able to afford the time to increase the CPU sensitivity for those 30 where we would not have wished to do so for each of the 300.

A modest improvement in sensitivity would be to include in the calculation the amount of interference time required by the input/output units to transmit data to and from memory. Later on, this interference can be taken into account when calculating CPU requirements. To calculate interference time, we need to have in the program the amount of memory time required for each record transaction. This time represents only that required by the control path to do its job, once initiated. It does not contain any time that the CPU may have spent to initiate the transaction. Assume that in our original example we had a configuration that required 10 μsec interference for each *four* characters transmitted with regard to magnetic tape, and 10 μsec for *each* character transmitted with regard to unit record equipment. We can construct a timing table to determine the amount of interference as shown in Figure 4.23.

Since by definition this time is overlapped, it will be contained within the overlap portion of the system time. Until the activity of the CPU is such that as much of its time as possible is overlapped, this interference time would

Device	Volume (char.)	Interference/char.	Time
Tape in	500,000	2.5 μsec	1.25 sec
Tape out	500,000	2.5 μsec	1.25 sec
Reader	32,000	10.0 μsec	0.32 sec
Printer	12,000	10.0 μsec	0.12 sec
Total interference			2.94 sec

Fig. 4.23   Interference timing table.

not affect the system's time. However, when the overlap time starts becoming saturated, then the presence of this interference would tend to allow less CPU time to be overlapped than if it were not calculated. On small scale CPUs, the relative proportion of interference becomes greater. In this event, interference should be carefully considered.

Of more importance is the ability of the model to take into account the amount of CPU processing required for the initiation of each read and write. In today's environment we generally have the actual device selection routines as part of the control program services. In fact, a complete access method may be imbedded in the control program in addition to merely the device selection routine. Before we have the model automatically insert these requirements, we should determine how much, if any, of the coding for these routines was included in the input application data. If the routines were included in the data, we should do one of two things. Either not have the model do the calculation of the access method time or remove that function from the application input. In a more sophisticated model, we perhaps could identify to the model that the input data did have access routines and/or device selection routines in it of a certain type and let the model itself strip out the CPU load.

The advantage of stripping the load due to access routines out of the input data is that the model can be programmed to include a variety of access methods. A library of access methods can be structured in the synthetic model so that the analyst merely has to select one or more of them to be used on any particular run.

4.4.4. Example of Record Blocking

Another reason for stripping the input/output instructions from the input is to allow estimates to be made concerning the effect of blocking and buffering. Assume that the original example had ten instructions in the input data for each read or write performed. The first thing to do would be to remove those instructions from the application input. Doing so would provide a CPU requirement as shown in Figure 4.24.

We will rely on the synthetic model to calculate the additional CPU requirement for accessing data. Let us now structure a synthetic model which

Item	Instructions	Adjusted	Incidence	Total
Each master (in and out)	50	30	1000	30,000
Each transaction	200	190	400	76,000
Each exception	50	40	100	4,000
Total				110,000

Fig. 4.24 Adjusted instruction count.

takes the basic application input data and has the capability to apply blocking and buffering. The application input now has the form shown in Figure 4.25.

Device	Volume
CPU	110,000 instructions
Master in-tape	1000, 500 character records
Master out-tape	1000, 500 character records
Transaction in-card	400, 80 character records
Exception out-printer	100, 120 character records

Fig. 4.25   Application input.

We have decreased the CPU requirements by eliminating the number of instructions per record that were concerned with reading and writing. We have augmented the information concerning card reading and printing to identify the record lengths involved. Let us assume that the analyst has declared to the synthetic model that he wants an evaluation based on a blocking factor of five for the magnetic tape input and output. The configuration information that we must have for this model contains the following:

CPU: Average instruction time: 100 μsec
                Interference per data byte transmitted
                    Magnetic Tape: 2.5 μsec/byte
                    Unit record: 10 μsec/byte

Magnetic Tape: Start/stop time: 5 msec
                Character time: 0.011 msec/byte

Unit Record: Card rate: 500 cpm
                Printer: 1000 lpm

The model structure will follow the same general lines as the primitive model explored earlier. We will maintain the same overlap factors as before. First the unit record subsystem has the same device requirements as before, namely, 48 seconds of card activity and 6 seconds of printer activity. Assuming full overlap of the printer operation, we have a class time of 48 seconds.

However, we have two additional calculations to perform in this case. First, the calculation of interference caused by the transmission of data with regard to the unit record equipment. According to the input data, we have transmitted some 44,000 bytes of information with an interference time of 10 μsec per byte. This comes to 0.44 seconds of additional CPU time which will be completely overlapped by definition. Second, we have to calculate the amount of CPU time required to initiate the reads and the writes. Let us assume that each read and write of unit record activity requires 12 instructions. Since these instructions represent activity to *initiate* the read or the write, they generally cannot be overlapped with the *device* that they represent. However, they can be overlapped on the same basis that the devices themselves are overlapped. So within this portion of the procedure we see that the reading of cards required 4800 additional instructions for the CPU which cannot be overlapped with card reading. The printer activity requires 1200 instructions which can be overlapped with the card reading, but not with the printer activity. Since the printer activity is completely overlapped with card reading, we can safely construct the synthetic model to overlap the additional instructions necessary to initiate printing within the act of card reading.

Upon exiting this portion of the procedure, we have the following information:

Subsystem time:	48 seconds
Interference overlapped:	0.44 seconds
CPU requirement, overlapped:	1200 instructions
CPU requirement, nonoverlapped:	4800 instructions

The information which is in addition to the subsystem time will be used later on in the combining algorithms.

In the magnetic tape subsystem, the procedure should take care of the blocking factor. The application requirement for both input and output is for 1000, 500-character records. The analyst has asked for a blocking factor of 5 on both input and output. The procedure then determines that for a blocking factor of 5, a 500 character record to the application turns out to be a physical record on tape of 2500 characters, not counting control characters. Even though we know that the same applies to both output and input, the procedure will determine the physical record length for each device involved. The tape passing time is therefore based not on 1000, 500 character records, but on 200, 2500 character records for both input and output. In this case, the input tape device time is 6.5 seconds, as is the output tape device time. Assuming the same overlap factor of 0.5, the subsystem time is 9.75 seconds.

Again, we have two additional computations to perform while still in the subsystem procedure. First, we have the amount of CPU interference due to the transmission of data. For each device we have 500,000 characters transmitted to or from memory. The interference rate for magnetic tape is 2.5 μsec per character. For the magnetic tape subsystem, the total interference is 2.5 seconds. By definition, this time is overlapped with the input/output operations.

Next, we calculate the amount of CPU processing to initiate a read or a write. Let us assume that the number of instructions involved is 15 instructions for each physical read or write and 5 instructions for each level of the blocking factor. So the reading and the writing will each have 3000 instructions which cannot be overlapped with the individual device and 5000 which can. However, we can have an algorithm which specifies that the number of nonoverlapped instructions can be overlapped to the same extent that the individual devices are overlapped within their class. Since we have an overlap factor of 0.5 for the writing of magnetic tape, we can apply the same overlap factor to the 3000 instructions involved with the initiation of tape writing. The first 3000 instructions associated with reading will be considered non-overlapped. The other 5000 are overlapped. The output of this portion of the procedure will be as follows:

Subsystem time: 9.75 seconds

Interference overlapped: 2.5 seconds

CPU requirement overlapped: 11500 instructions
(5000 + 5000 + 1500)

CPU requirement, nonoverlapped: 4500 instructions
(3000 + 1500)

We now turn to the procedure for calculating the CPU time for the application. In the primitive example, we had the CPU's processing requirements as a single number: total number of instructions required. In this model, we should maintain several different categories of CPU load as shown in Figure 4.26.

Generally overlappable: 110,000 instructions
Restricted overlappable: 4,800 cannot overlap unit record
                           4,500 cannot overlap tape
Overlapped within class: 1,200 overlapped within unit record
                           11,500 overlapped within tape
Overlapped interference: 0.44 sec. within unit record
                           2.50 sec. within tape

Fig. 4.26   CPU load table.

The generally overlappable category is from the input of the application program. There are no forcing conditions on that activity, so that block will be treated by the overlap factor for the CPU. In the restricted case, we have instructions which cannot be overlapped with the activity of the associated class. The 4500 instructions which cannot overlap tape can overlap the unit record activity.

Another point to consider at this time is that the two classes of restricted overlappable and overlapped within class contain the instructions related to input/output processing. If we wanted a more general model, we could allow for different CPU performance characteristics for this type of programming as opposed to merely using the same characteristics used for the general coding of the application. In fact, the load characteristics could be expressed in some unit other than number of CPU instructions required to perform the function. We could express the load as a number of entries to a particular type of I/O routine, or we could have expressed the load in terms of amount of time required.

We now convert all load entries to time. As before, we will use the average instruction time of 100 μsec per instruction. This gives us a load table as shown in Figure 4.27. We maintain the same general categories as we did before.

Generally overlappable:	11.00 seconds
Restricted overlappable:	0.48 seconds cannot overlap with UR
	0.45 seconds cannot overlap tape
Overlapped within class:	0.12 seconds with unit record
	1.15 seconds with tape
Overlapped interference:	0.44 seconds within unit record
	2.50 seconds within tape

Fig. 4.27   CPU time table.

In combining the various elements, we make two passes to establish total system time. On the first pass, we consider only the generally overlappable portion of CPU time. On the second pass, corrections will be inserted to account for the other three categories.

Our subsystem times at this point are as follows:

CPU	11.00 seconds
Magnetic tape	9.75 seconds
Unit record	48.00 seconds

The combining algorithm will operate again as shown in the timing table in Figure 4.28. Again, the unit record factor was forced to zero because that class has the greatest time.

In preparation for the second pass, it will be useful to portray the above information in system profile form as shown in Figure 4.29. (Remember that the profile is in summary form.)

The region A to B is the time that the CPU is the only class in operation. The region B to C is the time that magnetic tape is the only class in operation. Implicit within the algorithms is that the calculation of residual time is a calculation of the element of a class which cannot be overlapped with pre-

Class	Time	k	$1 - k$	Residual
CPU	11.0	0.8	0.2	2.2 sec
Magnetic tape	9.8	0.8	0.2	2.0 sec
Unit record	48.0	0	1.0	48.0 sec
Preliminary total				52.2 sec

Fig. **4.28** Preliminary timing table.

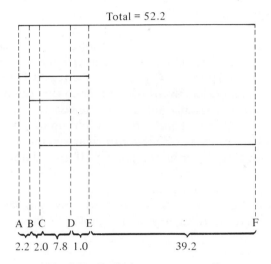

Fig. **4.29** Preliminary system profile.

vious classes. (Naturally, the forcing of the zero factor for the class with the greatest time does not apply.) The region C to F contains all of the other elements of the classes. The points D and E are established on a preliminary basis. The point D is the end of the magnetic tape summary and is 7.8 seconds from the point C. The point E is the end of the CPU summary and is 8.8 seconds from the point C. The region E to F is the area when the only operation is in the unit record subsystem. The time of this region is 39.2 seconds.

The basis for the correction pass is to insert the additional CPU times in their proper region. The primary approach is to insert as much as possible into the region C to E, thus causing the point E to move towards point F. If at any time point E becomes equal to point F, then further corrections must be added into the region A to B. The region A to B is also augmented whenever an element of time is forced into the region because of a restriction. In light of this approach, let us examine the additional CPU times that must be inserted into the profile.

The first entry is the 0.48 seconds which cannot be overlapped with the unit record subsystem. This restriction precludes the region C to F because that class is operating in that region. The region B to C is excluded because of the implicit assumption of residual time calculation (i.e., no CPU in operation). Therefore, this element of time must be added into the region A to B, increasing both the region time and the total system time.

The second element is the 0.45 seconds which cannot be overlapped with magnetic tape activity. Only the region B to D is excluded. We can add this element of time to the region D to E, thus moving the point E towards point F. The third element is the 0.12 seconds of time which is overlapped with unit record. This is also added to the region D to E.

The 1.15 seconds which is overlapped with magnetic tape should go into the region C to D. The net effect of the insertion is to displace an equal amount of time from the region C to D into the region D to E. Therefore, the computing procedure simply adds that time to the region D to E. Similarly, the interference times are added to the region D to E. At each point of addition, the model should check the relationship of point E to point F. Although we have no problem with this particular example, we should remember that the point E is bound by the point F. If any addition to the region causes E to exceed F, then the excess time must be added back into the region A to B. The adjusted profile appears in Figure 4.30.

Here we see that CPU only has increased to 2.7 seconds, tape only remains as 2.0 seconds, and the remainder of the profile is 48 seconds. The total

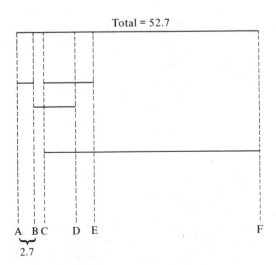

Fig. 4.30   Adjusted profile.

system time produced by the model is 52.7 seconds. For reference, the point D is 7.8 seconds from the point C, and the point E is 13.5 seconds from the point C.

4.4.5   Direct Access Device Subsystems

Up to this point, we have discussed subsystems which are sequential in nature. The algorithms which are used by the direct access procedure are more complicated. For each file (or data set) description we need the following information:

The nature of the file:
    Read only
    Write only—is write-check used
    Read/write—is this update-in-place

The size of the file:
    Volume extent
    Number of tracks or cylinders (depends on geometry of device)

The number and size of records transmitted

Distribution of transmitted records across file volume:
    Linear distribution
    Some other distribution

Access method used (file organization):
    Random
    Sequential
    Indexed sequential

For each of the access methods, we must prepare procedures in the model which take into account the geometry of the device as well as any particular control program philosophies which may effect the operation. For example, there may be a philosophy in the control program which calls for the issuance of two seeks for each record transmitted. Although this example may seem strange at first, if we consider that the access method is designed to operate in a multiprogramming environment, the issuance of the seek for the record and the actual read or write of the record may be separated in time considerably from one another. To make sure that no intervening operation disturbs the position of the arm between the seek and the read, a second seek is issued as insurance. If the arm is in position, the time of the second seek is near zero. (Its time is in terms of microseconds rather than milliseconds.)

Some of the algorithms which could be utilized in a synthetic model are now considered. For the random access method, we have to construct an average access time as well as a record fetch time. Record fetch includes the rotational delay of the device and the data transmission time. To structure the bounds of the access time, we need to know the physics of the access arm. If it has the ability to make relatively high speed track to track movements we need to take that into consideration. The general algorithm also takes into consideration the number of tracks and/or cylinders that contain the data set. If the file of interest is contained in, say, 10 cylinders, we would not want to use an access time calculation which covers 200 cylinders. The input to this particular algorithm is generally a table of equations which expresses the access characteristics of a device for a given number of cylinders. This table would then form the boundary conditions of an average access time calculation.

There are two approaches in calculating the average access time. The first is to simply use the average time for the relevant block of cylinders at all times. Every time we require an access within the block, that number would be used as the average access time. Another way to calculate the same item is to include some randomizing formula which will select an average access time from within the set of boundary conditions. Depending on the type of randomizing algorithm, this approach may add to the computation time of the synthetic model without really improving its accuracy. We shall use the simple average access time within the boundaries.

When calculating the record fetch time, we are faced with the same decision in the calculation of average rotational delay. We can either use one-half of the rotational period as the average, or we can use a randomizing formula to take some proportion of the rotational period. In a synthetic model, the simple average will probably suffice.

The computing procedure for the random access method would be as follows:

A. Given the number of cylinders involved, select average access time for the data set.

B. Determine procedure to use from the nature of the file. One of the following alternatives will be used.

    1. Read only.
       (a) Calculate the data transmission time given number of characters in a record and the speed of the device.
       (b) Add average rotational delay of device.
       (c) Add average access time obtained in A.
       (d) Calculate interference from number of characters and interference characteristics of data path.
       (e) Calculate CPU initiation requirements given in configuration information.

    2. Write only—use same procedure as for read.

3. Write-check—(a) through (c), same as above.
   (d) Add a rotational period.
   (e) Calculate interference on twice number of characters (once for the write and once for the read back, depending on CPU).
   (f) Calculate CPU initiation requirements given in configuration information.

4. Update-in-place.
   This uses the same computing procedure as write-check. Write-check first writes the record and then reads it back, while update-in-place first reads a record and then writes it back. If item (f) differs, a separate CPU requirement would be given for each class. If we use update-in-place with write-check, we use a similar procedure, but add two additional rotational periods in step (d) rather than one. We also calculate interference on the basis of three times the record length.

After a record time is calculated, the procedure then multiplies the various elements by the number of records involved to obtain a file activity time. This may or may not represent the device time which will go into a subsystem timing procedure. We may be faced with more than one data set on any given device. If this occurs, we must alter our combining approach depending on the concurrent use of two or more data sets on one device. If we had three data sets which were not used within the same time span, then we could simply calculate three different data set times and add them together to obtain the device activity time.

If more than one data set were active on a device at a given time, we have to take into account the mutual interference of arm motion between the two data sets. Even though each data set could be neatly contained in a small number of cylinders, the access arm in fact would have to move from one data set to another while they are in concurrent use. To take account of this type of activity, the previous computing procedure did not multiply any of the elements by the number of records until the routine was almost over. At this point, the procedure must be given information about the number of data sets on a single device.

Assume that we have two data sets, A and B, on a device whose cylinder requirements produce an average access time within each data set of 25 msec. Further assume that data set A processes 5000 records and data set B processes 1000 records. If no other information is available, we must assume that the processing of the two data sets is concurrent. In this case, probably all of the 1000 records for data set B will be fetched following a fetch to data set A rather than B. This means that we must use a larger average access time for data set B than the one produced for its volume extent. If we, again, have no more information on the spatial relationship of the two sets, we should use the average access time of the device while operating in its full volume. If we have information or can make assumptions about their relationship, then we can again get the relevant average access time from the device table.

Similarly, a number of accesses (equal to B) for data set A will be affected by the larger average access time. This is because every time the arm was moved into the volume extent for B, it had to be moved back into the volume extent for A.

At the point of calculating data set times, the procedure will have to augment a number of records by the difference in average access used within the routine and the average access that should be used for that number of records. So if we had at the exit of the routine for the calculation of data set A a record time based on an average access time of 25 msec, and an average access time of 50 msec for interaction with data set B, we would add 25 msec to the record time for 1000 of the 5000 records. The remaining 4000 would use the time calculated by the routine. In the case of data set B, all 1000 of its records would be augmented by the appropriate access time.

If there were more than two data sets, a similar calculation would be performed for each data set, taking into account all other activity.

Turning now to the sequential access method for direct access devices, the procedure takes into account the number of cylinders which contain the data set, the number of records involved, the distribution of the records across the data set, and the device geometry. Assume that we have the following information provided as input:

Number of cylinders: 10

Number of records processed: 5000

Distribution of records: Assume a level distribution of record activity across the entire data set

Device geometry: Track to track access time is 10 msec

With a level distribution of activity across the data set, we can assume that there will be a track to track access every 500 records. The remainder of the records are assumed not to require any arm motion.

The procedure will treat the calculation of record times in essentially the same way that we saw for the random access method. However, it will apply a track to track access time to 500 records, and a zero access time to the others. There is also allowance for the interference due to the concurrent operation of other data sets on the same device. In this case, it will first proportion the number of interfering records across its own distribution. So if we have 1000 records which require the full average access time of 50 msec, they will be distributed on the same ten-to-one ratio that was used for the distribution of sequential seeks. 100 of the 500 records which utilized a track to track seek time of 10 msec will have 40 msec added to their record time.

900 of the 4500 records which had a zero seek time will have 50 msec added to their record time. In this way the model keeps track of inter-data set interference.

Other access methods can be included in a synthetic model. Let us consider the addition of an indexed sequential access method. The purpose of such a method is to process all of the transactions sequentially, but avoid the necessity of reading every record from the data set as is required in a pure sequential access method. For each new transaction, the key field is compared to the boundaries of the present arm position to determine whether an arm movement is required. If the transaction is within the present position, the transaction is completed using sequential techniques. If the transaction is not within the boundaries of the present position, then the access method goes to an index to determine where to position the arm so that the new boundaries will contain the record of interest. Here, we can structure an algorithm which takes into account the same type of information as for the sequential access method. The primary difference is that every time we should move to a new arm position, we must first return to the index track, read a record, perform some nonoverlapped processing, and then move the arm to a new position to continue with the search for the record of interest.

To illustrate this approach, assume that we want to process 100 records against an indexed sequential file. Assume that the records on the file are 500 characters long and that we have a level distribution of the processed record across the data set. Assume that we have a direct access device which contains five records on a track and that there are 20 tracks in a cylinder. This gives us 100 records in a cylinder. Let us further assume that we have a total of 1000 records in the data set so that we will utilize 10 cylinders for data storage. Assume that we have allocated additional tracks at the beginning of the data set to take care of the index. So we have a total volume extent of 11 cylinders. The access method will first go to an index track to determine an arm position, position the arm, select the track head, and then start searching the records from the first record of the track until it finds the record of interest. On the next transaction, the new record is compared to the present boundaries to find if it is in the same cylinder. If it is, the new record is compared to the present one to determine a match. If there is, the transaction is completed and we then take the next record request. If there is not a match with the present record, then the search continues sequentially in that cylinder until the record of interest is found. If the new record were not within the boundaries of the present arm position, the access method would go back to the index cylinder to find the correct arm position and continue as outlined above.

In addition to the information outlined above, we need one very important piece of information to satisfy an algorithm. When we are in search mode, sequentially reading each record to locate the record of interest, is there sufficient processing power in the system to allow the reading of at least the key field from each record (if not the entire record), the comparison of that field with the key field from the transaction record, and the reinitiation (or re-select) of the unit so that it can read the next record from the direct access device before we have passed the point of the beginning of the next record? This question is further compounded when we distinguish between the five records on the same track and, going to the next track, within the cylinder. In some systems switching the track read/write heads within a single cylinder requires the CPU to perform the instructions which command the switch to occur. Again, the analyst must know whether sufficient processing power is available to perform the key comparison or the head switching; an extra revolution of the device is necessary to perform its function. It would be bad enough to take an extra revolution for head switching, but if we had to have an extra revolution to read each record the degradation would be intolerable.

For this example the procedure would first determine that, with our level distributions, we will be looking for 10 records in each cylinder. This means that we will resort to the index track 10 times to determine arm positioning. Within a cylinder, we will search an average of 10 records for each record of interest. Let us make some further simplifying assumptions. Assume that while searching, only the key field is read into memory, and assume that that field is 20 characters long. This field length will be used for the calculation of memory interference. Further assume that the system has the capability to compare fields without resorting to the CPU but that we do require some CPU processing to switch heads. Let this amount of processing be the time, S. We shall also assume that the time, S, is short enough to allow us to switch heads in time to read the next record without taking an extra revolution of the device.

Given the above assumptions, we have the following outline:

A. Arm positioning.
    1. Move arm to index track.
    2. Search index track for boundaries of argument.
    3. Matching argument, read in positioning information.
    4. Move arm to new position.

B. Record searching.
    1. Read key field.
    2. Wait for next key field.

C. Record found.
    1. Read entire record into memory for further processing.

D. Summarization.
    1. Summarize arm positioning elements, device time, interference, CPU requirements, etc. Multiply by 10.

2. Summarize search procedure by same elements. Multiply by 900.
3. Summarize record found procedure by same elements. Multiply by 100.
4. Summarize this section.

In structuring the detail, the analyst has flexibility in deciding what sensitivities to insert into the procedure. Probably the most critical assumption regards the amount of processing required to re-select the heads when a new track selection is required in the cylinder during the search operation. An error of a few microseconds in the amount of processing required can cause the device to take an additional revolution before reading the next record. Quite literally, a 1 microsecond error can cause an additional rotation which may be on the order of 25 milliseconds.

4.4.6 Summary Notes on Synthetic Models

Other sensitivities can be structured in a synthetic model. The model can account for such items as time for job initiation and termination, inter-job set up time, tape rewinds both intermediate and final, media switching time for reels, packs, and other media, and operator messages and response times. A synthetic model can also take into account certain attributes of the size of processor storage. If each application had as part of its input the amount of storage required for its program, the model could be given the task of determining optimum blocking and buffering arrangements of input/output with the remainder of storage. If the model were to do this, it could more accurately reflect the advantage of having larger amounts of processor storage.

Before leaving this section, let us keep in mind that the basis of the synthetic model is to build up an estimate of system time by taking the various subsystem times and combining them with assumed overlap factors. The subsystem times are in turn built up from device times, which are structured from the data set activity on the device. All of this information is presented to the synthetic model in summary form. When we reduce any set of activity to summary form, we tend to lose the interaction between the various elements.

Even though we do have restrictions in the methodology and use of a synthetic technique, it does offer the advantage of producing estimates of system time with a very fast calculating procedure. It will take more time than profile conversion, but should provide more accuracy. Its major disadvantage is the amount of detail which must be obtained about the application programs, the control program philosophy, and the configuration. Once established, however, the study of many options can be executed at a high rate of speed.

PROBLEMS

1. For the sort table given in Figure 4.1, how long will each of the following take?
   (a) Ten passes of 10,000 records, channels switched.
   (b) One pass of 100,000 records, channels switched.
   (c) One pass of 100,000 records, 1 channel only.

2. Given the following compile time factors,

$$K = 2.0 \text{ sec.}$$
$$R = 0.006 \text{ sec.}$$
$$T = 0.024 \text{ sec.}$$

What is the machine time requirement of the following load?

Number of Jobs	n	p
10	200	0
20	250	1
40	400	2
20	800	6
10	1000	9

3. Given the system profile in Figure 4.5, what is the relative system throughput of each of following?
   (a) CPU improvement of 5.0.
   (b) Magnetic tape improvement of 3.0.
   (c) The combination of the two above.

4. Given the system profile in Figure 4.5, what CPU improvement factor alone is required to achieve a relative system throughput of 2.0? (Why not?)

5. Consider the example given in Figure 4.12 with the assumptions in the surrounding text. What is the effect of each of the following changes?
   (a) Changing access time only to a minimum of 20, an average of 40, and a maximum of 100 msec.
   (b) Changing rotational period *only* (not transmission rate) to 20 msec.
   (c) Changing transmission rate *only* to 400 kb per second.
   (d) Changing all three of the above at the same time.

6. For the synthetic summary in Figure 4.21, assume overlap factors of 0.5 for each subsystem. What is the system time?

7. For the example introduced in Figure 4.14, assume that the transaction file is on a magnetic tape (rather than card reader) with a blocking factor of one, that the output is on magnetic tape with a blocking factor of five, and that tape units of the original type are involved. Assuming subsystem overlap factors of 0.5,
   (a) What is the system time of this configuration?
   (b) What is the relative system throughput compared to the original in the text?

5 SIMULATION TECHNIQUES

Simulation is widely used as an investigative tool in many areas. It is used in the design and evaluation of communications and electrical networks, continuous-process activities such as refineries, traffic control patterns, and production machine loading, as well as in many other applications. Webster's definition of simulation, in particular the verb simulate, is: "to assume the appearance of; without reality." Looking further into Webster and also Roget, we find many disturbing synonyms, such as feign, imitate, resemble, mimic, and pretend. Things get worse when we see the list also includes counterfeit, falsehood, and even hypocrisy. Many people who have been misled by the erroneous use of simulation prefer the latter list.

These words, of course, apply to the verb in the most general way. In the first place, simulation is used to achieve the effects of reality even though the simulative process may be quite different. Secondly, digital simulation is only one of many methods of simulating. There can be mechanical analogs, electronic analogs, or manual methods of simulation. We can perform physical simulations with equipment which approximates reality such as airliner cockpit mock-ups or the Link trainer. The digital computer offers flexibility to the analyst in that prepackaged routines may be established for future use, and perhaps most important, the change of a simulated process involves only the recoding of instructions to new algorithms.

We are concerned here with the use of simulation programs to be used as tools in the evaluation of digital computer systems. Simulation may be used at various levels of evaluation. We can simulate the entire computer room where the computing system is only a part of the operation; the complete computing system subsystems, such as the direct access file compement; or even the inter-register working of the CPU. During design stages, simulation is used to evaluate the interaction of the basic elements that go into the logic of the CPU registers.

It should be noted that there are essentially two types of simulators, deterministic and probabilistic. In the deterministic simulator, discrete information is given which is acted upon by precise formulae to produce a definitive answer. Any inaccuracy would be introduced by either an input error or an error in the formulation. The probabilistic simulator is one which takes input which is known to be variable, processes algorithms which try to take into account the variability, and produces an answer that is acceptable. It is important to note that, given an answer from a probabilistic simulation, that answer is not a *proof* of the process, but a *presumption* of the process. (In other words an answer says that *if* a process works, here are its characteristics.)

Probabilistic simulation is most often used in situations where critical input characteristics are unknown or, more importantly, are known to be random. Input to classical simulations has been in the form of probability distributions. The processing of the algorithms are often invoked through the use of random number generators. The ability to perform this type of calculation is important to such fields as terminal load design and prediction of availability of complex systems. These applications have the characteristic that certain events will probably occur, but there is no way of predicting exactly when they will occur.

In the field of evaluation, simulation techniques which combine deterministic and probabilistic approaches are often used. They have the characteristic of applying precise data to known conditions. Of course, if sensitive data are not available, then either averages or probability functions are applied. Examples of this type of simulation are trace driven simulation and the algorithmic timer.

5.1. BASIC SIMULATION TECHNIQUES

In the synthetic technique, we saw that the procedure was to build up information in a hierarchical form from a data set, to a device, to a subsystem, and finally to a system. The basis of a simulative approach is the change of state of an *entity* at a point in time. Such a change of state is called an *event*. (Furthermore, a procedure can look for more than one event within a particular time frame.) An entity has attributes and a family tree. It is useful to structure two types of attributes, permanent and temporary. There may be many attributes within each type. A permanent attribute is one which stays with the entity throughout the process. A temporary attribute is one which changes during the process. An entity can pick up and lose temporary attributes during the process. The family tree simply says that an entity may belong to a set of members, and/or have members of its own set. (Even entities have organization charts.) Entities use *facilities* which may be thought of as a separate class of parameters in a simulation. Naturally, entities can call on other entities as well.

Entities can be created by input to the procedure, or can be created by the procedure itself. The procedure can also purge, or destroy an entity or any temporary attribute of an entity. It can also change its set association. So we see that throughout the simulation, the procedure giveth and the procedure taketh away.

There are two basic techniques which are employed in the method of stepping the time increment in the simulation. One method is to advance the simulated "clock" by a set, regular increment throughout the entire simulation. At each clock "tick," the simulation procedure examines the activity lists to determine whether any processing need be done for any entity. The other method is to use a variable time increment. In this case the simulation procedure examines its activity list to determine the time of the next event. When this is determined, the clock is advanced to that time.

The regular interval technique has the advantage of requiring less information about the various activities which in turn calls for less storage in the computer performing the simulation. It has the disadvantage of possibly stepping through long periods of time at an interval very much smaller than that required. For example, if the simulator happened to be calculating at a particular instant the wait status of a system while waiting for the completion of an input transaction, quite a bit of real computer time could be used. One can imagine the result if the transaction period is expressed in milliseconds and the clock interval is in microseconds.

The variable clock technique has the advantage of taking less computer time for situations like the example given above. It has a disadvantage of requiring more data about the transactions being simulated, and therefore requires more storage in the computer performing the simulation. There are two distinct schools of thought concerning which is the better method. Each has its place, and furthermore can operate with acceptable efficiency in the optimum environment of the other.

5.2. PROBABILISTIC SIMULATION

To explore probabilistic simulation, we shall use the simple application of message switching. Furthermore, we shall assume that a network analysis has already been performed so that we can restrict our study to that of loading effects on the computer, or switching center, itself. In other words, the number of lines and number of terminals on each line, as well as the class of service and speed of terminals, is a constant for this study. There will be three distributed inputs to the study: the message arrival time, the message length, and the number of addressees.

In a simple message switching application, a computer is used as the switching mechanism for the message traffic as shown in Figure 5.1.

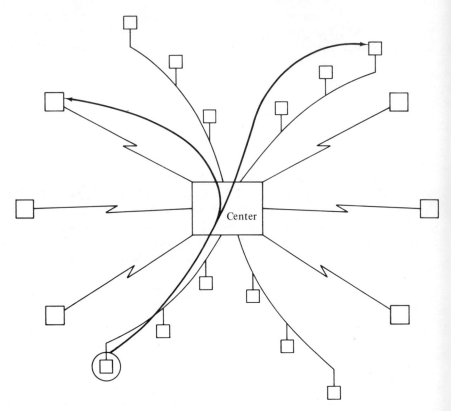

Fig. 5.1   Message switching.

An operator at some terminal sends a message into the center with a simplified address code for each addressee. The computer refers to an address file to determine the full address and routing for each addressee and then transmits a copy of the message to each addressee. Furthermore, for control purposes, the computer logs onto tape a complete copy of each incoming message and a copy of the header information for each outgoing message. Each log entry is augmented with control information provided by the center, including time of day information. (This log tape is used for audit purposes as well as recovery purposes. Recovery is invoked in case of an error which cannot be overcome using the active file information.) Naturally, the system should be processing many messages simultaneously.

The message center configuration is shown in Figure 5.2. Here we see that the transmission control unit and all of the communications lines and

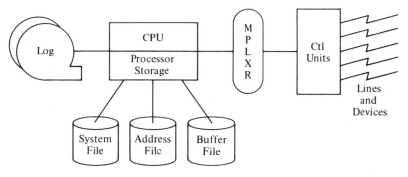

Fig. 5.2 Switching center configuration.

terminals are considered as a single unit in the configuration. The multiplexor is the interface between the processor's storage and the transmission control unit. In the configuration, there are shown the principal files utilized in the application. There are two magnetic tape units allocated to the log file. This is to avoid a shutdown of the system when a log tape is filled up. Without multiple log tapes, the system could come to a stop while the log reel is rewound and a fresh tape mounted by an operator. The system file is assumed to be on a direct access device. The purpose of this data set is to hold all of the system programming necessary for processing. Normally, the main program is always in processor storage, but in case of error, a new copy of the program could be read quickly into the system. This file could also contain routines which are so seldom used that they are not retained in processor storage, but are read in when needed.

The address file is also on a direct access device. This file will be used in a random way to obtain complete address and routing information for each addressee on a message. Finally, there is another direct access device allocated for message queues. If we run out of buffer space in the processor storage, then messages will be queued up on the device. Not shown in the configuration are other units which we reasonably expect to see on the system. The operator's console, the reader, printer, punch complement of equipment, and other direct access devices and magnetic tapes are not considered in this particular study. In such a center, there are usually additional terminals which have special attributes allocated to them by the program. These terminals are used by the center's staff to broadcast general messages or provide trouble shooting assistance to personnel on the system. Their activity will be considered as part of the general message load, outboard of the multiplexor.

Having covered the intent of the application and the system's configuration at the center, we should turn our attention to just what and why are we going into a simulation program. To determine the "what" to simulate, we should first understand the "why." Since there are many options open to the analyst in structuring a simulation, he should fully understand how the output of the simulation is to be used. For example, if we perform the study merely to determine whether a particular configuration will be able to process the message requirements, the analyst may make simple structures in the model which do not allow for sensitivity studies to be performed on some of the units. On the other hand, if the study is being performed to obtain an optimum configuration, rather than one which merely performs the function, then the analyst can provide in the model sensitivity to the variables of the units which would changed. Let us assume that in this study, we do wish to obtain an optimum configuration for a given load (message traffic).

Now we come to what we want to simulate. Our first concern is to determine the information of value to the study. (These are generally called value parameters.) We can provide as output of the simulation process the answer in terms of a throughput characteristic. In a message switching application, the obvious one is messages per hour. However, this answer may only be a reflection of the requirements of the communication network rather than any noticable effect of the switching center. For example, the total load on the network may be 1200 messages per hour. If we expressed the *answer* in terms of messages per hour, 1200 may just be the answer that we get out of the simulation. Of course, if we were concerned with the question of whether the system could merely support the application, then that would probably be a satisfactory answer. We could then try various configurations until we found one which started degrading the message rate. We could then assume that the lowest cost system which did not degrade throughput was the most acceptable system. Such a stochastic approach could require a surprisingly high amount of computer time to perform the number of simulations required to reach that decision.

Since we do know that we want to optimize the configuration, either in terms of cost, or perhaps cost plus some given expansion factor, we can provide additional output to aid in the decision process. The first item that we can obtain from the simulation is the response time of the center. This would involve the complete processing cycle of the application. We can have the model provide the time from, say, the time of the last byte (character) of information from an incoming message to the time of the last byte of information of the last outgoing message associated with the input. Furthermore, we can have the model keep this response time distributed across many other factors such as message length and/or number of addressees. We could take one more step, and have the response time distributed across message length *within* number of addressees. This latter approach could be very useful if we wished at a later time to assume a different distribution of incoming messages. If we do not use such a distribution of response time, it is a simple matter to collapse the greater distribution into one of the others with an adding machine. Of course, going all the way, we could have the model produce both sets of distributions, but we should be cautious in overloading the number of functions that we want in a model. The overload is not in terms of whether the model is capable of performing its function, but more in terms of the amount of computer time that will be required to process the model.

A second very important value parameter to obtain from the model is the distribution of queue lengths on the various facilities. If we see a relatively large queue length building up on the message buffer direct access device, since the processor storage message queue was almost always full, then we can see that a possible way to improve throughput and reduce response time would be to allocate more processor storage for the function of message queue.

Therefore, we shall ask the model to provide as output an expression of message rate, a distribution of system response times, and a distribution of queue lengths. This information would allow us to determine the optimum system in the least amount of time, and probably by far the least amount of computer time spent in processing the model.

To obtain the above information, we should know more about the application processes than the brief description of a message switching application given earlier. First, let us consider the main components of the programs that are in the simulated system.

In Figure 5.3, we see that there are six principal sections in the program. These are the poll routines, the process routines, the interrupt routines, the interrupt return routines, the control program services routines, and the error routines.

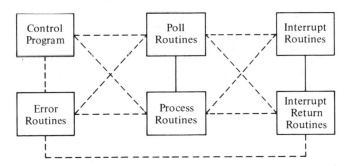

Fig. 5.3   Principal program sections.

The poll routine is normally entered by having an internal interval timer interrupt whatever is in process to give attention to polling. The assumption of the setting of the interval timer is that the time increment is much larger than the amount of process time normally needed in the poll routine. The poll routine also includes the message log activity.

The process routine is the one which takes an incoming message, determines the number of copies to be dispatched, looks up the relevant addresses, and dispatches the messages. As long as there are messages in the system, this is the normally active routine.

The interrupt routine is the section of the program that is invoked whenever an interrupt occurs. The cause of the interrupt can be the interval timer, an input/output interrupt, an error condition, or an interrupt caused by one of the other routines to obtain some control program services. This routine determines the cause of the interrupt and the necessary action to take because of the interrupt. If there is more than one interrupt present, this routine determines the order of processing.

The interrupt return routine is the section of the program which is responsible for returning to the correct point as a result of some interrupt. Since during the process of an interrupt, additional interrupts could have taken place, this routine checks to see that all interrupts are properly handled. This routine also checks to see if any routine is waiting for the results of some action, such as a direct access read. It checks the posting of status notices and updates relevant tables and status conditions so that routimes can proceed when able to do so.

The control program services routine provides the normal types of functions for the rest of the programs. Classical among these services are the input/output routines required by the rest of the program. Other services provided by these routines could be the management of the processor storage space for buffers and/or program routines, as well as management of the data and space on all auxiliary equipment. Other functions in control program services will be described as needed.

The error routines are concerned with recovery of the system in case of failure. Depending on the type of failure, that routine determines what must be done to recover from the error. Of course, in the case of "catastrophic" failure, i.e., the error routine itself is unable to function for any reason, the system operator must intervene to get the system back on the air. Depending on the expected incidence of failure for the various error conditions, most, if not all, of the error routines may be stored only in auxiliary storage rather than in processor storage.

The collection of programs such as control program services, interrupt routines, interrupt return routines, and error routines are normally related together under the general concept of the "control program." There routines are normally provided by the supplier of the equipment as part of a support package. The poll routine (in the general sense that is used here) and the process routine are generally provided by the user, although major elements of the poll routine may be provided by the supplier. These latter two routines are normally referred to as the "problem program," in that those are the routines which are solving the particular problem for the user. The control program merely provides assistance on general functions.

Let us now examine the detail of the problem programs. First, we shall look at the general flow of the poll routine.

In Figure 5.4, we have the poll routine flow chart. As discussed earlier, the normal entry to this routine is through the use of the interval timer. This is to ensure that the correct poll rate is maintained for the number and class of lines on the system as well as number and type of terminals. Within the general concept of the poll routine are such concepts as poll initiate, negative poll, poll restart, and other functions associated with the maintainence of communication lines. Of interest to us is a particular function called message overflow. This means that an incoming message is longer than the amount of buffer space which has been allocated for the message. Looking ahead to the distribution of message lengths, we have a situation where the "average" message length is 200 bytes, the 90th percentile is 450 bytes, and the maximum allowable is 1050 bytes. We will allow the number and length of buffers to be a variable to obtain the optimum size. (Clearly, if we allowed the size of each buffer to be the size of the maximum length record, we would probably be wasting a large amount of processor storage.) If in the case of message overflow, there is no additional processor storage available, the system must halt input until it can reclaim sufficient storage to allow further message input. This would be considered the pathological case.

In the next block, we see the determination of message complete. This could either be an incoming message or an outgoing message. If we have an incoming message, after logging the message, the first thing the routine tries to do is determine whether there is any work in process. Remember, if there are any messages queued in the system, the process routine is normally active. The reason for checking whether there is work in process is that if there is not, we would want to transfer immediately to the process routine. If work is in process, then we will have to queue that particular message in either processor storage or on the direct access device.

If we have completed an output message, we want to log out the relevant information and release the space occupied by the message. Having done so, the routine checks to see if there are any further messages waiting for output buffer space which can go into the space just released. It should be noted that there are two basic philosophies of output buffer space which could be employed. One is to associate buffer space on a one-to-one basis with a particular communication line. This would be queueing to a line. We could have an output buffer pool which would be used by all lines. In this case, there would be a subsidiary queue for lines and terminals. Here, we shall assume

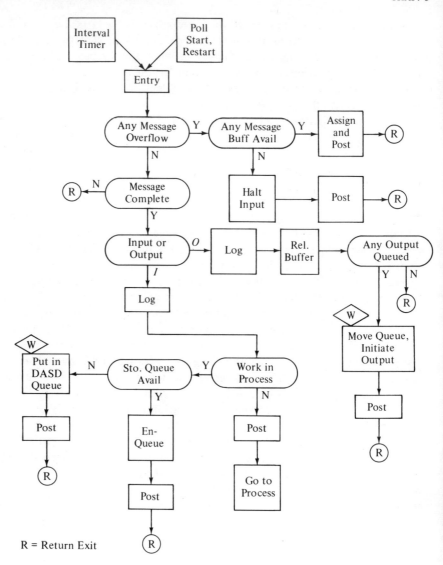

Fig. 5.4   Poll routine flow chart.

that we are using a segmented pool of buffers for output to simplify the example.

At various points in the flow chart, we see the posting of conditions to reflect the change in status of the availability of various facilities. These postings will be used by the interrupt return routine to determine which routines should receive priority in processing before arbitrarily returning to the routine which was interrupted. For example, if the input had been halted, then any item which indicated that the routine could obtain more buffer space would immediately cause a return to that routine because of its highest priority. After that routine then enabled input to continue, we would go once again to the interrupt return routine to see what was next most important. In Figure 5.5, we have the flow chart for the process part of the program.

The normal method of entering this routine is the discovery that upon completing message input that there is nothing in process. Once entered, we will stay in this routine, except for interruptions, as long as there are messages any place in the system. The inner loop of the routine is to look up address and routing information for each of the addressees on the message. As each address is obtained, the routine augments the header information and attempts to move the message over to an output buffer. If no buffer is available, the process routine comes to a temporary halt, waiting on the availability of a buffer. After all outgoing messages have been dispatched for an incoming message, the routine then checks to see if there are any messages in the queue on the direct access device. The reason for checking the device first is to maintain a first in-first out (FIFO) processing order for the messages. (If processor storage were exceeded, the application would dump its present contents onto the device.) If this were not done, a message could be delayed for an inordinate amount of time while later messages are processed first. At this point, there could be a priority selection routine for different classes of messages. Again, for simplicity, we will assume that in this example all messages are of the same priority. If there are no messages in the direct access queue, the routine checks to see if there are any messages in the processor storage queue. If there are, it obtains the earliest message and returns to its process entry. If there are no messages in that queue, then there are no messages in the system to be processed. In that case, the process routine simply goes into a wait state until there is more work for it to do.

In setting up the simulation model, we can first consider some of the entities that we have in the model. The first entity is the CPU itself. Its permanent attribute is processing time. It has a temporary attribute in whether it is processing or not. If it is not processing, it is considered to be in the wait state. (In this model, we will not take into consideration another time that the CPU is not processing, namely, when the system is in a "manual" or "stopped" state. In this event, the system is not operating at all.) The CPU belongs to a higher entity called "the system." The CPU also has entities which are contained in its own set. The first level of these entities would be the major routines of the program. Each one of these would have in turn entities of their own set which would be the various function blocks of their flow charts.

Another major entity under "system" would be the buffers. The hierarchy

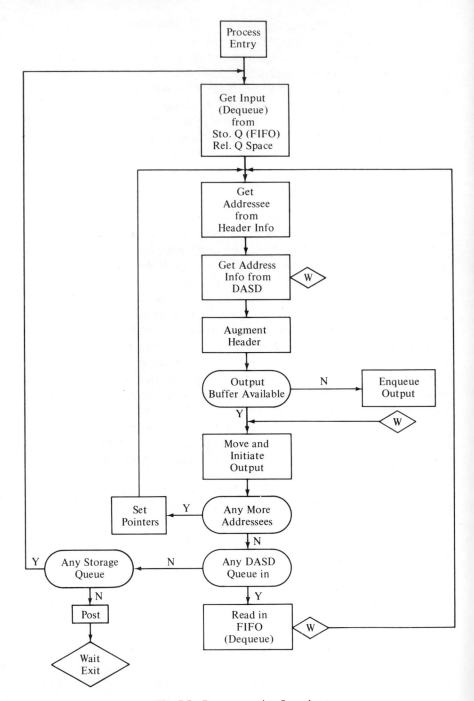

Fig. 5.5 Process routine flow chart.

of buffers is as follows:

Entity	Item
B	Buffers
B1	Input buffers
B2	Message buffers
B2.1	In processor storage
B2.2	On direct access device
B3	Output buffers
B4	Address buffers
B5	Log tape output buffers

For any given run of the model, each buffer set would have a permanent attribute of length and number. In this model, we assume that buffers are pre-allocated to function rather than using a completely generalized buffer pool.

At some time or another, each of the above entities will possess temporary entities, namely, messages. As a message progresses through the process, it will belong in turn to the relevant entities above. A message will also possess entities, namely, addressees. These entities will also proceed through the system and be related to different sets at different points of time.

Each message will have attributes of length and number of addressees generated for it by the model. These two attributes will be used to determine which entities will be involved in which events.

The primary source of events will be the message arrival time. This arrival time is considered to be an external source to the model in that the information is supplied as an input driver. In letting the computing procedure generate message arrival time for the model, we can use a variety of generation routines, depending on the nature of the data that we have on message traffic. Assume that we have an average message rate of 20 incoming messages per minute. We could have a generator program produce a message arrival on a level distribution or some other distribution. If we had a statistical distribution of message traffic, then we could have the generator conform to that pattern. If we do not have a good statistical distribution, we could allow a random generator to create the arrival rate, being constrained not to exceed the line capacity while operating within minimum and maximum boundaries. The primary event generator can be structured to conform to our knowledge of the input data. For simplicity, let us assume that we have a level distribution of arrival times for the messages (in other words, we will use average arrival time), but will let the message length and number of addressees be randomly distributed within a given distribution curve.

Given this input, all other events will be created by the model from information given to it concerning entities and event rules built into the model.

The facilities which we have at our disposal will be the various device characteritics which the entities will use to determine completion time. For example, we will have an entity called the address file. It will have an attribute of time of address fetch for an address record of given length. We will structure four subentities under address file, one for the CPU time requirement of the access method, and one each for the variable channel, control unit, and device time required to read the record into storage. During this time, there will also be an attribute which forces the CPU into wait state while the record is being obtained. The variable device time will be calculated from the facility of a direct access device. This facility will have the attributes of access time, rotational delay, and record transmission rate. For each reference to the file, a time will be calculated for the fetch time. Other event generation rules will be discussed as they arise.

We shall have the model account for the elapsed time from the arrival time of a message (last byte read in) until the last byte for the last addressee is transmitted. These times, incidentally, would correspond to the times obtained from the log tape in actual practice. We want to have this time distributed by message length and number of addressees. At this point we can use one of two approaches within the model. If we want to merely see a *summary* of this distribution, we could set up the complete matrix of distribution in the model and let the model tally the various incidents. However, if we wished to see a time dependent distribution of the response times, we could ask the model to create a simulated log tape of header information only. If this were done, various analysis programs could be used to examine the data after the model has been run to completion. Since we may wish to have a distribution of response times on a time basis, we shall have the model provide a simulated log tape for post-analysis.

We shall also have the model maintain the amount of time that the various facilities are used in the simulated system. This is so that we can determine utilization of the various components of the configuration. Finally, we shall have the model also keep track of the various queue lengths which are involved. This will allow us to determine bottlenecks in the system. Although either utilization or queue length would guide us to probable bottlenecks, the presence of both sets of information will provide much more guidance.

In Figure 5.6, we have the major process sections of our model. There is, first, an initialization routine which gets the operation off the ground. Since we have two major event generators, one from the outside and one from the inside, we start both of them off before going into the main portion of the model. Firstly, we generate from a time zero the time of arrival of the first message. Secondly, on the same basis, we generate the time of the next interval timer interrupt. These two times are then posted to the "next event table," and control is passed to the event processor. Every time a new event time is posted to the next event table, a routine "sorts" the table so that the earliest event in time is available to the event processor.

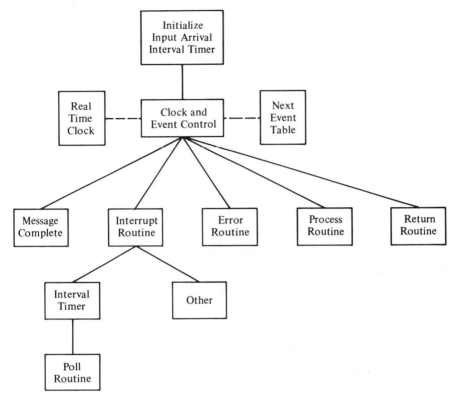

Fig. 5.6 Major sections of model.

The major routines to which the clock routine exits are the message completion routine, the interrupt routine, the error routine, the process routine, and the return routine. Under the interrupt routine, there is also identified the interval timer routine which leads into the poll routine and all other interrupts. Although only one block is indicated for these routines, there are in fact many blocks involved. For example, the process routine section could provide an entry for each of the functions shown on the process routine flow chart.

The first function of the "clock and event control" routine, shown in Figure 5.7, is to maintain the simulated clock of "real time," which would be the operational time of the simulated system. Its second function is to determine from the next event table which of the event routines to invoke to calculate the time of some next event.

Let us explode the process routine in the way the simulator would handle it. Since we have some amount of choice in setting up the model, let us first examine the flow chart of the original application. In Figure 5.8, the flow chart is repeated with block identification to aid in the discussion.

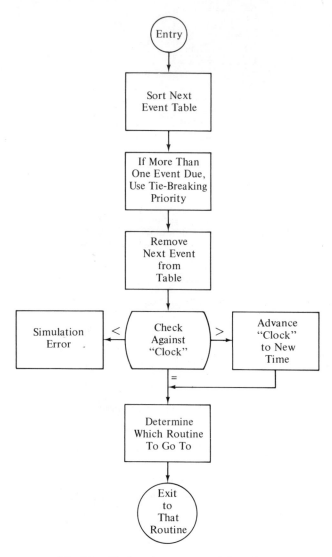

Fig. 5.7   Clock and event control flow chart.

The first entry into this routine is made when the message complete routine has determined that an incoming message is completely in processor storage and that the process routine is idle. From that point on, the routine will remain active as long as there are messages in the system to process. If at any point there are no messages in the system to process, the process routine simply waits for the next message and entry from the message complete routine as was done in the first entry.

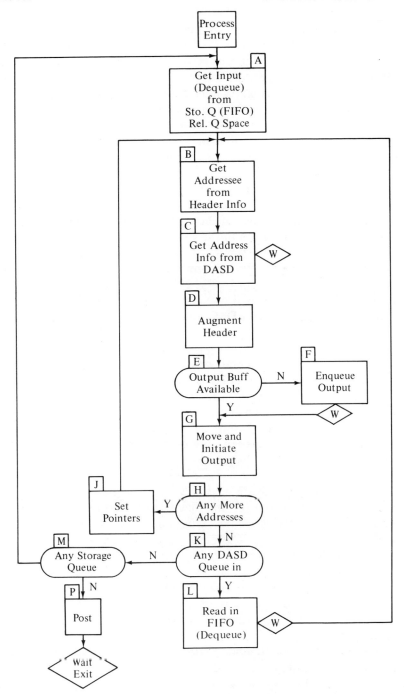

Fig. 5.8 Process routine flow chart with block identification.

Blocks A, B, and C represent an amount of process that can take place in a sequential fashion. However, in Block C there is a request for another facility, the address file stored on a direct access device. The real CPU cannot proceed in its major function until that record has been brought into storage. Therefore, our simulation program must allow for a discontinuous action of the CPU. Here, we must calculate the time of initiating the Block D by simulating the expected time to fetch an address record in from the device. In our simulation program, we will assume the use of a subroutine to provide the elapsed time for the act of fetching the address record. This time is then added to the entry time of Block C to give the event time of Block D. This time and event identification will then be placed in the next event table of the simulator, and control will be returned to the clock and event control routine.

When Block D is at the "top" of the next event table, the clock and event control routine will pass control to the routine that simulates this section of code. Given such an entry, the simulator then would take the effect of Block D and Block E into account. Block E, however, has a branch point depending on the availability of an output buffer. If one is not available, the process must wait until one is available. If one is available, we can calculate the entry to Block H as the sum of Blocks D, E, and G. If an output buffer is not available, the entry to Block H is the sum of Blocks D, E, and G, plus Block F. Following this path introduces another concept in the simulation program. At this point, we assumedly cannot predict the time of entry into Block H until we know the time that a buffer is free. In this simple application, the first time an output buffer is not available, the main process routine stops. Therefore, to calculate the entry time of Block H, we must conditionally post its event until the buffers are known to be available.

When Block H is at the top of the next event table, the simulation program can then take it into account. Here, we have a decision point with regard to the number of addressees. If there is another addressee, we can calculate the time it will take to get through Blocks J, B, and C. Again, we can use a subroutine to obtain the amount of time that a fetch from the address file will take. Given that time, the simulation program can set the new entry time of Block D, as was done before. The next event table is updated and control returned to the clock and event control routine.

If we did not have any more addressees, we would determine whether there are any messages in the queue on the direct access device. If the answer is yes, we can calculate the effect of Blocks K, L, B, and C. Block L involves a reference to the device message queue. This reference will be calculated through the use of a separate subroutine for handling timing for that file. In this sequence, we also use the subroutine to obtain the time of an address fetch from its device. All of these times are then added together to establish the next entry time for Block D. The next event table is updated and control returned to the clock and event control routine.

If there are no messages in the device queue, the simulator then determines whether there are any messages in the processor storage queue. If there are, the timings for Blocks K, M, A, B, and C are calculated. The entry time for Block D is calculated and posted, and we return as before.

If there are no messages in the storage queue, the simulator simply times out the Blocks K, M, and P. The simulator then obtains the arrival time of the next incoming message and sets that as the next entry time of Block A. After posting to the next event tables, the program returns to the clock and event control routine.

At this point, we see that rather than having one event routine for the process portion of the simulation we have three, namely, Blocks A, D, and H. The number of event blocks can be increased or decreased as desired.

Let us now structure the flow charts of the simulation program to indicate how it actually goes about its task.

In Figure 5.9, we have the flow chart of the routine which will simulate the effects of Routine A. At the entry to the program, we first make sure that a temporary variable TEMPA is set to zero. This will be used in determining the next event time. In the next block, we add the CPU times of Blocks A, B, and C to TEMPA and a variable called CPUTIMER. This latter quantity will be used at the end of the simulation to determine the utilization of the CPU. We then use a subroutine to obtain the amount of time required to fetch an address record into processor storage from a direct access device. (Although we will discuss this subroutine later, it should be noted that it will also be adding time to the CPU time as well as timers for channels, control units and devices.)

In the next block, we calculate the time of entry into Block D by adding together the current time, TEMPA, and the record fetch time from the subroutine. We then post all information for Block D to the next event table and exit the routine (back to the clock and event control routine).

This was a rather straightforward routine which simply added up relevant times and posted the results. Since the simulation of Routine D is a little more complex, reference numbers have been added to its flow chart, shown in Figure 5.10.

As before, upon entering the routine, we make sure that the quantity TEMPD is set to zero. In Block 1, the times of blocks D and E are added to CPUTIMER and TEMPD. In Block 2, we check to see if an output buffer is available. The way this is performed is to use variables which have been created for the model. The nature of the variables is to describe the output buffer arrangement which would be used by the real system.

Assume that there have been allocated n buffers of m bytes each for the purpose of output buffering of messages. The allocation scheme for each output record is to determine the number of buffers required for the particular length of the record, l. (This is accomplished by using integral division and

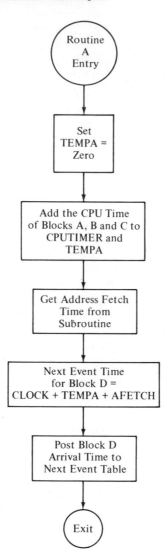

Fig. 5.9 Simulation of process routine A.

adding one to the result.) The number of buffers required, NR, is then compared to the number of buffers available, NA. If NR is less than NA, then the buffers can be allocated. The number of buffers available is reduced by the number allocated. As buffers are released, the number of buffers available is increased by the amount released. (There would be a check in the procedure to ensure that adding buffers back would not exceed the original number given as a parameter to the model.) Furthermore, we can assume that the buffer requirement need not be contiguous and that data chaining is used to link the various buffers of a single record.

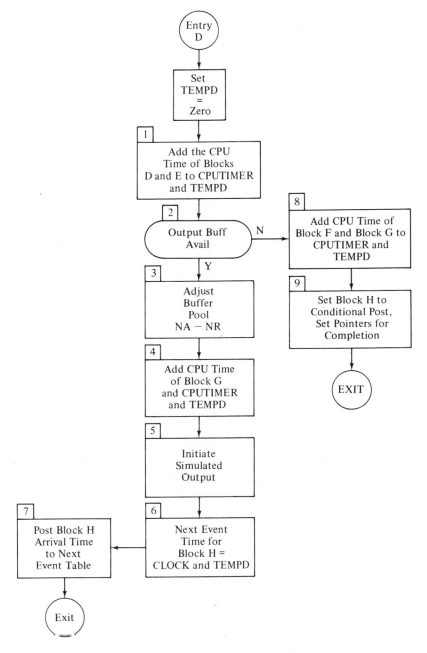

Fig. 5.10 Simulation of process routine D.

If the required output buffers are available, we go to Block 3, where the number of available buffers is reduced by the requirement. In Block 4, the CPU time of Block G is added to CPUTIMER and TEMPD. In Block 5, we use a subroutine to simulate the initiation of an additional output message. This subroutine also calculates the completion time of the output message and posts that in the next event table. In Block 6, the new time of entry for Block H is calculated. In Block 7, we post the information on Block H to the next event table and exit the routine.

Having taken this path, we could go directly into a calculation for a Block H entry. Because the other path of calculation in this routine can result in a delayed entry into Block H, we close off the processing at this point.

Returning to Block 2, we now follow the path that occurs when there is not sufficient buffer space to hold an output message. In Block 8, the times of Block F and Block G are added to CPUTIMER and TEMPD. In Block 9, we set up Block H as a conditional posting to the next event table. We cannot use the time of completion of the next output message because even though buffer space would be released, we do not know that there would be sufficient space available to cover this particular requirement. The model will cause a pointer to be set in the message completion routine to have it do the calculation necessary to provide a new entry time for Block H. Having conditionally posted, the routine exits.

In Figure 5.11, we have the flow chart of the simulation of Routine H. Again, a temporary variable, TEMPH is set to zero. In Block 1, we start off by determining whether there are any more addressees associated with the input record. If not, we step to Block 2 to determine whether there are any messages in the direct access queue. If not, we step to Block 3 to determine whether there are any messages in processor storage queue. And again, if not, we step to Block 4. In Block 4, we add the CPU times of Blocks H, K, M, and P to CPUTIMER (TEMPH was not used on this path). In Block 5, the model obtains the arrival time of the next message to be used as the next entry time of Block A. In this case, we can use the next message arrival time, because there would not be any message scheduled if there were any buffering problems on input. In Block 6, we set the next entry time. In Block 7, the information is posted to the next event table and we exit the routine.

Returning to Block 1, if there were additional addressees, the model would step to Block 8, where the number of addressees would be reduced by one. In Block 9, the CPU times of Blocks H, J, B, and C are added to CPUTIMER and TEMPH. In Block 10, we obtain the time of fetching an address record from the same subroutine that was used in the simulation of Routine A. In Block 11, the current clock time is added to TEMPH, including the time of fetching the address record to create a new entry time for Routine D. In Block 12, the information is posted to the next event table, and the routine exits.

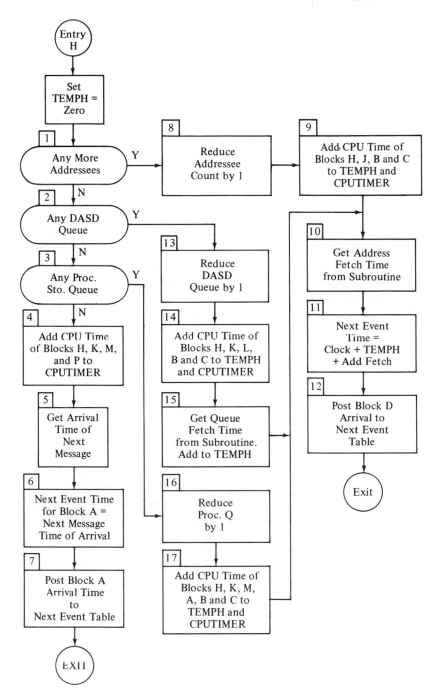

Fig. 5.11 Simulation of process routine H.

Returning to Block 2, if there had been a message queue on the direct access device, the model would step to Block 13 where the queue would be reduced by one. In Block 14, the times of Blocks H, K, L, B, and C are added to CPUTIMER and TEMPH. In Block 15, the time of taking a message out of the device queue is calculated. This will also be structured as a subroutine, not because other routines will be using it, but because the queue insertion routine must be closely allied with the processing of this activity. We would structure the routine so that there would be an entry point for inserting in the queue and another entry point for removing items from the queue. Since the queue is really a read/write file, there could be possibilities of conflict. Therefore, the subroutine will keep track of the accesses to the file for either enqueuing or dequeuing. Following Block 15, the model goes to Block 10 for the completion and exit of the routine.

Returning to Block 3, if there were a queue in processor storage, the model would transfer to Block 16, where the queue would be reduced by one. In Block 17, the model adds the times of blocks H, K, M, A, B, and C to CPUTIMER AND TEMPH. The model then goes to Block 10 for the completion of the routine and exit.

Let us next turn our attention to another event routine of the model, the output message complete routine. Although the event block in Figure 5.4 was identified as merely message complete, there are in fact two such blocks: one for input and one for output. In the original application, whenever an output message was completed, the following actions would be taken as shown in Figure 5.12.

In Block Q, the header information is written on the log tape and the buffer space for that record is released. In Block R, the routine checks to see whether there is any output waiting for buffer space. If not, the routine simply exits. If there is output queued up, then, in Block S the routine checks to see whether there is sufficient space in the buffers to take another output record. If not, again, the routine simply exits. If there is buffer space available, the routine allocates the space, moves the output record into the buffer area, and initiates another output. Finally, in Block U, the routine posts all of the transactions that it has made. Involved in the posting is the setting of a signal that says that the CPU is free to proceed and how buffer availability was changed. The buffer availability tables were updated in Block Q when the routine released the space. In Block Q, there is a possibility of delay if the log tape is in current operation. If it is, then this routine will have to wait until the tape is free so that the header record can be written.

In our simulation model, whose flow chart is shown in Figure 5.13, we start as usual with setting a temporary variable, TEMPMO, to zero. In Block 1, the model checks to see if the log tape is in operation. This is accomplished by checking a signal which is controlled by the log tape initiation and completion routine. If the log tape is not in use, the model steps to Block 2 where

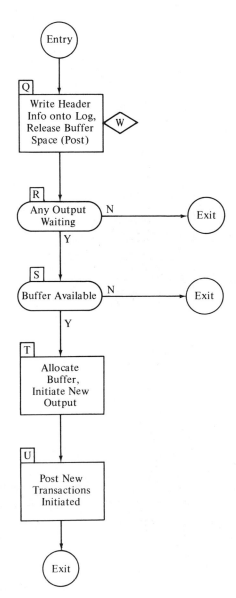

Fig. 5.12 Output message complete routine.

the CPU times of Blocks Q and R are added to CPUTIMER and TEMPMO. In Block 3, we use the tape initiation subroutine to obtain the relevant times to start the log tape in operation. For the timing of this block, we do not need to have the complete write time, only the initiation time. We assume that once we have initiated the log tape, other operations can proceed parallel with

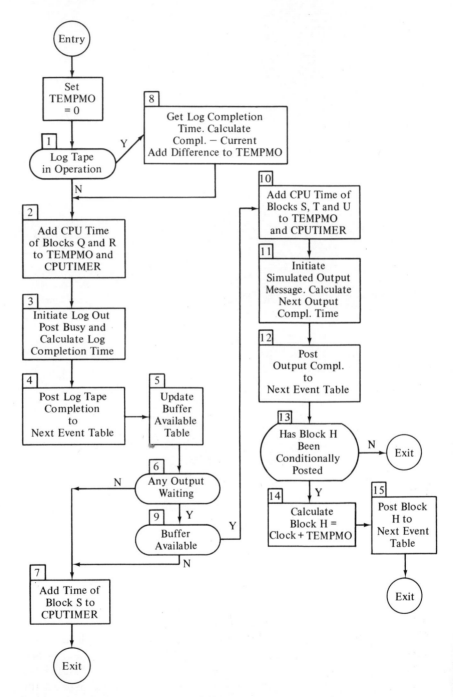

Fig. 5.13 Simulation of output message complete routine.

that operation. The initiation routine also turns on the busy signal so that if there is another requirement for logging, the utilization of the device can be checked as was done in Block 1. The completion time of the log tape is calculated for posting to the next event table. In Block 4, we post this completion time.

In Block 5, the buffer availability table is modified to represent the release of buffer space. In Block 6, the model checks to see if any output is waiting. If not, the model goes to Block 7 where the time of Block S is added to CPUTIMER. Notice that in this case, we did not use the contents of TEMPMO in the final exit. It was used, however, in the subroutine indicated by Block 3.

Returning to Block 1, if the log tape is in operation, Block 8 obtains the completion time so that an adjustment may be made to TEMPMO. This would represent the CPU's going into wait state because the log tape was not available.

Returning to Block 6, if there were output waiting the model would step to Block 9 where it would perform the matching of available buffer space to required buffer space. If sufficient buffer space is not available, then the model goes to Block 7 for completion and exit of the routine. If space is available, then, in Block 10, the model adds the times of Blocks S, T, and U to CPUTIMER and TEMPMO. In Block 11, a subroutine is used to simulate the initiation of an output message. Not only are the relevant times produced, but the completion of the next output message is calculated for posting. In Block 12, the next output message completion is posted in the next event table. In Block 13, the routine checks to see if there has been a partial posting of Block H. (This would have occurred in the simulation of Routine D.) If not, the routine merely exits. If there is a conditional posting, then, in Block 14, a completion time for Block H is calculated. In Block 15, Block H is completely posted to the next event table, and the routine exits.

Another section of the model to consider is the termination routine. We saw that to get the model started, we initially calculated the event times for the first message input and the first interrupt of the interval timer. But the question now is, how do we turn the thing off? There are many ways of terminating a simulation. For the application just described, we would probably want to stop the run when a certain amount of simulated time had elapsed. We may want to simulate 1 hour, 24 hours, or 1000 hours. We set the time of termination in the initiation routine. Another block is inserted in the initiation routine which causes the termination to be included in the next event table at a predetermined time. When the real time clock reaches that time, the termination routine will find itself at the top of the list. The clock and event control routine simply passes control to the termination routine just as it did any other routine.

Other ways of terminating involve the use of conditions generated within the model. For example, if we wanted to terminate after processing 1000 input messages, we would modify the input message completion routine to keep track of the number of incoming messages. When it reached 1000, that routine would then create a new entity, the termination routine. It would then post this to the next event table with a time indication of when to stop processing.

The termination routine would cause all of the variables such as CPUTIMER and other elements to be read out. It would also cause the simulated log tape to close as well as all other data sets.

Since we wanted a distribution of all queues in the system, each of the routines which handled a queue, either enqueuing or dequeuing, would have additional routines to record the queue change and the simulated time at which the queue was changed. This information would be carried as an additional data set of the model. The termination routine would see that any buffered information would be properly read out to auxiliary storage before having the data sets closed. In this way, we can collect all of the information which we desired from the model.

The preceeding examples have been included to provide a moderate amount of direction in structuring a simulation model. The completion of the model is left as an exercise to the student.

There are a number of special compilers available with their own particular languages to assist the analyst in programming a simulation model. Some of these will be covered in the bibliography. Although a special simulation language will materially assist in programming, most simulation models can be programmed using almost any of the general programming languages, or combinations of those languages with assembler coding.

5.3. TRACE DRIVEN SIMULATION

As the title implies, there are two elements to trace driven simulation, the act of tracing applications and the act of simulating the applications on some other system. Trace routines, as such, will be discussed in a later chapter. For the time being, assume that facilities exist which can provide the desired input to the simulation routines.

The input to the trace driven simulation model is in the form of event time and identification. There is usually an editing routine which takes the direct output of the trace and formats the information into the way that the model can handle the input. For example, a trace routine would have entries for reading a record as: time x, start read of record on unit A; and later on at time y, stop read of record on unit A. The editor would change those two entries to one entry of the form: at time x, start read of record from unit A, which lasts for time w, or $y - x$. Some amount of processing is required in the edit run for the routine to scan, identify, and associate the various trace entries into this type of format.

Many trace driven models have as their input merely the time and type of event. In other words, the traced input has information on *what* happened in the observed system rather than information on *why* some particular action took place. If there is no information provided by either the trace or by the analyst, the model is limited in what assumptions it can make. It is limited in how far it can go in restructuring data sets or how far it can go in assuming degree of overlap. Naturally, the more detail that can be supplied by the trace input or the analyst's input, the more the model can do.

To indicate various levels of detail which may be simulated, let us take three cases. This examination is to understand the approaches that *may* be taken. The structure of a simulation model will be given following these examples. The assumption is that the observed application and system configuration are identical in each case, but the level of detail obtained by the trace routine differed. The underlying method in each case is that an element of computing, say, 100 milliseconds, is broken down into component parts. Further assume that only two components are in process during this time, the central processor is in operation, and an I/O call is being made. System "A" will be the observed system, and System "B" will be the "target" or simulated system. The assumed component characteristics are shown in Figure 5.14.

	System A	System B
CPU performance factor	1.0	3.0 (B is three times as fast)
Rotational device characteristics		
Average access time	70 msec	70 msec (B has same characteristics)
Average rotation delay	40 msec	20 msec
Transmission rate	100 kb/sec	400 kb/sec
Average I/O performance factor	1.0	2.0 (B is twice as fast)
All other attributes are considered equal.		

Fig. 5.14 Component characteristics.

The assumptions of CPU performance and average I/O performance are considered to be supplied from some other source, such as the various unit performance techniques discussed in previous chapters.

CASE I

Assume that the trace produced activity from System A as given in Figure 5.15. The central processing unit is the sole activity from 0–25 msec; therefore, it would be dominant as far as systems improvement is concerned. At 25 msec, I/O is initiated. Since the I/O improvement factor of 2.0 is less than the

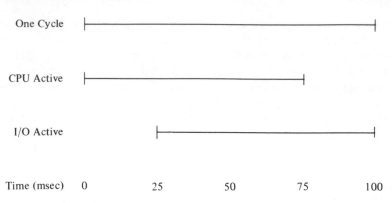

Fig. 5.15   System A cycle trace—Case I.

CPU improvement factor of 3.0, the system improvement will be governed by the lessor performance. From 75–100 msec, only I/O is operating, so that time will be influenced by the I/O improvement factors initiated at time 25. The resulting profile for System B would be as shown in Figure 5.16.

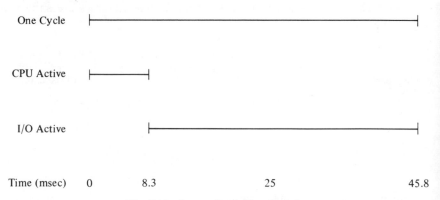

Fig. 5.16   System B profile—Case I.

CPU time from 0–25(A) was mapped to the time 0–8.3(B) by applying the performance improvement factor of 3.0. From 25–100 in System A is dominated by the performance improvement factor of I/O activity. Therefore that entire block of time is mapped to the time 8.3–45.8(B). The total cycle of System A has been reduced to 45.8 msec on System B. The principles shown in this short calculation are repeated for each modicum of time in a general simulation.

CASE II

Assume that the trace produced activity from System A as given in Figure 5.17.

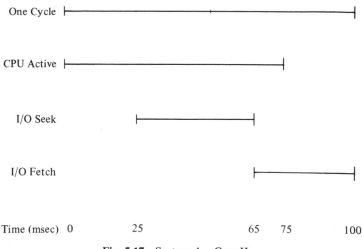

Fig. 5.17   System A—Case II.

The distinction between the trace for Cases I and II is that the I/O activity has been broken into two parts, the seek time and the record fetch time. Record fetch time is assumed to include rotational delay as well as the record transmission time. To perform this calculation, we must have an assumption for the average performance increase for the function of record fetch. Again, assume that from some other source, a factor of 3.0 is obtained as described in previous chapters.

Examining System A's profile for dominance, we observe the following:

From 0–25,   CPU dominant

From 25–65,   I/O seek dominant

From 65–100,   I/O fetch dominant.

Applying respective improvement factors, the resulting profile for System B would be as shown in Figure 5.18. CPU time from 0–25(A) was mapped to the time 0–8.3(B) by applying its performance improvement factor. The time 25–65(A) was mapped to the time 8.3–48.3(B). Seek time was *not* improved. The time 65–100(A) was mapped to 48.3–60(B) by applying the I/O fetch improvement factor of 3.0. In this case, the total cycle was reduced to 60 msec on System B.

CASE III

Assume that the trace produced activity from System A as given in Figure 5.19. The difference in this case is that the I/O fetch has been broken down into its two parts of rotational delay and data transmission. Again, examining

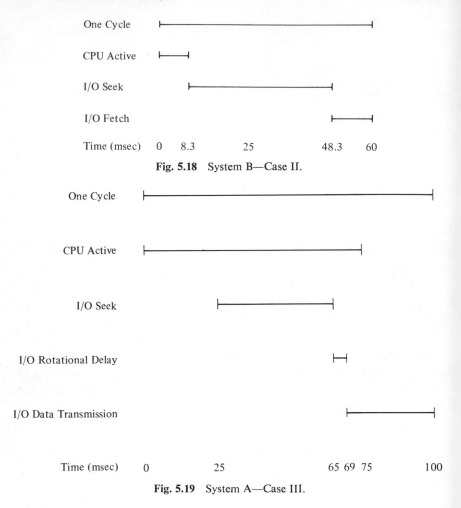

Fig. 5.18   System B—Case II.

Fig. 5.19   System A—Case III.

the profile for dominance we observe the following:

From 0–25,   CPU dominant

From 25–65,   I/O seek dominant

From 65–69,   I/O rotational delay dominant

From 69–100,   I/O data transmission dominant.

Applying respective improvement factors, the resulting profile for System B would be as shown in Figure 5.20. CPU time from 0–25(A) was mapped by applying its performance factor. (The time 25–75 is mapped for reference.)

The time 25–65(A) was mapped to 8.3–48.3(B). This was because of the

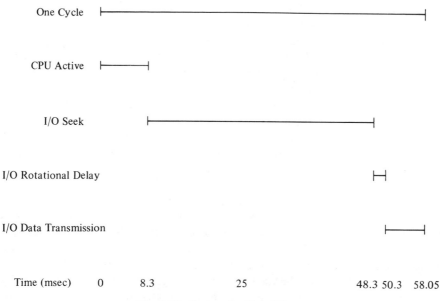

Fig. 5.20   System B—Case III.

seek performance. The time 65–69(A) is mapped to 48.3–50.3(B). This was due to the improvement factor for I/O rotational delay. The time 69–100(A) is mapped to 50.3–58.05(B). This is due to the improvement factor for I/O data transmission. In this case, the apparent total cycle on System B is 58.05 msec.

However, let us examine one anomaly. The observed rotational delay on System A was 4 msec. Case III simply used the relative performance factor of the *average* rotational delay of the device of the two systems. If the seek had completed such that the requested record were immediately under the transmission heads, then the rotational delay would have been zero and the resulting cycle time would have been 56.05 msec. On the other hand, if the seek had completed such that the requested record had just missed the transmission heads, then a full rotation would have taken place prior to the transmission of the record itself. The total cycle time would then have been 96.05 msec.

In the three cases above, we have seen three different answers obtained by merely assuming different levels of input detail. For the observed time on System A of 100 milliseconds, we obtained answers for System B as follows:

Case I	45.8 msec.
Case II	60.0 msec.
Case III(a)	58.05 msec.
III(b)	56.05 msec.
III(c)	96.05 msec.

In Case III, we had a wide divergence of answers because of the way of handling rotational time. The original time of 4 milliseconds observed in System A is very much less than we would expect from its device. In the general case, we could expect observations from future cycles to be much larger so that over the entire problem, the average of the access times would approach the device's average access time. However, in many applications this will not occur. This is because the applications have been reprogrammed, adjusted, and finely honed so that the process requirements fill up most of the latent rotational time. In other words, we could be observing an application where the rotational delay is always on the order of 4 milliseconds rather than the 40 milliseconds which we expect from the characteristics of the device itself. Methods of handling this situation will be discussed later.

Ignoring Case III(c) for the moment, we see that we have a range of answers from 45.8 msec to 60 msec. At this point, we do not know which is really the correct answer for the application, but we have some confidence that the answer lies within that range. If we go back and include Case III(c), we can be very confident that the answer lies within the range. If the range of possible answers is too broad to be of use, then we should use other techniques in conjunction with the trace driven model to improve the range of answers. The technique to use depends on the importance of the job or application which has been traced. If the application is a minor one, we could drop back to the technique of profile conversion or the use of synthetic model to form another estimate of job time. If the application is major, we could use either probabilistic simulation or job run timer (to be discussed later) to get a confirming estimate of run time.

To illustrate the function of the editor and simulation model, let us examine how the observation (trace) of System A above would be processed. There are two modifications of the cases above. First, there will be more than one cycle observed just to provide a better feeling of the structure. Second, we will assume a trace program that provides more information than any of the trace programs assumed in the three cases. The improvement is more realistic in that we could reasonably expect a trace routine to provide the added output. Specifically, for each I/O operation, we will augment the time with unit number, track or cylinder number, and in the case of read or write, the number of bytes.

To understand why certain information is maintained by the editor routine, there are two major premises concerned with the model. First, any I/O device initiation (seek, read, write, etc.) depends on the CPU performance since the last I/O completion. Similarly any CPU initiation (after the first one) depends on some I/O completion. A CPU initiation is a change from wait state to active state. Furthermore, for this particular application, we will assume that we have obtained information from the analyst that each seek is separated from its associated read or write. This means that the channel and control unit would be free to perform functions for some other device while a seek is in process. Along with this information, we have the further information that whenever a seek is completed, some amount of processing will be required by the CPU to determine that the seek has completed and to initiate the read or write of the data.

The trace output would have information as shown in Figure 5.21.

Time	Item
T(0)	CPU active
T(25)	Seek unit A, track XXX
T(65)	Seek unit A, track XXX complete
T(65)	Read unit A, track XXX, 3100 bytes
T(75)	CPU wait
T(100)	Read unit A, track XXX complete
T(100)	CPU active
T(125)	Seek unit A, track XXY
T(175)	CPU wait
T(185)	Seek unit A, track XXY complete
T(185)	CPU active
T(186)	Read unit A, track XXY, 3100 bytes
T(187)	CPU wait
T(247)	Read unit A, track XXY complete
T(247)	CPU active

Fig. 5.21   System A trace tape output.

At T(65), we see that the seek complete and the initiation of the read occur in the same time observation. However, in the sequence T(185) to T(186), we see that the action occurred in two different time frames. This is to indicate that we can have actions which are really separated by some finite amount of time appear to be concurrent because of the precision of the reading. We also see that at time T(185), the CPU became active in order to handle the completion of the seek and the initiation of the read. Back at T(65), the CPU processing to perform that function is implicit in the CPU active state.

The editor routine will scan the trace output tape to develop the following edited input to the simulation model. In Figure 5.22, we have the result of the edit pass.

Notice that although the editor calculates the duration of the various events, it leaves the completion as an event in itself. Although, strictly speaking, this is not necessary for the model to operate, in many instances the model would have to recalculate that time to determine overlap between the various units. Here, we have the editor simply leave that information in the input.

To demonstrate the simulation model itself, we will consider that it will operate in two passes. On the first pass, the model will adjust the various initiation, duration, and completion times for the target system.

Time	Item
T(0)	CPU active for 75 msec
T(25)	Seek unit A, track XXX for 40
T(65)	Seek unit A, track XXX complete
T(65)	Read unit A, track XXX, 3100 bytes for 35
T(75)	CPU wait
T(100)	Read unit A, track XXX complete
T(100)	CPU active for 75
T(125)	Seek unit A, track XXY for 60
T(175)	CPU wait
T(185)	Seek unit A, track XXY complete
T(185)	CPU active for 2
T(186)	Read unit A, track XXY, 3100 bytes for 61
T(187)	CPU wait
T(247)	Read unit A, track XXY complete
T(247)	CPU active

Fig. 5.22   Edited trace output.

On the second pass, the model will collect unit utilization figures for the various components. Although the model is demonstrated in two passes, it is common to have the entire operation in one pass. In Figure 5.23, the output of the first pass is given.

Time	Item
00.00	CPU active for (a) 25 msec, (b) 24.33
8.33	Seek unit A, track XXX for 40.00
24.33	CPU wait
48.33	Seek unit A, track XXX complete
48.33	CPU active for 0.67
48.33	Read unit A, track XXX, 3100 bytes for 39.42 (31.67 + 7.75)
49.00	CPU wait
87.75	Read unit A, track XXX complete
87.75	CPU active for (a) 25.00
96.08	Seek unit A, track XXX for 60.00
112.75	CPU wait
156.08	Seek unit A, track XXX complete
156.08	CPU active for 0.67
156.41	Read unit A, track XXY, 3100 bytes for 11.34 (3.59 + 7.75)
156.75	CPU wait
167.75	Read unit A, track XXY complete
167.75	CPU active . . .

Fig. 5.23   First pass for target system.

At time 00.00, there were two calculations for CPU time.

(a) The first calculation is based on the duration of the original system and the improvement factor of the target system. In this case we had 75 msec divided by an improvement factor of 3.0.

(b) The second calculation decreased the first by 0.67 msec. This was due to the fact that at time 48.33, the model forced the CPU into an active state to handle the seek complete and the initiation of the read. In the observed system, this was assumed to be contained in the original 75 msec. The model does not want to count this time twice. In this simple example, the result is the same, 25.00 msec. In a more complex analysis, the distribution of CPU activity could influence the direction of the timing.

At time 8.33, we have the initiation of the seek. The model calculates the time of I/O initiation by collapsing the observed time from last I/O completion. (In this case the time zero is considered an I/O completion.) The original system delta was 25.00. Applying the improvement factor of 3.0, we obtain a target system start time of 8.33. The duration of the seek can be calculated in one of two ways. We can apply an improvement factor to the duration of the original seek, or we can calculate a seek time for the given track address. If we use the latter approach, the model will keep track of each arm of each device in the system. Since the original device characteristics indicated that we have the same geometry for the devices, we will use the improvement factor approach. In this case, that factor is 1.0.

At time 24.33, the CPU goes into wait state. This was calculated from the (b) routine of the first step. At 48.33, the seek is completed as calculated in the seek step. Also at 48.33, the CPU becomes active for 0.67 msec. The model was programmed to insert a CPU active time at the completion of an I/O operation if the CPU were not in active state. The fact that the time should be 0.67 rather than any other number is supplied by the analyst. (He could have obtained this time by observing the fact that on the original system, at time T(185), the CPU became active for 2 msec for the same purpose.)

At time 48.33, the read is initiated. The model calculates a time of 39.42 msec for this activity. This time is the sum of two portions. The 7.75 msec is obtained by simply taking the number of bytes transmitted multiplied by the time per byte (inverse of 400 kb/sec). The 31.67 is obtained by a calculation of rotational delay. The algorithm uses a residual approach. It considers the fact that a rotating device has some index point which is the start of its formatted read area. In this case, the model considers that at simulated time 00.00, the index point is under the read/write heads. Since that is the point that must be under the read/write heads to perform a read or a write, the model keeps track of the position of the index point. It can do this by taking the time of the simulated clock to the modulus of the rotational period.

The difference between the modulus time and the next period start is the residual amount of time that will be used as rotational delay. This is given as $P - (T(ModP))$. In this example, the read was issued at time 48.33. The rotation period is 40. 48.33 (mod40) = 8.33. The difference between that and 40 is 31.67 msec.

At time 49.00, the CPU returns to wait state. At 87.75, the read is completed as calculated by the read initiation step. Also at that time, the CPU becomes active again. Because of the observed coincidence of the CPU's becoming active at the time of I/O completion, the model assumes that the same relationship is maintained in the target system. In this case, there is only one calculation for CPU active, namely, the 25.00 msec which would be obtained from the original duration and the improvement factor. This is because on this cycle the CPU in the original system was brought out of wait state to process the completion of seek and initiation of the read.

At 96.08, another seek is initiated. The time of initiation and duration are calculated as before. At 112.75, the CPU enters wait state.

At time 156.08, the seek is completed. Also at time 156.08, the CPU becomes active. This time, however, it is active because the trace of the original system observed this change of state. The duration of activity is calculated by taking the original duration divided by the improvement factor. There is no adjustment back to the duration of time calculated for the initiation at 87.75, because we observed the proper relationship in the original system.

At time 156.41, another read is initiated. The duration of the action is calculated as before. From the transmission rate characteristics, we obtain the time of 7.75 for the transmission portion of the read. The residual calculation gives us a rotational delay of 3.59 (40 − 156.41(mod 40)). At time 167.75, the read is completed and the CPU becomes active to continue the process.

During the calculation of the first pass, other items were also computed. These were especially the channel and control unit times for the I/O activities. The (artificial) second pass is to accumulate the information produced by the first pass to provide utilization figures for the various units of the system. Considering only those items which would be relevant to this pass, we have the information as shown in Figure 5.24.

The figures for channel and control unit utilization assume that only one millisecond of time is required in the channel and control unit to initiate a seek command. It also assumes that the channel and control unit are tied up for the full duration of a read or write, including rotational delay.

Summarizing the above information, we have the following utilization times from which utilization percentages may be calculated:

Total Clock	167.75 msec
CPU	50.67
Device A	150.76
Channel	52.76
Control Unit	52.76

Time	Item
00.00	CPU active 24.33 msec
8.33	Seek unit A, track XXX device 40, chan. 1, control 1
48.33	CPU active 0.67
48.33	Read unit A, etc. device 39.42, chan. 39.42, control 39.42
87.75	CPU active 25.00
96.08	Seek unit A, track XXY device 60, chan. 1, control 1
156.08	CPU active 0.67
156.41	Read unit A, etc. device 11.34, chan. 11.34, control 11.34
167.75	CPU active . . .

Fig. 5.24 Input for Pass 2.

It should be re-emphasized that breaking the model into two passes was artificial in order to demonstrate the functions involved. Normally, all processing would be done in one pass. In Figure 5.25, the principal flow chart for a one pass model is given.

At the start of the program, all counters, flags, triggers, and conditions are set to the proper setting. The next step is to read the edited input tape that was produced from the trace output tape. Although there is only one read indicated, some of the routines have to read further inputs in order to search ahead for information required. Having read the input, the type of input is determined. Of the various types a special stop signal is to indicate an entry into the termination routine. The termination routine would gather together all of the relevant summaries including CPU and other device utilization figures.

If the type of activity is a CPU initiation, control is given to that routine. If it is an I/O initiation, it is given to that routine. If it is a completion, either an I/O device or the CPU entering wait state, control is passed to a special routine which posts and checks information for the other routines.

In Figure 5.26, the main flow chart for the CPU initiation routine is given. In Block 1, the routine checks to see if a special CPU activity was created by one of the I/O routines. The model has the capability to insert the CPU load required to handle I/O completion. Every time an I/O event is handled, a special CPU initiate is placed into the input stream. If we do not have a special event, the model steps to Block 2 where a new CPU duration is calculated. The calculation is simply to apply the new CPU improvement factor to the old observed duration. This now becomes the new CPU increment. This increment is added to the time of the last I/O completion to obtain a new wait state entry time (Block 3). The increment is also added to CPUTIMER

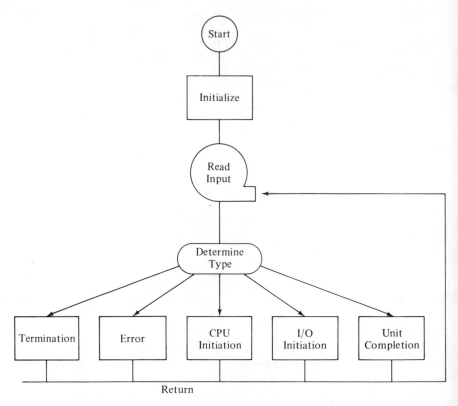

Fig. 5.25   Model of trace driven simulator.

(Block 4) for the purpose of calculating unit utilization. In Block 5, all of the relevant information is posted, and the routine exits.

If in Block 1 there had been a special insertion, the model would step to Block 6 where a routine would check to see whether any adjustment was necessary to previous CPU calculations. If no adjustments are necessary, the model steps to Block 2 and completes the routine. If adjustments are necessary, Block 7 obtains the amount of CPU time required to handle the termination of an I/O event. In Block 8, this time is subtracted from CPUTIMER. The additional load required is placed in the location holding the new duration of CPU time, and the routine steps directly to Block 3 for completion. (Note that no other duration time is calculated.)

In Figure 5.27, we have the main routine for handling an I/O initiation. In Block 1, the new device initiation time is calculated by first determining the amount of time since the last device completion in the original system. This time is then compressed by the CPU improvement factor. This new delta is then added to the last device completion time of the simulated system

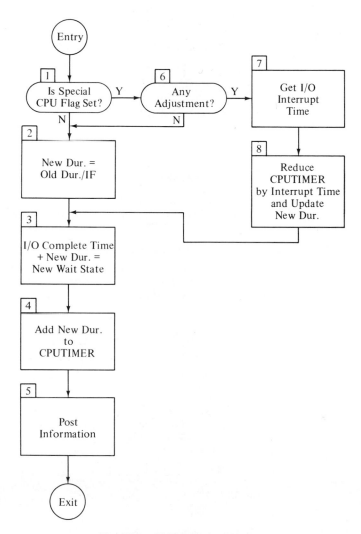

Fig. 5.26 CPU initiation routine.

in Block 2. This becomes the new I/O initiation time. In Block 3, this time is posted to the various tables which will require its use. Inherent in Block 3 is the determination of which device, control unit, and channel are involved in the operation. The posting of the device start time must be relevant to the device, channel, and control unit. In Block 4, the model determines whether the simulated facilities are busy. If any of the facilities, device, channel, or control unit, is busy, the model will then go into a delay routine which will calculate a new start time for the facilities involved. If the facilities are not

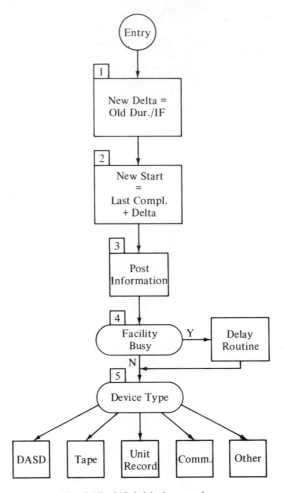

Fig. 5.27   I/O initiation routine.

busy, the model steps to Block 5 where a particular routine will be invoked depending on the type of I/O activity. The possibilities given here are direct access devices, magnetic tapes, unit record equipment, or communications equipment. Other device routines could be added as necessary.

In Figure 5.28, the details of the direct access routine are shown. In Block 1, the type of action is identified. The possible actions for a direct access device are seek, read or write, write–check, or sense. Write–check and sense are not detailed.

If the type of action is a seek, the duration of seek is calculated in Block 2 by simply applying the seek improvement factor to the duration of the original seek. If some other duration calculation routine were desired, it would

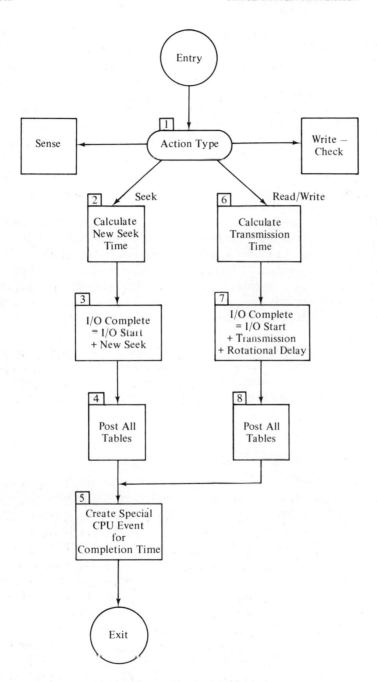

Fig. 5.28   Detail of DASD initiation.

replace this particular block. In Block 3, a new I/O completion time is calculated by adding the new seek duration to the new I/O start time. In Block 4, all relevant information is posted to the proper tables including unit utilization information. In Block 5, the internal CPU event is created and placed in the input stream. After that the routine exits.

If the type of action is a simple read or write, the model starts off in Block 6 where the data transmission time is calculated by combining the number of bytes transferred, given by the input stream, and the transmission rate, given as a parmeter. In Block 7, a new I/O completion time is calculated by adding the transmission time and rotational delay to the new I/O start time. In Block 8, all relevant information is posted. The model then transfers to Block 5 for completion and exit.

The above examples and skeleton of a simulation model have been provided to demonstrate the nature of trace driven simulation. As before, the completion of the model is left as an exercise to the student.

The trace driven model is often used to determine the effects of particular multiprogramming or multiprocessing approaches. The input for such models is obtained by observing several applications' operations and then bringing the characteristics of each application into the model according to some scheduling algorithm. The editor which precedes the actual model run is generally used to combine the programs on a single input data set. In modeling complex systems, we do revert to something of a two-pass system in that the edit function takes account of many of the rules and procedures that are under study. The combining portion of the model then takes over after the edit pass.

5.4. CPU TIMING SIMULATORS

A special situation of the trace driven simulator is one in which the concentration is on a central processing unit and its associated processor storage. This technique is used when there are elements within the units which are extremely sensitive to the sequence of instructions and/or the location of the data. Since the time step of the simulation is at about the level of a CPU minor cycle or less (expressed as nanoseconds or sometimes even picoseconds) the amount of real time simulated is usually quite short. The input to the simulator is an assumed stream of instructions. The simpler timers require that the instruction stream be "rolled out." That is, that any loops which may have been in the original program be given as a sequential string of instructions. For example, a six instruction loop which is assumed to have been executed 1000 times would be presented as a stream of 6000 instructions. More sophisticated timers accept loops in the input stream, providing information is also given as to the number of times the loop is traversed. The timer program itself will then do the unrolling.

The basic principle of the timing simulator is the same as the trace driven simulator. The primary differences are the time step as was previously mentioned and the detail of the physical elements being simulated. Whereas the previous example used blocks of computing time as an entity, a CPU timing simulator may use the gating of information into an intermediate register as an event block. This type of simulator is most often used by the designers of products.

To illustrate a CPU timing simulator, assume that a designer has the option of designing a CPU in one of two different methods. The first method will involve a rather classical approach in that each instruction will be completely executed and then the next instruction will be taken for execution. The second approach will involve a "pipelined" design in that while an instruction is being progressively processed, the next instruction is in some stage of processing. The polynomial evaluation problem will be used as an example of input to the simulator. It should be noted, however, that in practice a large selection of problems is used to investigate alternate designs.

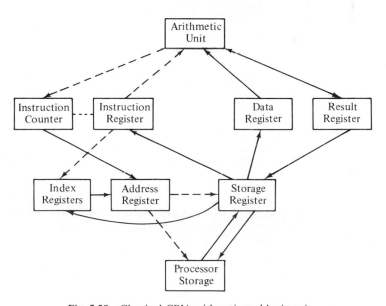

Fig. 5.29   Classical CPU arithmetic and logic unit.

In the first design, we have the CPU arithmetic and logic unit as shown in Figure 5.29. In this case, each instruction is completely executed before the next instruction is taken. The instructions that are relevant to the polynomial evaluation are given in Figure 5.30. In the real world, all instructions of the processor would have their execution times identified.

Instruction	Time
Load	2 cycles
Floating Add	2 cycles
Store	2 cycles
Floating Multiply	6 cycles

Fig. 5.30   Classical instruction times.

The polynomial evaluation problem is given by the formula

$$Y = (((K4*X) + K3)*X + K2)*X + K1)*X + K0.$$

The coding for this problem for these particular CPU designs is as follows:

Address	Instruction
1	Load index register 1 for value of X and Y
2	Load index register 2 for the K values
3	Load X(1) to FP2
4	Load K4(2) to FP0
5	Multiply FP0 by FP2, result in FP0
6	Add K3(2) to FP0
7	Multiply FP0 by FP2, result in FP0
8	Add K2(2) to FP0
9	Multiply FP0 by FP2, result in FP0
10	Add K1(2) to FP0
11	Multiply FP0 by FP2, result in FP0
12	Add K0(2) to FP0
13	Store Y(1)

Assuming that the polynomial evaluation is a subroutine, both locations of X and Y are described by an index register. The location of X would be described by index register 1, and location Y would be described by an offset to index register 1. The locations of the Ks would be described by suitable offsets from index register 2.

In either design, we have a CPU that has the capability of multiplying a floating point register against floating point register zero without disturbing the original contents of the other floating point register. The result of the multiplication is found in register zero. If the sequence of instructions is timed out by the timing rules as presented in Figure 5.30, we have the timing calculation as shown in Figure 5.31.

For the second approach, we will consider one way of producing a "pipelined" design. The CPU arithmetic and logic unit is shown in Figure 5.32.

In this case, an instruction progresses through the various stages of processing, allowing subsequent instructions to be partially processed behind

Instruction	Type	Time (in cycles)
1	load	2
2	load	2
3	load	2
4	load	2
5	multiply	6
6	add	2
7	multiply	6
8	add	2
9	multiply	6
10	add	2
11	multiply	6
12	add	2
13	store	2
Total		42 cycles

Fig. 5.31   Classical timing of instructions.

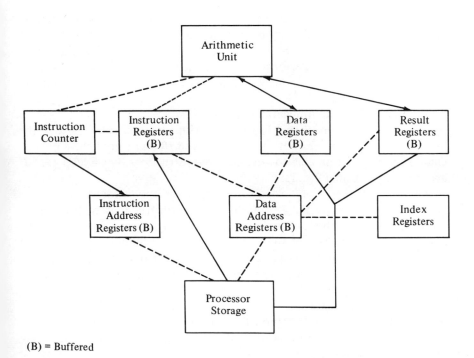

(B) = Buffered

Fig. 5.32   Pipelined CPU.

it. In this design, the instruction counter (IC) generates the address of the next instruction. Unless a branch (transfer) or interrupt occurs, the addresses are generated sequentially. In the instruction register (IR) the operation is decoded and any data fetch from storage is initiated. In the arithmetic unit (AU) the instruction is executed. After execution, the result of the operation is placed in one of the result registers (RR). The design has the following timing rules. One cycle is required to progress from IC to IR. Similarly, one cycle is required to progress from IR to AU. The arithmetic unit has a variable amount of delay, depending on the operation. The operations that we have in our sample program and their delays are shown in Figure 5.33. After the correct delay, the result is placed in RR.

Load	1 cycle
Add	1 cycle
Store	1 cycle
Multiply	4 cycles

Fig. 5.33   Arithmetic delays.

The simulator must be programmed to produce results as shown in Figure 5.34. This is the timing chart for the sample problem.

In Cycles 1 through 4, the first instruction progresses through the various parts of the CPU. As Instruction I1 leaves a facility, I2 enters the facility. On Cycle 4, Instruction I3 requires the use of Index register 1 in order to perform the data fetch of X. Since the index register was loaded on that cycle, the instruction is able to perform its address generation. If the index register had not been loaded, then there would have been a hold on I3 until the index was available.

On Cycle 7, the multiplication of Instruction 5 started its first cycle of operation. It is not until Cycle 11 that the arithmetic unit is free to take the next operation. Therefore both the IC and the IR must hold their present contents without being able to advance any instructions. On Cycles 12, 17, and 22, a similar hold occurs.

On Cycle 26, there is indicated some next instruction address generation. At that point, we have finished addressing the instructions of the sample problem. However, the sample problem is still in progress in the pipeline. It is not until Cycle 28 that the store of result Y is completely finished. In the general case of pipelined designs, Cycles 1 to 3 would be considered the "filling" stage of the process. Cycles 26 to 28 would be considered the "draining" stage. In developing sample problems to test pipelined design, the problem should be of sufficient length (number of instructions) to minimize the filling and draining effects. In this example, irrespective of the number of instructions processed, there will be six cycles involved in filling or draining. During the fill or drain, it is obvious that the full effect of the pipeline design is not being utilized.

Cycle	IC	IR	AU	RR
1	1	empty----------.		
2	2	I1	empty-------	
3	3	I2	load	empty
4	4	I3	load	Index 1 loaded
5	5	I4	load	Index 2 loaded
6	6	I5	load	X in FP2
7	7	I6	mult.	K4 in FP0
8	7	I6	mult.	
9	7	I6	mult.	
10	7	I6	mult.	
11	8	I7	add	K4*X in FP0
12	9	I8	mult.	+K3 in FP0
13	9	I8	mult.	
14	9	I8	mult.	
15	9	I8	mult.	
16	10	I9	add	*X in FP0
17	11	I10	mult.	+K2 in FP0
18	11	I10	mult.	
19	11	I10	mult.	
20	11	I10	mult.	
21	12	I11	add	*X in FP0
22	13	I12	mult.	+K1 in FP0
23	13	I12	mult.	
24	13	I12	mult.	
25	13	I12	mult.	
26	next	I13	add	*X in FP0
27	–	–	store	+K0 in FP0
28	–	–	–	stored in Y

Fig. 5.34 Pipelined designed timing chart.

In Figure 5.35 the flow chart of the CPU timing simulator is shown. Upon starting the model, Block 1 initializes all relevant conditions in the model. In Block 2, the cycle counter (CC) is updated. In Block 3, there is one of the two methods of terminating the simulation. The analyst can put a limit on the number of cycles that he wishes to simulate. If that limit is reached, the model transfers to the termination routine. This type of termination is often used with models which "roll out" instructions within the model itself. However, additional information should be given to the model concerning rules of rolling out. In this model, we will assume that all instructions have already been rolled out.

A cycle limit is also used to provide a level of intermediate output. Rather than having every cycle printed, we could print every 10 cycles. In this case, rather than going to a termination routine, the model would go to an intermediate print routine. It would generate a new limit before exiting the routine.

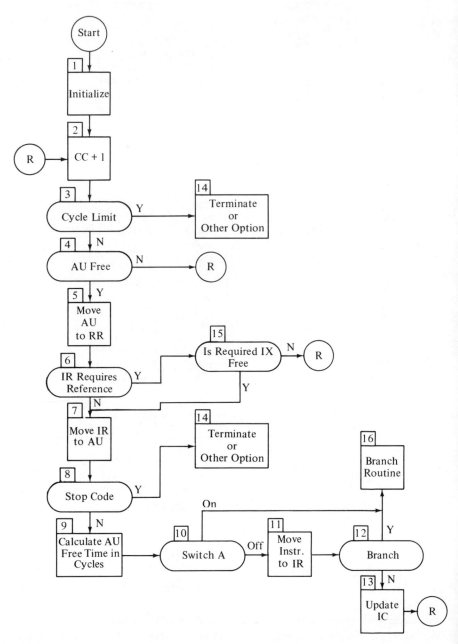

Fig. 5.35   CPU timing simulator.

In Block 4, the model checks to see if the arithmetic unit is free to take another operation. If it is not, the model returns to Block 2. If the arithmetic unit is free, then in Block 5 the "result" is moved to the result registers. There is no checking in this model to see if the result registers are free because that is assumed to be implicit in the instruction sequence.

In Block 6, the model checks to see if a data fetch or store is required in the instruction register. If one is required, the model steps to Block 15 to see whether an index register is required for the data address generation. If one is required, the model checks to see if the contents of the index register are available. If they are not available, the model steps back to Block 2. If there is no data reference or if all information is available for such a reference, the model steps to Block 7, where the instruction is moved from IR to AU. In Block 8, the model checks to see if the operation code is really a special stop instruction inserted by the analyst. This is the second way of terminating the simulation. The analyst simply puts a specially coded instruction at the end of the instruction stream as a signal to the model that all instructions have been processed. Depending on the design of the model and the design of the CPU under study, the analyst may have to "pad" additional instructions in the sequence following the stop signal. If the stop signal is present, the model goes to the termination phase.

In Block 9, the model calculates how long the arithmetic unit will be tied up, depending on the operation code of the instruction. This information is posted for use by Block 4. Block 10 is a switch controlled by the branch routine. If the switch is "on," the model steps to Block 16. If the switch is "off," the model steps to Block 11. In Block 11, the model moves the instruction called for by the instruction counter to the instruction register. In Block 12, the model immediately checks the operation code of the instruction to see if it is a branch type instruction. If it is a branch instruction, the model goes to Block 16 for further handling. If it is not a branch instruction, the model steps to Block 13 where the instruction counter is updated and returns to Block 2.

In Figure 5.36, the detail of Block 16 is shown with its relationship to Blocks 10, 11, 12, and 13. At the start of the model, switch A (Block 10) is turned off so that the model normally goes to Block 11. The first time a branch is encountered would be in Block 12. Blocks A through E are subsections of Block 16.

When a branch is encountered, the model steps to Block A where the model checks to see if the conditions for branching have been met. Naturally, an unconditional branch will be able to branch immediately. If an indexing operation is involved, the routine performs whatever index activity is called for, checking that the index register has been loaded in time, and then makes the decision on branching. If the branch is an arithmetic branch, the routine checks to see if the arithmetic unit has completed the cogent operation to

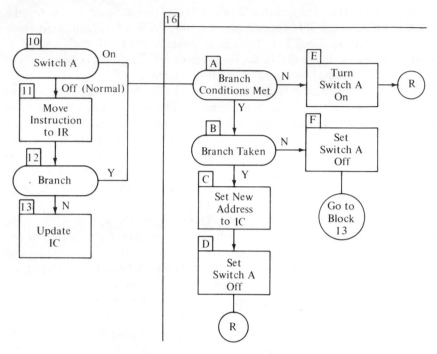

Fig. 5.36   Branch routing detail.

allow a decision to be made. If the branch result is known, the model steps to Block B, where the model determines whether the branch is taken. If not, the model steps to Block F to reset Switch A (if necessary) and then back to Block 13. If a branch is taken, the model steps to Block C, where the "branch to" address is placed in the instruction counter. In Block D, the routine makes sure that Switch A is turned off and exits the routine.

If, for any reason, information is not yet available for the branch decision to be made, the model steps to Block E where Switch A is turned on. The routine then exits.

The purpose of Switch A is to inhibit the fetching of an instruction to the instruction register. This in turn stops the instruction counter from progressing. Whenever Switch A is turned on, the model steps directly to Block 16A to see if sufficient information is available to make a branch decision. This path is followed until all information necessary to make the decision is available. At that time, the model exits through the path 16B.

This has been a demonstration of a simple model simulating a rather simple pipelined design. For a more complex design, the same basic principles apply, the model merely becoming more complex. The underlying theory of a CPU timing simulator is the interrogation of conditions within the model to see whether instructions can progress. A timing simulator does not actually execute a simulated program, it merely produces a timing estimate for the running of a program. If there are many data dependencies in the design of the system under study, then a more complex model may be necessary.

5.5. SYSTEM EXECUTION SIMULATORS, EMULATORS, AND INTERPRETERS

Another type of simulation is the act of producing operational results as some other system would have done, rather than merely projecting how some other system would perform. Although this class of simulation is not an evaluation technique, it is included here to distinguish it from simulative evaluation techniques. The system execution simulator and the interpreter are first cousins (or even closer kin) to each other. The word interpreter has generally been associated with the execution of a program and its associated data when the program is presented in a form other than the natural instruction set of the computer. When a separate translation act occurs without the computation or processing of the program's data, that is of course the act of compilation. The interpreter essentially translates and executes the program with its data at the same time. The structure of such a program uses the same techniques as an execution simulator.

The system execution simulator (referred to as system simulator) also operates on a program and its associated data to perform the expected results, but it does it as if some other system had actually been performing the work. In performing the work, the simulator accepts the input in the same form as the other system (the target system) would have accepted it. The simulator program takes care of the interpretation of the instructions of the target machine as well as performing all necessary data conversions. Rather than simulating the detailed intra-CPU conditions of the target machine, the system simulator produces the result with proper retention of intermediate data that each instruction of the target machine would have produced. Timing characteristics of the target machine may or may not be included in the simulator routines.

System simulators are used in two principal activities. The developer uses them to project the expected performance of new products and the user installations use them to execute programs written for older (or other) systems in their own installation. In the user case, this allows the execution of programs on new equipment without the necessity of reprogramming and/or converting data files for operation on the new equipment.

The general organization of a system simulation program is to have the target system's program and data in processor storage for execution. A typical storage map is shown in Figure 5.37.

The simulator program occupies lower storage where most systems have

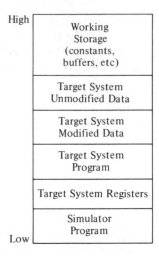

Fig. 5.37 System simulator storage map.

special sections of storage set aside for such items as interrupt routines, initial program load routine, and other special functions. The next level of storage would be allocated to keeping the "pseudo-registers" of the target system. This would include the target system's instruction counter, instruction register, index registers, condition registers, and arithmetic registers. On each simulated instruction, the simulator sets the pseudo-registers to the proper setting and/or result.

The next area of storage is a mapping of the target system's own processor storage. In this area, the target program and data are held. It is also usual to have the information in this area in slightly different form than would have been observed in the original target system. If the system doing the simulation had a 64 bit word organization, and the target system had a 36 bit word organization, the simulator can distribute the original 36 bits across the 64 bits in such a way as to optimize the performance of the simulator.

Since the simulated target storage is usually in a modified form, most system simulators allocate space in which to read in or write out information from the original media. The target system's program and data are originally read into this area. The simulator then modifies that information and moves it into pseudo-storage for actual execution. Similarly, output produced by the target system is passed through this area for conversion.

There is also some working storage for the use of the simulator, itself. In the system configuration, there are also set aside some of the auxiliary devices for the simulator's own use. These are in addition to the units required by the target system.

The emulator is essentially a system simulator which utilizes special hardware capabilities of the running system to make the act of simulation faster. Even though phonetically similar, the word "emulate" has a different origin.

To emulate is to equal or exceed. Thus the goal of a system emulator is to be as fast or faster than the target system. To achieve this goal, special hardware is generally employed. The emulation hardware can take many forms. Some of the forms are as follows:

(a) Inclusion of some of the instruction set of the target system within the emulating system.

(b) Inclusion of special registers which would be used as the target system would have used them.

(c) Inclusion of special instructions whereby sequences of instructions used by the simulator routines can be replaced by one instruction in the simulator routines.

The emulator has the advantage of high speed, but has the disadvantage that the special functions are generally designed to one target system or set of compatible target systems. The simulation of various other systems merely requires the loading of a particular program into the running system. (This naturally assumes that the simulator programs are available.) To orient emulation to various other systems either requires the designing in of all functions required for all systems or a hardware change for each system.

5.6. JOB RUN TIMERS

Although not a separate technique, there is special interest in the pre-packaged simulation of a particular type of application. The package can be either probabilistic or deterministic. In the run timer, various configuration options are usually packaged in the program's library. Inherent in the program are usually the times of various control program services which would be unique to the particular programming system that the application would be performed under. These services would normally include such items as the input/output control system, job scheduling algorithms, processor storage management, and general data management for all devices.

The analyst provides input to the timer by specifying his object code, I/O activity, and a skeleton of the requirements for control program services. The input takes the general form of the application's skeleton program. Some timers allow or even require the actual skeleton instructions to be provided by the analyst. Generally, the timer operates merely from a given number of instructions, or a given CPU time for a particular CPU. The particular CPU must be part of the timer's library so that it can use improvement factors for projections to other CPUs as required by the analyst.

The analyst also specifies as input the target configuration. Included in the specification would be a description of all data formats. This data specification is usually made in a form similar to the way a programmer would provide the same information to the actual control program for the application. In this way, additional work for the purpose of timing is held to a minimum.

The timer usually provides all of the effects of initiation and termination of the simulated application. It also provides the effects of control program services. Depending on the type of timer, the analyst supplies input/output activity in a trace generated form, a distribution form, or a combination of both. In timing a communications program, the analyst may have the terminal traffic in distributed form and all other input/output in a determined form depending on the type of terminal traffic. The timer would generate terminal traffic using some randomizing algorithm that conforms to the distribution characteristics.

The job run timer can be as simple or as complex as desired. The general use of the job timer is to track the expected performance of an application as it is being developed. To achieve tracking, there may be several levels of timer, depending on the known qualities of the application. These levels can then be selectively used as the application progresses to a running state.

PROBLEMS

1. Assume that a simulator which uses a regular time interval of 10 microseconds requires an average of 300 microseconds for each time step. While stepping through a 70 millisecond seek, how long does the model take?

2. Structure a randomizing algorithm to produce message traffic that conforms to the following characteristics:

Minimum length:	100 bytes
Average length:	200 bytes
Ninetieth percentile length:	450 bytes
Maximum length:	1050 bytes.

3. For the traffic in Problem 2, what would be the optimum buffer size?

4. Complete the model in Section 5.2. (Depending on the use of this text, completion may be only to flow chart level, or to the level of a running program.)

5. For the model in Section 5.3, construct the flow chart of a routine that calculates seek time from track addresses rather than improvement factors.

6. For the model in Section 5.3, rotational delay was structured with the assumption that all devices had their index point under the read-write heads at time zero. Determine at least two other methods for establishing initial index point position.

7. Use the answers from Problem 6 to modify the model in Section 5.3 to calculate target system time.

8. If in the example of the model in Section 5.3, the seeks were chained to the

read-write (i.e., no CPU intervention, but continuous channel and control unit activity), what modifications to the model would be required?

9. Complete the model in Section 5.3.

10. Program the inner loop of a matrix inversion for a matrix of order 100. Assuming that divide is 2 cycles longer than multiply in each case and all other required instructions have add-type characteristics,
    (a) What is the CPU time assuming timing rules as shown in Figure 5.30?
    (b) What is the CPU time assuming timing rules of the model in Figures 5.32 and 5.33?

11. If the target system were extremely data sensitive, discuss what modifications to the model in Section 5.4 would be necessary.

12. Complete the model in Section 5.4.

6 A NOTE ON DATA ACQUISITION

In structuring an evaluation, one must not only consider the information gained from the output of the evaluation and the technique of the evaluation, but also the choice of the data which is used in the evaluation. In general, those calculations which are oriented to the evaluation of a specific application would require data which in some way represent the attributes of that application. On the other hand, calculations which are oriented to the "guideline" type of information would want to use data which cover the extremes of the expected range of interest with sufficient intermediate points to allow approximation.

Consider the case where the prime coefficients of the application of compiling are to be calculated. A way of doing this would be to structure a set of jobs which span the extremes of all of the known variables of the solution in such a way as to allow a regression analysis or some similar technique to be applied. In this case a wide range of jobs would be structured. The requirement of being average or even "typical" is not present in this case, because the result of the calculation is to cover as wide a range of variables as possible. A "standard" set of jobs could evolve in this circumstance, but it would be more a matter of convenience rather than representation. Although a calculation of "average" time would be a necessary ingredient in the process of the analysis, it would have little or no meaning in itself.

When considering the case of evaluating the potential of a system in a particular environment, steps should be taken to measure the attributes of the environment under study. Also, when establishing a "standard" environment, a measurement of critical attributes is a necessary ingredient to the study and classification of the attributes of that environment. Techniques of measurement of attributes will be discussed later.

Since there is a wide span of requirements for the data in evaluation, the question of the use of actual applications versus artificial applications immediately comes to mind. Just to clarify these concepts, an "actual" application is one which in some way or another is being performed in some installation as an element of productive work of that installation. An "artificial" application is one which is structured to give the system loading effect of some real application, but does not even pretend to produce all of the results of the real application. A word of caution should be noted. In attempting to obtain an actual application, one may in fact obtain many artificial attributes. To obtain an actual application, one must obtain not only the program of the running procedure, but also the data which goes with the procedure. In some cases, one must also obtain all other procedures and data which may be in some stage of concurrent processing with the job under study. To really obtain all of that information, one may in many cases face the requirement that the capturing of the data may involve up to 40 disk packs of information as well as about 100 reels of tape for just one day's observation.

A way of overcoming the gross data requirements of obtaining an actual application is to use an application program known as a "benchmark." A benchmark is some particular programmed procedure with some amount of associated data which has been chosen in such a way as to impart meaning to the originator of the benchmark. Two classical benchmark problems are Matrix Inversion for the scientifically oriented community and Payroll Gross-to-Net calculation for the commercially oriented community. A very popular benchmark for many people is the Sort application. For those communities which fall between or outside these two, other benchmarks can be established.

A critical point to keep in mind is that there is no requirement for a benchmark to represent any application or expected loading on a system; its only requirement is that it have meaning to the originator. For example, there have been cases where a procedure which was ostensibly performing some type of work was found to have inserted into it an unexpected and seemingly nonsense routine. An extreme example would be the calculation of all prime numbers from one to N (where N would force a floating point overflow in the machine in question) in the middle of a file update routine. If a follow-up investigation were conducted, the originator's answer could be that he wanted to include a test of the new system's floating point capability. Would such a program meet the requirement of being a benchmark? Yes, it would have meaning to the originator of the problem!

In selecting a benchmark, the originator tries to determine the application or set of applications that use a major portion of the computer system's time. Assume that such an application has the following characteristics:

Compile time: 10 minutes

Number of compiles per week: 3

Overhead per production run: 1 minute

Number of runs per week: 500

Time of production runs per week: 2400 minutes (including overhead).

In the actual application, compile time is on the order of 1% of the applications weekly time, and overhead is on the order of 20%. In many cases, the originator will structure the benchmark to include the compilation and a sample run. If a sample production run of 2 minutes were chosen, the benchmark itself would have the following characteristics:

Compile time: 10 minutes
Overhead: 1 minute
Production run: 1 minute (excluding the overhead).

The benchmark would then have the attributes that compile time is on the order of 83% of the application, overhead is 8.3%, and the residual production time is 8.3%. When mapping back the results of a benchmark evaluation, this change in characteristic must be taken into account.

The artificial program has the requirement that it meets in its principal attributes, the attributes of the applications which it is purporting to either represent or span. Notice that the artificial program does not necessarily have the requirement of representing the calculating procedure of any other particular program. It may be satisfactory that a set of artificial programs merely span all possible, or most probable, attributes of the set of application programs. In this way, the results of the evaluation can provide either tables or graphs which would allow simple interpolation to obtain expected performance for particular applications.

Not only can the artificial program be used to span an environmental situation, it can also be used to determine sensitivity to parameters. If the artificial program is constructed with this in mind, the structuring of the parameters can be much more easily accomplished. This is very helpful to developers when testing new products.

In Figure 6.1, the basic structure of the synthetic job is shown. The synthetic job starts with some amount of CPU activity and then initiates an I/O operation. Following the initiation, there is still some CPU activity followed by a wait for I/O completion. When the I/O operation is completed, more CPU activity is generated.

The pattern of CPU and I/O events is set by the analyst. There can also be flexibility in establishing the type of I/O activity in that various file structures and access methods can be incorporated into the synthetic job. In the

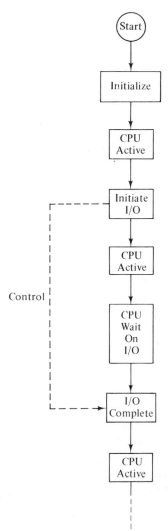

Fig. 6.1 Synthetic job structure.

initiation phase of the synthetic job, data files are generated utilizing algorithms that match the distribution of input/output. The file generator can match record lengths, blocking factors, key field descriptions, and other critical attributes. Any remaining portion of the records are generally filled in with dummy or random information.

In the synthetic job, the data access routines would generally be written in the same form as a real application would be written under any particular control program philosophy. The CPU activity is generally written as a macro-instruction, simply indicating that a CPU load is required for a given length of time or given number of instructions. The synthetic job processor then processes the sequence of CPU loading macros and I/O calls as if they were any other job. Quite often, a synthetic job has a pre-processing routine that translates these macros into some other language for subsequent compilation and execution.

Various techniques can be used to generate a CPU load effect. Perhaps the most common technique is to use a loop of known length, or time, which is then invoked a sufficient number of times to meet the description of the input macro. Notice that in this case there is no attempt to meet the internal computing pattern of any real application. There is generally no attempt to even meet the same instruction mix.

As stated earlier, the analyst can vary the attributes of a synthetic job to determine critical sensitivity points between the CPU and device activity. Simply changing the synthetic macros will produce a completely new type of job.

An alternative to obtaining actual applications, sample applications, benchmarks, or what have you, is to measure attributes of actual applications as they are being processed in their normal environment. For example, we have seen many predictive techniques which do not require specific information about the way a set of applications were performed in base systems. This is because there is sufficient knowledge about the set of applications obtained from other sources. The principal requirement is to know the incidence of use of particular applications. To obtain this type of information, simple, but highly productive techniques may be employed. Sticking with the example of compilation, if one is given the incidence of compilation on a base system, one may predict with a fair degree of accuracy the effects of using some new compiler in the system. Such an approach may be extended to a wide range of well-known applications.

6.1. MEASUREMENT INCENTIVES

There are two classes of techniques for the acquisition of data for evaluation purposes which are finding highly efficient use. One is the class of software measurement and the other is the class of hardware measurement. In the general case, almost all data acquisition may be performed with software techniques. The principal reasons for utilizing hardware techniques are ease of use, ease of installation, removal of overhead, and the ability to obtain data in a way which does not interfere with the workload in process by the host system. On the other hand, there are many attributes which are much more easily obtained by software techniques than hardware techniques. These attributes would be such items as job identification, data set identification, origin of requests for facilities, and other data dependent information.

In the general case, a hardware technique will more easily provide information as to *what* happened in a system, and a software technique will more easily provide information as to *why* something happened in a system. There are, of course, counterexamples to this general rule, depending upon the sophistication and complexity of a given technique, but for a guideline it will suffice.

Most of the software techniques have the attribute of inserting themselves in some way into the normal flow of programmed procedures to obtain the required information. The extent to which this technique is used depends very heavily on the type of information that is required of the measurement routine. If, for example, one merely wishes to determine the type of jobs which are being processed by the system, a relatively simple intercept of the job scheduling routine is all that is required. On the other hand, if one wishes to have a distribution of each execution of all types of instructions executed by some particular program, the measurement technique takes the form of the interpretive trace program with the consequent degradation of performance.

Hardware techniques generally sense electronic signals in the host system which when decoded by the hardware monitor circuitry provide the instrument with the capability to determine what is going on inside the system.

6.2. EARLY MEASUREMENTS

When the comparative efficiencies of computer systems started becoming more important to the users, measurements were made. These measurements usually took the form of "job times." In going over old records, it is interesting to note that these times were expressed in tenths of hours, obtained from the clock on the wall. Stop watches were also used to obtain basic information on job performance.

By the mid-1950's two primary techniques of measurement had evolved: the program-addressable clock, and the technique of counting entries into program routines, or counting the number of passes through a program loop. There is another programmed technique which is used in measurement: the instruction trace. The origin of this technique, however was for debugging and not especially for measurement. This was a technique which essentially put the machine into interpretive mode so that all information about the processing of instructions and related data could be captured and recorded. Within a few years, these techniques evolved into the basis for today's programmed measurement techniques.

The program-addressable clock is today available in many forms. The precision and accuracy have gone from fractions of a minute to microseconds, or sometimes, nanoseconds; and the implementation may be external to the main computing system or integral to it. It may be called by many different names, but the basic facility is still the same.

On the other hand, the technique of counting entries into routines or the number of times through a loop has had a change in evolving into today's techniques. Where once the main consideration was simply the number of entries, per se, today it is also often necessary to determine what caused the entry as well. Where once a simple identification of a particular routine was sufficient, today we find that a cause and effect relation must be established. Of course, this added information does take additional computing time from the system as well as processor and auxiliary storage for the retention of the information. This additional time and space is generally known as "overhead." The worth of this overhead is determined by the worth of the information being collected. This is determined by the interest of the one who is concerned with the data requirements.

In addition to the time and space requirements for programmed measurement routines, there is also the time and effort required to insert them into the system, or systems, under observation. It is important to note that by the term "system," we definitely mean the combination of the equipment and the programming support, popularly known as the "hardware/software" combination. In the general case, it is more feasible to add software measurement techniques to either a single system, or very few systems, than to add these to a large number of systems that come in a variety of configurations, installed in a variety of environments. This is especially true if only a relatively simple set of measurements is required. When circumstance indicates that programmed techniques may be unfeasible, hardware techniques should be considered.

As background to a decision to use hardware measurement techniques, let us consider a historical example.

When IBM announced the 709 as a successor machine to the 704, one of the main attributes of the system was the presence of overlapped channels. Through this overlap of channels, it was possible to speed up the tape input/output operations by a factor of 2 to 4, depending upon the logic of the problem and the number of channels that were on the machine. Unfortunately, for all concerned, this increase in capability of a single function was interpreted to mean the *total* capability increase of the system. In other words, the functional increase was interpreted to mean a relative system throughput increase. As we now know, this was a completely erroneous assumption.

When IBM announced the 7090 as a successor to the 709, its primary attribute was an internal performance increase of about six times over the 709. Again, a single function increase was interpreted to mean the relative system's throughput increase. But in this particular case, there may have been a little more basis for this erroneous conclusion. It was the general consensus of the scientific computing population (although there were enlightened exceptions) that the measure of internal performance did, in fact, represent the measure of a system's throughput capability. Most people felt that the 7090 was used to solve problems which had very little input/output with much internal computation. When conversions to 7090 were made, the throughput improvement did not come up to the expectations caused by the ratio of internal performance.

Prior to the announcement of the 7094, IBM wished to take extra action for its users to ensure in some way that no erroneous or misleading measure of throughput was inferred from published equipment characteristics. It was therefore decided that in addition to the normal equipment characteristics being published, there would also be available guidelines to relative system's throughput performance.

Laboratory studies indicated that although the basic data to predict the throughput performance was very simple, it would be difficult to obtain on a wide basis. The information required was the same as described in Figure 4.4 in Chapter 4. Laboratory study again indicated that the more feasible solution lay in the acquisition of data by hardware techniques. To obtain data, two "Machine Usage Recorders" were built for installation in Los Angeles and New York. The first installation was at the Western Data Processing Center of the University of California, Los Angeles, in October, 1961. The second installation was at the IBM Data Center in New York, in March, 1962.

The major considerations in using a hardware monitor to obtain the required data were first, ease of use, and second, economics. The study program indicated that a relatively large number of programs from a large number of users was required for examination. The problem was further complicated by the fact that the programs were currently running under about a dozen different "control programs" and, of course, almost every customer examined had some local variation to his control program. Looking back on the situation, although the original criteria were ease of use and economics, to solve the problem in any other way may have been well nigh impossible.

The functions and the method of connection are explained in Chapter 8 on instrumented measurement. The monitor simply counted computer cycles spent in various operations. The information that it accumulated was sufficient to establish the system's profile given in the previously referenced Figure 4.4.

As a matter of interest, the error in predicting relative system's throughput was 0.8% with a range of +5%, when the jobs observed by a hardware monitor were eventually run on a 7094.

So in the early 1960's, we had the three basic forms of measurement techniques:

(a) Programmed Techniques.

(b) Hardware Techniques.

(c) Programmed Techniques with Hardware Assistance.

To summarize the predecessors of these three techniques, we have the technique of routine entries or loop count and program traces as the early programmed techniques; the machine usage recorder as the hardware technique; and the program-addressable clock as the hardware assistance technique.

6.3. MEASUREMENT REQUIREMENTS

There are two major areas which require elements of measurement of installed computing systems. The first area is that of accounting and control; the second is that of operational improvement.

6.3.1. Accounting and Control

The requirement for accounting and control is mandatory not only from the point of view of good business sense, but may in fact be a legal or contractual requirement. The operations management of a computing center must distribute the costs of the computer operation along some established principle. Although there are many different ways of doing job accounting, each satisfactory in its own environment, the underlying requirement for measurement is integral to each.

The complexity of the measurement requirement is influenced by the operating environment of the computer system as well as the accounting practices of the user. Consider that when computing systems were used by various groups on a distinct time of day basis, or block time basis, the distribution of costs was very simple. Time of day or scheduled hours were accounted for each user. Hourly rates for usage were established and charges for time used or scheduled were billed to the user. This was the simple life. The measurement technique was usually a time of day entered manually into the operator's log.

As the operation of the computer became more sophisticated, there evolved a requirement to account not to just the using group, but to the "job" that was performed. An obvious, handy, and satisfactory solution was the time card. As each job was introduced into the operation, a time card was created and carried with the other cards, tapes, instructions and other paper required for the performance of the job. When the job was entered into the system, the time card was inserted into a time stamp for "sign-on." When the job was completed, another time stamp was made for the "sign-off." This time card could be used many times during its accounting period for each time the job was performed. At the end of the accounting period, the card or cards for each job were tallied by rather straightforward accounting methods.

The next level of complexity arose when computing systems became capable of running many jobs from many different users in the same "batch." The time card approach was not satisfactory in that even if the system did signal when it had stopped one job and started the next, the operator could not respond to the signal in any meaningful time unless the computer came to a halt. That, of course, was considered unsatisfactory. Therefore, the task of job accounting was pressed onto the computer.

At the time of putting the job accounting requirement onto the computer, programmed techniques could quite easily determine almost every desired attribute of the job being performed except two: when did it START?, and when did it STOP? There was no inherent way for the computer to determine either time of day, relative time, or an interval of time. Lest we become jaded with our sophistication today, consider two imaginative techniques which were implemented.

On one system there existed the ability to cause a transfer to a known location every time a logical branch was encountered in the program in progress. (This was known as "trap transfer.") Along with this forced transfer to the known location, there was also information concerning the address from which the branch was taken as well as the destination of the branch. The measurement technique was to calculate the number of instructions between each branch by differencing the addresses that the timing routine kept track of. Assuming some "average instruction time," a simple multiplication would give the time of the program. Leaving out the problems of inaccuracies, the technique was not used very much because of the computing time it took to do the measurement. In fact, as the incidence of branches increased, the time to execute the measurement routine exceeded the time of calculation of the original job itself.

The other approach, which did see a little more use, was based on the use of one of the magnetic tapes of the computing system. A sequence of numbers was recorded on a full reel of tape. The computer had the capability to start the tape in motion in such a way as to keep it running continuously to the end of the reel. The computer also had the ability to read information into processor storage in such a way as to keep putting the data from the tape into the same addressable location. This could be accomplished with a relatively small amount of computing time. The result provided for a location in processor storage which was continually being updated in a regular manner. The inaccuracies caused by the variation in the speed of the tape were less than the accuracy requirements for satisfactory accounting routines. The problem of accounting for the time that the tape took to rewind after reaching the end of the reel was handled in one of two ways. Sometimes the rewind was initiated in hopes that there would not be a job termination during that period. If a job termination did occur, half the rewind time, assumedly known, was simply added to the job. The other half of the time was accounted for on the next job. The natural assumption was that if a job were over-charged one day, it would be undercharged the next. The other method of handling the rewind of the timing tape was to simply terminate operations until that had been accomplished. For an installation manager to decide between which method to use for handling the rewind, he essentially had to make a trade off between systems efficiency and greater accuracy of account-ing. That same decision is still being made today.

The program-addressable clock was developed and implemented on sys-tems to provide job accounting information for a stream of jobs in a sequen-tial batch process. The job-to-job monitor simply read the clock between each job. Differencing these readings provided job time. Timing information was then provided with the job itself and/or on a separate "accounting card."

The next level of complexity, which is common, is the time sharing or multiprogramming environment. Because the facilities of the computing system are used a little bit at a time on different programs, the sequential technique of differencing job start and job stop times do not represent any use of the computer's facilities, other than the time that job was in the system —somewhere. Some measurement technique is used to accumulate the small increments of time in which the various computer components are utilized in the performance of a particular job. The algorithms of such techniques are quite varied. They try to take into account the amount of CPU time used by the problem, or on behalf of the problem as well as other timings of compo-nents such as processor storage, channel activity, control unit, and device activity. There are generally two categories of times associated with the tech-niques, *allocated* time, and *utilized* time. Allocated time is usually associated with a component such as a magnetic tape unit that is allocated to a job for the complete duration of the job. Allocated time would be used because no other job can use that facility as long as it has been allocated. The amount of utilization by the job does not enter into the accounting algorithm. Utiliza-tion time is generally used when a facility such as the CPU or channels can be operating on behalf of more than one job during the execution time of a job. In the case of a direct access devices, we often find that two times are maintained, an allocation time for the amount of space involved, and a utili-zation time of the amount of time that the device itself spent in operating on the job's behalf. Similarly, the system's processor storage is generally accounted by the technique of a time-space allocation.

There are two principal problems which should be addressed when con-sidering allocation and utilization measurements of components. The first problem is generally called "repeatability," that is, the ability for the *account-ing system* to provide the same economic algorithms for a given job when that job is repeatedly used with no explicit change to its own timing characteristics. In other words, if we have a particular job which is not sensitive in time to any variations of data, we would normally expect to have the same computer charges for the job each time it is run. There is a degree of error in our expectations, in that even if the job had been run on a system which did not have any of the complex control program philosophies, there would be variations in the running time of the job. The obvious deviation in job time would be due to the incidence of errors which the system is able to overcome by various methods. (There have been a few cases observed where there is a slight variation because of the relationship of the job's start time to the angular position of the index point of a rotating device. In other words, the program was never able to get into synchronization with the device.)

The repeatability problem is magnified because most accounting routines or measurement routines provide information as to what *actually* happened rather than what we would like to see happen. Consider the simple example in which a single job has a requirement on a direct access device in that all of the information required is stored in a narrow set of tracks. If the seeks to that data set had a direct influence on the job's time or even utilization of channel, control unit, and device, with a narrow band, the seek time for each record would be relatively small. If that same job were then thrust into a multiprogramming environment which contained other jobs, then that relatively short seek time could be increased by a considerable amount. Consider the effect on seek time if, while the original job were in process, there were also a job which had a data set requirement at the opposite end of the track geometry. Further assume that each job had its seek requirement interspersed with another. The net result would be that a much longer seek time would be utilized on behalf of the original job. On this simple example alone, an individual user of the system could be charged more for the running of his particular job because the installation management decided to improve the costs of jobs, *overall*, by installing a multiprogramming control program. Of course, the intent of installing multiprogramming is to lower the cost of each job. Depending on the accounting scheme, where the individual user had the system on an exclusive basis, he would probably be charged based on the allocation of the system. Under multiprogramming he would be charged on the utilization of the various components. It should be clear, however, that the utilization of components will vary, depending on the presence of other jobs in the system. Within multiprogramming systems, we quite often find scheduling and priority algorithms which may be utilized to hold conflicts on components to a minimum.

Although the above example is concerned with the obvious attributes of a direct access device, There can be other variations in component utilization. If techniques are used in the multiprogramming system which allow one job to push another "out of core," then there will be additional CPU, channel, control unit, and device activity because of the push. A normal procedure is to charge that additional time to the job which did the pushing.

The use of processor storage is usually accounted for on a time-space relationship. However, there may be a desire to let the cost of processor storage be a variable in some proportion to the amount of storage utilized. The philosophy behind such an approach is that if an individual job requires a "small" amount of processor storage, then there is more potential for other jobs to be processed concurrently. As a single job requires more storage, the potential for other jobs is lessened. In some multiprogramming systems, there are "threshold" amounts of processor storage. This would be the minimum amount of storage to perform any job, irrespective of its explicit storage requirement. Every time a single job's storage requirement crosses over an accumulation of thresholds, that job eliminates the ability of the system to start any other job. Installation management may wish to penalize a job because it preempts the presence of other jobs. In this case, the economic algorithm may involve a cost that increases as the square or even cubic power of the amount of processor storage allocated to a single job.

The second principal problem associated with accounting routines is usually the amount of accuracy involved in the data acquisition portion. It is possible to change the state or utilization of a component in a very short time. In the case of the CPU itself, every few microseconds it could be working on a different job. Since the CPU is still considered to be the primary element in the system, most accounting routines accrue its time from job to job. In the case of a control system which allows the dynamic allocation of processor storage, there may be some approximations to a single job's use of that component. The approximation is generally concerned with the level of precision that the accounting routines track the allocation of storage. We normally think of a job as requiring a certain amount of storage in order for it to be executed. In a dynamic storage allocation system, however, the system allocates to the job only that amount of storage to allow its execution *at that time*.

In Figure 6.2 there is a profile of storage requirements as a single job is executed. In a precise time-space allocation, the accounting routine would account for the area under the profile. If however, the accounting routine were to take the highest amount of processor storage used over the entire job span, the area would be $x(4)$ multiplied by $t(6)$ as shown in Figure 6.3.

If the job were arranged in discrete steps such as "compile" phase, and "execute" phase, the accounting routine may take into account areas by each step. Consider that in our example, the particular job is arranged in their steps; Step 1 from $t(0)$ to $t(2)$, Step 2 from $t(2)$ to $t(4)$, and Step 3 from $t(4)$ to $t(6)$. The accounting routine would then produce the areas as shown in Figure 6.4. Step 1 would have the area $x(1)$ multiplied by $t(0)$ to $t(2)$; Step 2 would have the area $x(3)$ multiplied by $t(2)$ to $t(4)$; and Step 3 would have the area $x(4)$ multiplied by $t(4)$ to $t(6)$.

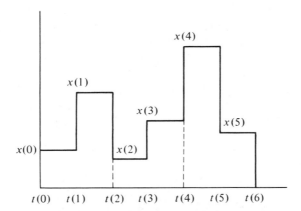

Fig. 6.2   Storage profile.

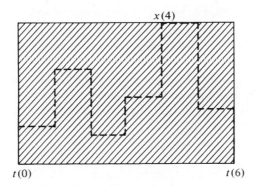

Fig. 6.3   Total job time-space area.

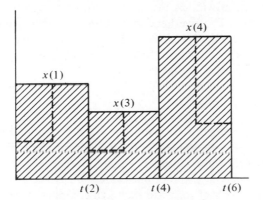

Fig. 6.4   Job step time-space area.

If the accounting routine were to track the jobs in such a way as to establish a time-space relationship every time the space allocation changed, the results would again be the results shown in Figure 6.5.

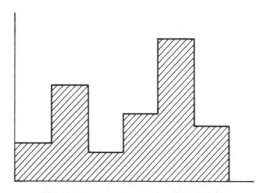

Fig. 6.5   Actual tracking time-space area.

The only thing that would preclude such an accounting routine would be the amount of time required to do the accounting each time a change occurred. In a dynamic multiprogramming or time sharing system, although an individual job would not change its space allocation, the conglomeration of jobs and control program functions would cause an allocation change at a remarkably high rate. If we add an even moderate overhead to do space accounting to a high rate, the cost of precision can rise to an unacceptable level.

The general problem of an accounting routine is that precision of information is obtained at an overhead cost. The greater the precision, the greater the cost. In establishing accounting routines and economic algorithms, a study should be made concerning precision versus cost. In many cases, simple approximations can provide as much useful information as exhaustive data acquisition routines. The overhead of the measurement routines must be distributed to the users on the same basis as general overhead in a computing installation. The better the overhead can be reduced by direct distribution, the better costs can be controlled.

6.3.2. Operational Improvement

The second requirement to measure for is the determination of utilization of the various systems components. The reason for the measurements is to take action to improve operations. It should be repeated at this point that a system component may be a unit of hardware such as a central processing unit or a disk drive, or a unit of software such as a compiler or a control program facility. Merely the determination of utilization of a component is seldom in itself sufficient. The important attribute to determine is whether the component is being used properly and efficiently. This determination must also be made in such a way as to establish a particular component's influence on the rest of the system. As an extreme example, the utilization of a disk drive may be very high with respect to total time. But if the reason for this high utilization is that almost all active data sets are housed on the single device and that the result of that assignment is the most economical method of processing the job, then the utilization may be satisfactory. On the other hand, if the assignment causes excessive job time, then there is probably room for corrective action.

The incentive to perform measurements may come from several different circumstances, but in general, the origin of the circumstance is that the operation is running out of capability. Quite often the lack of capability is obvious as in the example of not enough hours left in the day to get any more work done. On the other hand, a bottleneck may develop slowly over a period of weeks as in the example of a communication oriented system becoming saturated with work. The subtle bottleneck may manifest itself by showing up as a slow down of the input card reader.

For developers, measurement is integral to the planning, design, development, implementation, and testing of new products. Requirements for new products are determined in many ways, most of which are outside the scope of this text. However, measurements are made to determine bottlenecks of existing systems in order to plan improvement programs. The nature of the measurements is to determine both the efficiency of the product in a field environment and the utilization of the product. Efficiency measurements are normally made during the development and testing phase of a product, but manufacturers are constantly on the lookout for field environments which are substantially different from the laboratory testing environment to see if the characteristics of the product are adversely affected.

The more important aspect of field measurements is to determine the utilization of a product. If the product has a high utilization and is critical to the amount of work the computer system can do, then it would be a natural target for product improvement. On the other hand, merely determining that a product has a low utilization does not eliminate it from consideration. Further investigation must be made to determine whether there is some characteristic about the product that causes its utilization to be low. The incentive for the user of the system to measure performance is to determine whether there are improvements that can be made that lie within the user's power. The foremost ability within a user's power is the ability to obtain a totally different system to perform the present or projected workload. The second level within the user's power is to obtain new and/or different components that would produce better performance. The third level, which one might consider to be the normal or most popular level, is to modify the way in which installed components are being used.

One example of modification would be the determination that one of the channels on the system is loaded disproportionately to the other channels. Relief of this situation might be obtained by moving some of the devices from that channel to some other channel. The moving would be accomplished by re-cabling the units, and changing relevant addresses to correspond to the new arrangement.

Another example of modification would be the optimal placing of data sets on a device. Consider an installation that had placed all of the system data sets to optimize a single language processing system. If it were discovered that there was a large use of other languages, the arrangement of the data sets could be reoriented to produce the best results for the entire workload, not just that portion represented by the original language.

There are many options available to a user for a single set of system components. Measurement can assist in the determination of the optimum allocation and utilization of the components.

Although not mentioned earlier, the cost of making any changes must be taken into consideration. It is easy to conceive a situation where added equipment would greatly enhance a computer system's capability to do work, but the expense of doing so would be prohibitive. Since there are so many different methods of determining costs, both direct and indirect, techniques of *cost* comparison will be avoided.

7 PROGRAMMED MEASUREMENT TECHNIQUES

Most programmed measurement techniques are based on either an "intercept" concept or a "sampling" concept. The intercept basis is one in which additional coding is inserted at key points in the system control program and sometimes the problem programs. The sampling basis is one in which at a certain time or when some other criteria for sample is met, an added program takes control to scan the status of activity within the system. The underlying premise of either programmed measurement technique is that the status of required events are interrogable by an instruction sequence.

7.1. INTERCEPT TECHNIQUES

Preliminary to considering the intercept technique, let us examine two organizations of programs within a computer. In Figure 7.1, there is shown a typical example of the organization of programs under the so called "load and duck" control program or job monitor.

The load and duck monitor takes complete control of the system only between jobs or job steps. Other than that it has no control of the system. During the execution of problem programs, control program services such as IOCS may be available for the control of channel programs, but the problem program itself may (and usually does) perform many of the channel control services. Use of the interval timer is distributed throughout the control program and the problem programs. If there is any consistency of use it would probably be due to rigid management controls at the installation. Applying intercepts to this type of organization could be quite difficult. To intercept at the time of job scheduling would be relatively simple, but to

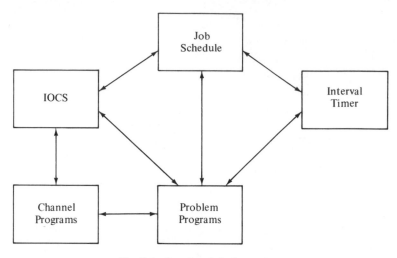

Fig. 7.1   Load and duck monitor.

intercept at a more detailed level would probably involve changes to almost every application program under study.

An example of a trace routine in such an environment would be the use of the "Select Trap Trace" routine on the 7090. When the routine was entered into the system, the 7090 entered a mode of operation in which each "select" (I/O initiation) instruction was trapped (forced interrupt) to a specific location rather than being executed. At this location, there was a transfer into the select trap trace routine. The routine then interrogated the channel command stream associated with the select instruction. From this interrogation, the trap routine was able to obtain not only the unit address and channel identification from the instruction, but also the number of characters involved in the transmission.

The problem in the use of the routine was that in many cases the command sequence was not in a straight forward manner. Many times, the command sequence depended on the context of the data that was obtained from the device. In some cases, the command structure was such that the sequence of events depended on the timing characteristics of the individual unit. If either of these situations were encountered, the trace routine would not be able to obtain a complete picture of the information. The only alternative would be to incorporate a unique trace routine in the particular command structure of the particular program under study.

After the select trap trace routine had obtained as much information as was possible, it then caused the execution of I/O in a normal manner.

In Figure 7.2, there is shown a typical organization of a "load and control" monitor. In this case, the monitor not only performs the functions of job-to-

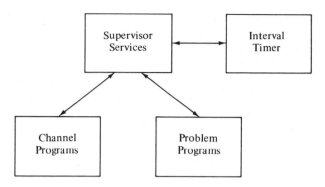

Fig. 7.2 Load and control monitor.

job control and IOCS services, but in fact controls all facilities of the computer at all times. Functions included in supervisor services are such things as the management of all I/O activity, management of device and processor storage allocation, management of tasks in the problem programs, and management of the internal timer. There are, of course, many more functions provided in today's control program which are not mentioned here. Intercept routines would be applied as shown in Figure 7.3.

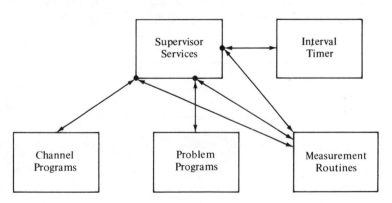

Fig. 7.3 Intercept points.

The principal advantage is that most, if not all, of the intercept points may be made at the system program level rather than modifying each application program. Another advantage of establishing simple intercept points is that when the measurement routines are not to be invoked, the intercept points may be directed to the normal functions that would have been called on if there had been no intercept. This would reduce the added time of the intercept point to near zero as far as system's time is concerned.

Let us now examine the intercept requirement for the trace output used in Section 5.3. Assume that the system control program actually starts the CPU activity, initiates the I/O operation at the request of the problem program, and receives control back from the application program when the application cannot proceed until the completion of the I/O operation. Also assume that there are routines which produce clock time through the use of the internal timer. (Whether the timer is an interval timer or a time of day clock is transparent at this point.) Further assumptions for the control program will be made as needed.

The measurement routines required for Case I involve intercepts within the supervisor at the following points.

CPU task initiation

I/O request handler

I/O operation initiation

I/O operation termination

CPU task wait

Interval timer readout control

The sequence of measurement routine usage for Case I is indicated with reference to Figure 7.4, which is a reproduction of Figure 5.15.

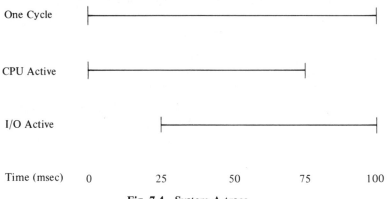

Fig. 7.4 System A trace.

At the initiation of the application task, an intercept out to the measurement routine is made before control is passed to the problem program. The measurement routine takes a timer reading and stores the reading along with the information that this was a CPU initiation for a particular task. For convenience, we shall call that time "zero," whatever the true clock contents may have been. At the time of 25 msec in the example, there is an I/O request by the problem program. At the intercept to the I/O request handler and at the intercept to the I/O operation initiator, control is again passed to the measurement routines so that time and event information may be stored. In this simple example, intercepting both the request handler and the I/O operation initiator is redundant because of the implied concurrency of the two events. However, in systems where I/O requests may be queued before initiation, there may be noticeable differences in the time of the events.

The next occurrence in this example was the inability of the application task to proceed until the requested I/O operation was completed. An intercept at the supervisor service which causes that task to wait again causes the measurement routine to note the time and event information. Finally, the completion of the I/O operation causes a return of control to the supervisor. An intercept in the I/O termination routine causes the measurement routine to note the time and event information of the I/O completion. The intercept at task initiation notes the time and event of task restart. At this point, the cycle is completed.

Going to Case II of the previous example, there is a requirement that the completion of the I/O seek be made known to the supervisor program. In most systems that act is made known to the channel program. If it is, an intercept point can be established within the channel program. Optionally, the channel program can be made to notify the supervisor program that such an event has taken place. If notification is made to the supervisor, then an intercept point may be established there.

Case III, as structured, indicates a situation just beyond the capability of programmed measurement routines in most systems. Case III called for a distinction between rotational delay of the device and the act of actual data transmission. Such a distinction is normally not available for programmed interrogation. If this is the case, the programmed measurement routine cannot obtain the information demonstrated in Case III.

Although the trace routine cannot provide in general the *specific* information required in Case III, alternate information can be provided. The number of control and/or data bytes for each I/O operation can in general be obtained by an intercept routine. This is accomplished by the routine's interrogation of the channel command structure associated with the I/O action. Given such alternate information, a projective routine, such as the trace driven simulator, can combine the number of bytes with the transmission characteristics of the observed device and calculate to some degree of accuracy the portions of time for data transmission and rotational delay within the time of data fetch. The input to such a routine would appear as input for Case III with the added information of number of bytes. In the examples given, Case III identified that the I/O fetch occured in the time from 65 msec to 100 msec. If the intercept routine indicated that 3100 bytes had been transmitted on that I/O activity, the projective routine can first determine that for the observed device, the transmission time as such was 31 msec. Subtracting that time from 100 msec, the routine can assume that the rotational delay was from 65 to 69 msec. This has now achieved the input in a form which Case III expected.

7.2. SAMPLING TECHNIQUES

The basis of the sampling technique is that at a regular interval, or at a certain time, or that when a combination of events occur which meet some criterion, control of the system is passed to the measurement routine. This routine would then note the time and scan the system to determine the status of events. Typical events of interest to the sampling routine would be the following information just before the sample is taken.

CPU active or inactive

Location of the instruction being executed

Location of the data being referenced by the instruction

The instruction itself

The operating status of channels, control units, and devices

The locations of the currently operating channel programs

The origin or destination of the data concerned with I/O

All of the above information is obtained at the time of the sample. The set of data collected is sometimes known as a system's "snapshot." This data would be used in analytic or simulative programs which are based on sampled-data techniques.

In systems which involve such concepts as dynamic processor storage allocation because of either multiprogramming or time sharing, the particular instruction, or location of the instruction does not have as much meaning as the particular section of code or task which is currently in operation. Similarly, equivalent information is desired concerning the I/O activity. In such systems, the control program usually has tables of events maintained within its own operation to keep track of the various activities. Under such a control program, the sample routine would then interrogate the various tables of the control program to determine which tasks are active for both the CPU and the I/O equipment. In this way, the analyst can determine, on a task or job basis, what is going on within the system.

Even in systems operating in this mode, designers would still have an interest in the distribution of operation codes and logical separation between instructions and their required data. Therefore, task and job information is usually collected in addition to the earlier information such as instruction location, data location, operation code, etc.

The user can determine through an incidence analysis which jobs or tasks within a job are taking the greatest amount of time. If a particular section of code were predominant in the execution of a job, then the user could examine that particular section for improvement, rather than attempting to improve the job by recoding the entire problem. The user can also determine whether the system's options are optimally arranged within his particular system. If for example, there were certain control program services which could be retained in either processor storage or on an auxiliary device, the user could determine which set would best be held in storage because of the incidence of use. Similarly, relative location of data sets on auxiliary devices can be optimally determined. This may be determined by examining not only a frequency analysis of individual data sets but by also examining the time sequence relationship between references to data sets. If, for example, it was determined that there were two data sets on the same device that were in conflict (bouncing between them on every other reference), then those two data sets would be candidates for separation on individual devices. On the other hand, if the two data sets were not in conflict (used in different phases of the job on a mutually exclusive basis) then they could well be allocated to the same device.

The sampling technique has the advantage of generally reducing the amount of time to obtain sufficient information when compared to the intercept technique. Of course, the amount of data may not be the same, but it is assumed that sufficient data is obtained for further processing. It should be noted that the sampling technique can produce a considerably greater volume of data than the intercept technique. This is accomplished by merely stepping up the sampling rate. The disadvantage is that the time requirement for the measurement routine would increase proportionally with the increase in sampling rate.

When a sample routine is used for the purpose of determining use of data set activity, a relatively low sample rate may be used. Typically, fetching data from a high speed drum would be on the order of 10 msec (assuming multiple tracks worth of data). Fetching from a direct access device would have an even greater amount of time for each activity. If the total duration of the observation were on the order of an hour or so, the sample rate could be set to a speed of once every second to obtain satisfactory results. Even though this sample rate seems low in relation to the items being sampled, if the incidence of the items is high, they would generally be caught.

When a sample routine is used to determine module or task activity, the job under observation may last only a few minutes or even seconds. In this case, a higher sample rate on the order of once every 10 milliseconds would be a better sample rate. For very high speed systems, it would not be unusual to see a sample rate of once every millisecond or faster utilized in a sample routine. As stated before, however, when the sample rate becomes high, equivalent information may be obtained through the use of an intercept routine. Even though more intercept points may be necessary, the time for the program to acquire data may be much less.

We have been discussing the use of a sample routine which is invoked on the basis of time. It is also possible to invoke a sample routine on the basis of the occurrence or coincidence of events. Such a technique is commonly used in debugging systems. The number of iterations around a loop can have a limit established such that whenever that limit is reached, the routine transfers control to some other routine which provides to the programmer complete information as to the status of his program at the' time of sample. A similar technique can be used to invoke a sample routine for the purpose of obtaining information on system utilization. For example, a sample routine could be called in every time a certain number of references have been made to a system component such as the system's residence device. The reason for establishing such a sample rate could be the underlying assumption that the faster the rate of reference to such a data set, the faster the rate of changing conditions within the system.

To use another example, assume that the sample routine was in a control program which dynamically allocated processor storage. Assume further that there is one particular routine in the control program services which is entered every time any type of storage allocation change occurs. If an intercept routine were used, there would be an accurate track of the map of processor storage. If a time sample were taken, there may be the problem of setting the right sample rate to get the picture required. If a sample were taken on a certain number of entries to the routine, say 10, then a sample routine may provide sufficient information to the analyst with a time requirement one-tenth that of the intercept routine.

When using event occurrence to enter a measurement routine, the distinction between an intercept basis and a sample basis is minimized. The incidence of utilization of the measurement routine is the primary consideration.

Another advantage of the sampling routine is that it generally eliminates the requirement for placing intercepts in the various problem programs. However, if the basis of the sample is the occurrence of a certain combination of events, then some type of intercept or program control must be present. Normally the sample routine would be invoked by events in the control program rather than events in the problem programs. The major exception to this would be when the problem program is controlling a communications oriented operation. In this case, the problem program would probably reside in the system while other jobs are being processed through the system. The size of the communications program is almost incidental to the fact that it is continually being used throughout the day's operation. In this case, there could be combinations of events within the problem program which the analyst would want to use to determine the incidence of the sample routine. Modifications to the communications program would then be worthwhile to obtain the data of interest. Of course, in this circumstance, whether intercept routines or sample routines are used the effect is almost the same.

7.3. CAUSE AND EFFECT RELATIONSHIPS

The programmed measurement technique offers the outstanding facility of determining cause and effect relationships. In many systems today, the control program has the ability to know not only what particular service is being called, but also the knowledge of what routine or program requested the service. By further analysis of the requesting program, the "why" of the request can also be established.

Consider that the previous example in Figure 7.4 was a trace of an application program's request for data from an intermediate utility file. The example showed what would be the effect of putting the same application on another system, assuming that the application was invariant with regard to procedure. If the target system had sufficient processor storage so that the intermediate data could be held without utilizing auxiliary storage, then the simulation routine could calculate the effect of that projected situation by eliminating that I/O activity completely. However, if the cause and effect relationship is not known, then there is not much chance of the simulation routine's being able to project the effect of a change of structure.

In a simple environment, an analyst can usually determine which data sets are intermediate and therefore subject to elimination. When intermediate data sets are assigned to magnetic tape, merely identifying to the projective program the number of the tape unit would provide sufficient identification. In today's environment where more than one data set is on a direct access device, merely a unit identification is not sufficient. Further information must be established at least in regard to beginning and ending track of the individual data sets. If multiple data sets on a device are pre-assigned, then an intermediate file can be more easily identified by the analyst. If, however, the system has the capability of assigning data sets almost anywhere on a dynamic basis, the analyst may have a very difficult time in determining just where the various data sets were in the system.

The usual way to overcome the problem of data set identification is to have an intercept measurement routine identify an I/O activity by data set name. The data set name may be the one originally established by the programmer, or it may be a name generated by the system at the time of execution. If the system generates an artificial name at the time of execution, there would be a unique correspondence to the original name supplied by the programmer. To ensure continuity, the measurement routine would also intercept the control program service which generates internal data set names from given originals. In this way, a post-analysis routine can revert back to the original name for tracking purposes.

It is also useful to track the use of control program services by each of the jobs or tasks which are active in the system. As an example there could be a major program which was created by the continued building of additional routines on earlier established routines. Again assuming that the program operates in an environment which dynamically allocates processor storage on request from the problem programs, a situation could develop in which each routine in the program was requesting a storage allocation. If we further consider that a major program could contain 100 to 200 such routines, an excessive amount of time could be spent in merely requesting processor storage. Individual requirements could be consolidated into a smaller number of requests for processor storage allocation. If this were done, the execution of the program could be improved.

In general, the determination of an unusually high incidence of use of any system facility would lead the analyst into an examination of cause and effect relationships. If these relationships can be established with very little additional overhead at the time of measurement, the results would well justify the effort, overhead, and expense.

7.4. JOB IDENTIFICATION ANALYSIS

A simple, but very powerful application of a programmed "measurement" routine of the intercept variety is the determination of the identification of jobs that are processed through the system. When jobs were pre-batched onto tape for processing through a simple control program such as a job-to-job monitor, the identification of the job was usually determined at the time of transcription. This information was easily summarized for all work processed. In fact, this was usually done to allow the operators of the system to keep track of the jobs as they went through the computer room. When jobs are entered into the system directly as they arrive, the recording of the identification may never be externally displayed except during the execution of that particular job.

When the results of the job processing are placed on magnetic tape for off-line transcription for printing or punching or plotting, the job identification is naturally maintained with the output. When the output of the job is placed, for example, on a direct access device for transcription by the main system itself the job identification is also maintained with the output.

In the general case, there is ample opportunity to determine the identification of the various jobs as they pass through the system. The reason for establishing an intercept routine to capture job identification is to simply take advantage of one of the opportunities. The problem that the routine is trying to overcome is one of *retention* of data in machine readable form that can be used at a later time to analyze the work on the system.

Although the job ID may have been displayed on the operator's console or recorded with the output, those messages may not have been retained either by the system or on any media. In the case of magnetic tape output for off-line transcription, as soon as the output has been verified, that tape may be subject to reuse. If that occurs, naturally, all information previously on the tape is lost. In the case where a job's output is placed on a direct access device in order for the system itself to transcribe the information, as soon as the transcription has been verified, those records are subject to purging so that the space on the direct access device may be used for some other job. After that happens, the only place that the job identification is known is on the printed, punched, or plotted output that went back to the originator of the job, or maybe in the systems accounting log, if that log maintains job and step identification.

In the case of tape, the reuse of the reel may not occur for several days, depending on the requirements of the installation. In the case of direct access space, the purge and reuse of the space could be immediate. If verification procedures are not used, the purge could occur within milliseconds after the last output had been performed.

The purpose of obtaining job identification information is to allow the analyst to determine whether the system is optimally configured for the work load being processed. For example, a system could be configured such that some of the system data sets and library files optimized the use of a particular language. If the assumption were made that almost all of the compilations were performed in that language, there may not have been any consideration given to the placement of data sets for the compilation of other languages were they to occur. A job identification analysis may be used to verify such an assumption. If on analyzing job identification, it turned out that a reasonably high percentage of the work is performed in some other language, steps could be taken to optimize the arrangement of data sets to take into account the presence of the other language or languages.

A simple trace of job identification would include the job's own identification as well as an indication of various other attributes. If the job involves compilation, the routine would get the name of the language used. In today's environment, a job may consist of many different segments or steps. A typical three-step job would be a compile step, an editing step where the output of the compiler would be put into a form ready to load into the system, and an execution step where the compiled program actually performs its function on its own input data. Under the step concept a job can have many steps and combinations of steps. Furthermore, a job may utilize more than one language in compiling various steps. Therefore, the job ID routine would examine each individual step to obtain relevant information. Typical for each step would be the step identification, system programs used, the amount of input, the amount of output, and requirements for intermediate I/O.

Many systems operate in an environment where each job must have, along with all normal information, an estimate of job time or CPU time. In multiprogramming systems, CPU time is normally the cogent input. The originator of the program run has an incentive to be as accurate as possible. If the CPU estimate is too short, the system may cause an early termination of the program. This is because many systems use the CPU estimate (plus some tolerance) to determine whether a program may be in an infinite loop. The tendency, therefore, would be to over-estimate the CPU requirement. On the other hand, estimated CPU time is also used in systems to establish the priority under which the particular job would be scheduled. It is a normal practice to schedule "short" jobs in the prime hours of the working day and "long" jobs for second and third shift operation. If CPU time is used for this function, the originator would want to keep the estimate as low as possible.

If the job ID routine obtained the CPU estimate along with other information, it would probably be reasonably accurate because of the constraints above. Depending on how the job ID routine operates, it may be able to obtain actual information on what the jobs and their steps actually used in the system.

A job ID routine can operate at the initiation of jobs and steps, the termination of jobs and steps, or both. If the routine operates at initiation time only, then it can easily obtain information on jobs coming into the system, except that it would have to use estimates that the originator supplied with his other input. If the job ID routine operates at termination time only, it will be able to pick up what actually happened to the jobs in the system. The problem here is that what actually happened to a job in the system may not be the same as what was intended to happen. Consider a job with eight steps that gets an early termination in the first step because of an aborted compilation. The job ID routine would probably get information on the first step only because of the normal practice of skipping over all other steps in the input stream.

If time and space are available, the job ID routine could operate with both the initiation and termination of jobs and steps. This would provide the most accurate picture of what was intended and what actually happened. The only disadvantage to doing this would be the additional time and space requirements. However, those additional requirements may be justified by the value of the output data.

The way the job ID routine usually works is to simply interrogate the job identification and accounting information which is read into the system at the beginning of each job and step. (These cards are normally called job control cards.) The information is collected in some buffer space of the analysis routine. When the buffer is filled, the information is written out to some data set associated with the routine. Later on, this data set is retrieved for further analysis. It is normally placed on magnetic tape for ease of shelf storage. If it is originally created on magnetic tape, then there is a minimum chance of interfering with the other work in process. Placing the data set on a direct access device with other data sets increases the probability of interference.

Whether job identification information is obtained by normal accounting routines or special intercept routines, the main value is in the subsequent analysis and use of the information. A simple report could be an analysis of language utilization as shown in Figure 7.5.

Language	1	2	3	4	5	6-10	11-15	16-20	21-30	· · ·	Total
FORTRAN						I/T					
COBOL											
PL/1											
JOSS											
ALGOL											
Assembly											
.											
Total											

Job Distribution by Steps

I = Number of Jobs in Class
T = Computing Time of Jobs in Class

Fig. 7.5 Analysis of language utilization.

The major distribution is on the various languages used in the installation. In this particular report the distribution of jobs by number of steps is also desired. Within each element of the matrix, there is provision for giving not only the incidence (I) or number of jobs in the class, but also the amount of time (T) that those jobs used in the system. Various total lines and columns are available.

The analyst can determine how to handle multiple entries of a single job (e.g., a three-step job could be entered against three different languages) by determining what is of interest to the recipient.

In Figure 7.6, there is shown a distribution of job activity by number of data sets and "average" physical record length, greatest record length of any

Average Physical Record Length	Job Distribution by Number of Data Sets								
	1	2	3	4	5	6	7	8	$\cdots$
100					I/T				
200									
300									
400									
500									
1000									
1500									
.									
.									
.									

I = Number of Jobs in Class
T = Computing Time of Jobs in Class

Fig. 7.6   Data set analysis.

data set in the job, or some other criterion of interest to the user. There could also be a distinction between "user" data sets and "system" data sets.

Other reports which can be generated include a distribution of jobs by amount of processor storage assigned, a distribution of jobs by special print forms, or a distribution of jobs by number of private tape reels and/or disk packs. All of these reports are intended to assist installation management in the allocation of resources. The language utilization report may either confirm or influence the organization of the system residence facility. Data set analysis can influence the allocation of buffer space. Processor storage utilization can influence the selection of multiprogramming facilities.

In the above examples, the element of "job time" was included. In a multiprogramming environment several different concepts of time could be used. CPU time or time of the job in the system are just about the two extremes. Again, the analyst should determine what is of interest to the user and then select the most valuable parameters.

7.5. MODULE TRACING

Almost at the opposite end of the spectrum from determining job identification is the problem of tracing module activity. Here the word, module, is used to mean a portion of coding interior to a task or any other major section of coding of a program. The importance of module tracing is generally in regard to control program services or important modules of a problem program such as found in communications activity.

Since the module is interior to a task or job step, there is generally a requirement to intercept the module with additional coding which will cause a measurement routine to account for its use. The general method of intercepting the module is to put transfer instructions at the entry point and exit point of the module under study. If there is more than one entry point to the module, then an intercept can be placed at the first point of common code, or individual intercepts can be placed at each entry point. Generally, we would find an intercept point at the first point of common entry.

The purpose of module tracing is to determine the incidence and duration of particular sub-sections of coding within a program. The reason that duration would be measured is to determine the average or range of execution time if the module were sensitive to either the data or input parameters or environment parameters. Once the duration or average duration of a module is established, then the measurement routine would be used for the most part to determine the incidence of utilization of the module.

The method of intercepting the module, shown in Figure 7.7, is to replace

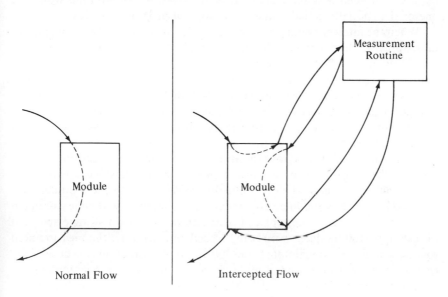

Fig. 7.7 Module tracing.

its own original instruction or instructions with an instruction which causes a branch or transfer to the measurement routine. If the system allows for simple entry points to the measurement routine or the ability of special instructions to interrogate registers which contain the transferred-from point, a simple transfer instruction can be used to transfer from the module to the measurement routine. Here, the assumption is that the location from which the transfer takes place uniquely identifies the module of interest. If this is not the case, then there is usually a pair of instructions placed into the modules of interest. The first instruction would be the one which causes a transfer of control to the measurement routine. The second instruction would be a null or no-operation (NO-OP) which contains module identification. If necessary, there would also be identification as to whether this was an entry point or an exit point of the module.

The instruction which causes the transfer is highly dependent upon the system and control program philosophy of the measurement routine. In general, it will be a linkage transfer that causes the transferred-from location to be put into some interrogable register. In this way, the measurement routine can determine where the module identification is located. In some systems the measurement routine is operating in a special privileged or supervisory mode of operation. In this case, the problem programs have to execute a special type of call instruction which transfers to the supervisor or control program through a common entry point. These calls are in themselves especially coded to identify the type of control program service which they require. For such a system, the call to the measurement routine would be one of the specially coded requests for control program services.

When the intercept point to a module is identified, one of two conventions must apply. Either the module has additional instructions added to its coding, or additional instructions replace some of its coding. If additional instructions are added to the coding, the only disadvantage is that the module is increased in its storage requirements. Although this seems like a simple change to the characteristics of the module, in some systems there may be a requirement for a re-compilation or re-editing of the module with all of its associated coding.

If the additional instructions to cause the intercept replace existing instructions in the module, then the measurement routine must ensure that the instructions are executed before control is passed back to the module. This means that for every module being measured concurrently, the measurement routine must maintain the replaced instructions in its own storage space. If for example, 100 modules were being traced concurrently, the measurement routine would have to maintain some 300 different instructions to successfully transfer control back to the module (2 for the replaced instructions and 1 to transfer back). If entry and exit points are traced, the number would double.

One of the problems with using a pair of instructions to transfer from a module to a measurement routine is the question: where is the NO-OP instruction that has the module identification? We could normally expect that if the intercept transfer instruction were in the location alpha, the NO-OP identification would be in the location alpha plus one. Unfortunately, many entries into subroutines have a convention that the entry into the subroutine is location alpha, and parameters are inserted by some other program into the locations alpha plus one to alpha plus N. If this type of entry philosophy is maintained, then the measurement routine would have some problems in determining the location of the identification of the module. Of course, if a convention were established that for all routines the entry point would be location alpha, the routine identification would be alpha plus one, and all parameters would follow that location, then measurement routines would have a much easier time in identifying modules.

The general method of establishing the intercept points is for the analyst to indicate to the measurement routine at an initializing point which modules should be intercepted and in what manner. This initialization procedure usually takes place at the time the modules are being edited together for loading into the system as a complete program. The intercept initialization routine replaces or adds instructions as required to the modules which will be traced. If instructions are replaced, the measurement routine stores the replaced instructions for subsequent execution. Following the initialization phase, the measurement routine simply waits for one of the modules to be encountered at which time the measurement routine is invoked.

Within the general subject of module tracing is the special category of tracing the use of control program services. If the system and control program have direct transfers into the various services, then there would be instruction addition or instruction replacement just as there would be for problem program modules. If, however, special instructions were utilized to call on control program services, a simple intercept routine could be established to catch all calls for control program services. Following the acquisition of data concerned with the call for services, the measurement routine could then direct control to the particular service which was originally requested.

A special case of requests for control program services would be the tracing of requests for I/O activity. This particular type of trace routine would be very popular because of the importance of I/O events with regard to CPU events. This trace would be especially important when assessing the effects of a multiprogramming system or time sharing system. Even though the incentive of such systems is to maximize the utilization of the CPU or job-elapsed time (not necessarily the same criterion), it must be recognized that the complement of I/O facilities is a critical factor in such an operation. In many cases, the complement of I/O facilities must be increased to achieve the desired result.

If we add the trace of CPU status (active to wait and vice versa), to the I/O trace, the complete trace is obtained for use by trace driven simulators as described in Chapter 5.

7.6. MULTIPROGRAMMING ACTIVITY
ACCOUNTING

In a multiprogramming or time sharing environment the distinction between job accounting and activity measurement is extremely slight. In multiprogramming merely accounting for the total elapsed time from initial entry of a job until final processing of the output has been shown to be an insufficient measure for most accounting purposes. Although economic algorithms may vary, they all require information as to what actually happened on behalf of the job while in the system. The differences in job accounting and activity measurement are principally in the areas of allocated devices. In job accounting, if a device is exclusively *allocated* to a particular job, the accounting structure would consider the device charged to the job because of its preemptive nature. In activity measurement, the analyst would also want to know the *utilization* of the device. In practically all other facilities, the information required for job accounting and activity utilization would be the same.

Intercept routines are generally used at all points concerned with the processing of a job. In the case of CPU time, whenever the control program turns control over to a particular task, the time of the task from that time until the task relinquishes control is accounted to the task. When the task calls for control program services, the time of those services is also accounted to the task.

One of the problems in accounting for CPU time is in the area of I/O completion routines. One method is to identify the I/O in relation to the particular job that requested the I/O activity. Another method is to distribute that time as a general overhead factor across all jobs that were processed.

Another problem in job accounting occurs when a job of higher priority forces a delay in a job of lesser priority. Again, an accounting routine can charge this extra activity to the forcing job or distribute the effects over all jobs. Whichever accounting method is used, the measurement routine must account for the time spent in various activities.

In the I/O area the measurement routines must account for the amount of time that common facilities such as the channels, control units, and devices are used on behalf of a particular program. If queuing occurs, the measurement routines must also account for the difference between request time and initiation time of the I/O. This time may be used to determine the cascading effects of CPU wait time. The problem being attacked here is the one where

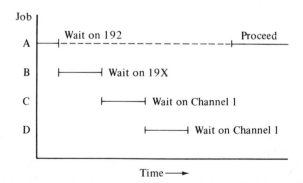

Fig. 7.8   Cascading wait effects.

a particular job is in wait state because it is waiting for some I/O completion (see Figure 7.8). Because I/O is in progress for that program, further I/O requests for that facility must be enqueued.

This causes another program to go into a wait state. There could be a cascading effect such that all programs in the system then enter a wait state. The *effect* is that there are many programs in wait state. The *cause* is that first program which preempted the necessary facilities. The accounting routines could charge the system wait time to the first program or, again, distribute the time across all programs as overhead. In either event, the measurement routines must account for the presence and cause of the wait state.

7.7. FACILITY REQUIREMENTS

Programmed measurement techniques do use facilities of the host system. They take not only the time to execute, but also space in processor storage, space in auxiliary storage, and time to read out the results of the measurement.

Processor storage can be considered in two parts: space for the control program and space for problem programs. Taking space in the control program reduces space for all problem programs which may be run in the system. However, taking the space as a region along with all other problem programs reduces the probability of conflict. Of course, when the measurement routine has been activated, it must obtain processor storage space from somewhere. However, when it is not in use, it may be easier to give back problem program space than control program space. For this reason, there is a tendency to merely put the intercept points with the minimum amount of coding in the control program's area. The rest of the measurement routine is allocated in the space for problem programs.

Another processor storage requirement for measurement routines is space for the buffering of measured information. This requirement can be reduced at the expense of writing shorter records onto the output device. The effect of writing shorter records is to require more of the system's I/O facility. Tradeoffs must be made between these two attributes for any particular situation.

Finally, there is the requirement for auxiliary storage for the output of results. To minimize interference with the system's normal operation, facilities may be uniquely assigned to the measurement routine. Sometimes the minimum interference which can practically be achieved is to allocate a magnetic tape drive for the output function. All other system's facilities must be shared with the applications under study. If the output is placed on a direct access device, there can be several hundred milliseconds of interference caused by an access arm moving out of its normal position.

An obvious method of reducing requirements on system's facilities is to defer as much of the massaging of the data as possible to a subsequent routine which can be executed at the convenience of the installation. Even this, however, should not be taken as a truism. Consider the example of obtaining a distribution of instruction codes executed. It could very well take more time and space to stream out the results of a trace program than to simply distribute the information obtained from the trace to a table contained in processor storage. Then at the end of the run, the table is simply read out.

The principal disadvantage of using programmed measurement techniques is that they do require system's facilities. It is possible that taking time or space from a system will cause a disproportionate interference with the normal operation. There is the pathological case of an allocation to a measurement routine reducing available processor storage thus causing one major problem program to go into a complex overlay structure. The result was that the program took twice as much auxiliary storage and ran four times as long. Hopefully, the occurrence of this phenomena is rare. But if one determines that the use of programmed techniques produces adverse situations which are not justified by the value of the data obtained, then other techniques should be examined.

PROBLEMS

1. If a measurement routine requires 10 msec of CPU time, what is the percentage of CPU degradation (additional overhead) if the routine is entered on an average of 10 times per second?

2. Given the following system profile:

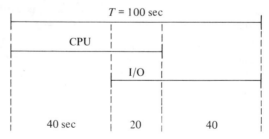

What increase in job time would be expected from the routine in Problem 1?

3. Assume that for every 10th entry of the routine in Problem 1, a record of 2,000 bytes must be written onto a tape that has a start/stop time of 5 msec and a 90 kb transmission rate. What additional effect will this have on the profile in Problem 2?

4. Assume that a sample type routine requires 10 μsec on a 1MIP machine. How much additional CPU time is required to obtain

(a) a 1% sample of instructions?

(b) a 10% sample of instructions?

5. Assume that a full interpretive instruction trace routine (100% sample) operates 20 times slower than CPU real time. For the routine in Problem 4, at what percent sample should the analyst consider the use of the interpretive trace routine rather than the sample routine?

Note: The following problems are optional, depending on facilities available.

6. Implement a job identification routine (to the step level, if applicable). Take a sample over one day's operation. Analyze results for the incidence of use of various system's facilities.

7. Implement a sampling measurement routine to obtain the items listed at the beginning of Section 7.2.

8. Implement a module trace routine that allows for the measurement of up to 32 modules concurrently. Use user name module identification at initialization time.

9. Implement an event trace routine to provide the information required by the simulator of Problem 9, Chapter 5.

8 INSTRUMENTED MEASUREMENT TECHNIQUES

In Chapter 6 we noticed the early forms of hardware measurement techniques; namely, the wall clock, the stop watch, and the time stamp. They naturally had the characteristic that they were observed or controlled manually with no relation to the computer system except through the operator. Today, we find the same functions that were performed by those devices incorporated into instrumented measurement techniques. The functions are known as "time of day" and "time interval." The primary differences are that the devices are connected directly to a host computer system and that control is derived by observing particular actions in the host computer rather than relying totally on an operator.

The hardware monitor can accumulate the time and the occurrence of many events simultaneously. Where time of day calculations and time intervals provide information on a job as a whole, the hardware monitor provides information concerning the activities of various systems components within the job.

It is useful to group hardware monitors into two classes; namely, summary type devices and dynamic type devices. The summary type device has the characteristic that it will accumulate the time or occurrence of a particular type of event for the total amount of time or total number of occurrences during the entire period of observation. It therefore provides the information as to how much or how often an event has occurred without regard to *when* it occurred. On the other hand, the dynamic type device accounts for the "when" of an event. It may or may not also include the timing characteristics that are present in the summary type device. In the general case, devices in use today tend to be of the dynamic type.

The primary physical differences between the summary and dynamic devices are the inherent speed and capacity of the device and the speed of the output media. It is interesting to note that a device which may be "dynamic" on a certain type of computer system, may not be fast enough in either inherent speed or output speed to function "dynamically" on a faster computer system. The inherent speed of the device also includes the ability to perform certain basic functions. Combinatorial logic is common with almost all devices. Functions such as "address comparators" or "sequence detectors" depend critically on the speed of the monitor in relation to the speed of the host computer system. Therefore, the classification of summary and dynamic is really based on the intended use of the hardware monitor taken in regard to the characteristics of the host computer system.

In Figure 8.1, the basic functions of a hardware monitor are shown.

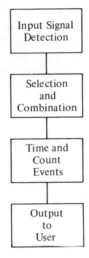

Fig. 8.1   Basic functions.

The first section of a hardware monitor is that of signal detection or "termination." In this portion of the device, the signals that are brought from the host computer are electronically reformed and reshaped for use in further sections of the device.

The second section of the monitor is concerned with the selection and combinatorial logic of the device. Here, the signals representing the various observed functions are combined by Boolean logic rules or other features that are used for signal selection. The third section is the storage portion of the device. Here a summary device counts events and times their duration. In a dynamic device, selected information is placed into the storage for buffering for output.

The final section of the monitor is the output section. This may take many different forms. There may be a simple display of the counter contents in either graphic decimal or signal light binary. The most common output is onto magnetic tape. Other types of output are the card punch, the cathode ray tube for photographic recording, the electrostatic plotter, direct access devices, or graphic consoles. It is possible to have various combinations of output capability.

8.1. SELECTION AND COMBINATION FUNCTIONS

In some form or another, there is usually provision for the basic combination of events by Boolean logic. Some monitors may utilize the natural capability of the circuitry, such as NAND logic, while others provide Boolean logic in "true" form. In the former case, the user of the device must be conscious of signal direction or "polarity" as well as the way in which logic stages tend to invert signals as they are combined. If a monitor is set up in "true" Boolean logic, the analyst need not concern himself with signal direction and signal inversion once the signals from the host system have been terminated correctly. He would then be concerned only with the true/false nature of the operation. In addition to the basic logic, additional functions may also be provided.

8.1.1. Basic Boolean Logic

For reference, the basic Boolean functions are described here.

The status of being "true" means that a signal is present, or active, or that we have the binary unit, one. The status of being "false" is that the signal is not present, or is inactive, or that we have the binary unit, zero. The AND function has a truth table as shown in Figure 8.2.

The output of the function is true only if all inputs are true. Although

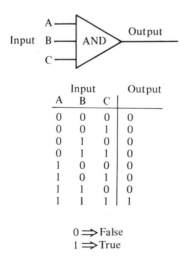

Input			Output
A	B	C	
0	0	0	0
0	0	1	0
0	1	0	0
0	1	1	0
1	0	0	0
1	0	1	0
1	1	0	0
1	1	1	1

0 ⟹ False
1 ⟹ True

Fig. 8.2   Boolean AND function.

there are only three inputs shown for demonstration, there can be any number of inputs to the function.

The Boolean OR function is shown in Figure 8.3. Here, the output is true if any one or more inputs are true. The NOT function, sometimes referred to as negation, complementation, or inversion, is shown in Figure 8.4. The output is true only if the input is false and vice versa.

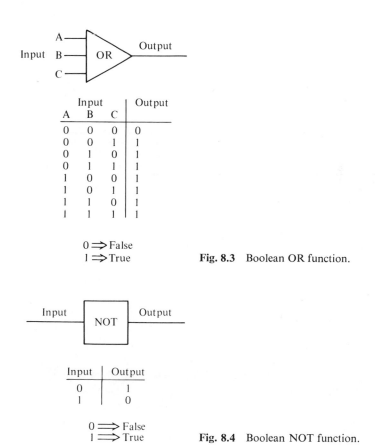

Input			Output
A	B	C	
0	0	0	0
0	0	1	1
0	1	0	1
0	1	1	1
1	0	0	1
1	0	1	1
1	1	0	1
1	1	1	1

0 ⟹ False
1 ⟹ True

Fig. 8.3 Boolean OR function.

Input	Output
0	1
1	0

0 ⟹ False
1 ⟹ True

Fig. 8.4 Boolean NOT function.

Although there are more functions and definitions to Boolean logic, these are the principal ones in use.

8.1.2. Latches and Decoders

An additional function of interest in the structure of the hardware monitor is the latch. In Figure 8.5, the timing of the latch operation is shown.

Once a latch is "set," it will have a true output until it is "reset." While

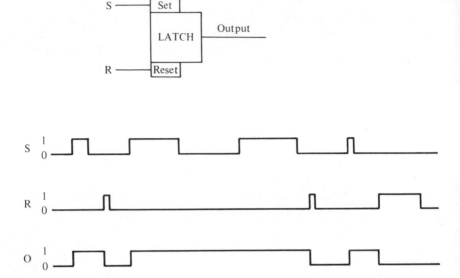

Fig. 8.5 LATCH function.

reset, the output is false until the latch is set. Notice that repeated sets, while already in a set mode, have no effect on the output. Resets have the same attribute. The latch is used in general to time the duration between two seperate events. It can also be used as a single bit of memory for more complex timing rules.

Another function useful in hardware monitors is that of the decoder. In Figure 8.6, a "four by sixteen" decoder is shown. In such a decoder, one and only one output is active depending on the combination of input signals. The signal input is usually coded in a binary progression for ease of output determination. There is often associated with the decoder input a "sample" signal or "strobe." This signal is used to activate the decoder. If this signal is not true, then there is no true signal from the decoder at all. When the strobe is true, the decoder will have one of its outputs true, depending on the status of the input signals.

The use of the decoder depends on both the characteristics of the host system and the ingenuity of the analyst. In some systems, such as the System/ 370, there is provision for a "memory protect" key which is associated with each program operating in the system. In such systems, it is common to find a system structure of four bits which define the areas of memory (independent of location) which each individual program is entitled to use. Asso-

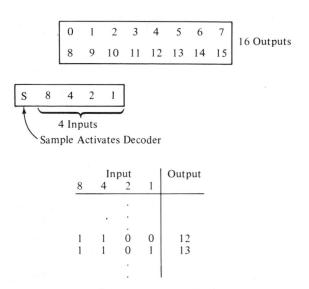

	Input			Output
8	4	2	1	
		·		
	·	·		
		·		
1	1	0	0	12
1	1	0	1	13
		·		

Fig. 8.6   4 × 16 decoder.

ciatcd with cach program would be a memory protect key which is used to determine whether a particular program can use a particular area of processor storage. The decoder can be used to track the activity of various programs within a system by determining which memory protect key is in active use. Assuming that we have such a facility within the host system, the memory protect key from the host system can be the input to the decoder. To cause an output from the decoder, the strobe can be activated by the function "CPU active" as shown in Figure 8.7. Therefore, any time the CPU is active, one of the sixteen possible outputs will be true, depending on which memory protect key is currently active.

If the four functions of CPU active, Channel 1 active, Channel 2 active,

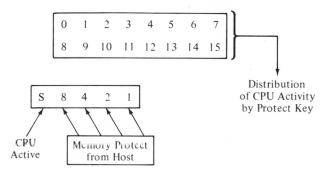

Fig. 8.7   Memory protect.

and Channel 3 active were the inputs to the decoder, and a continuously true function was the input to the strobe, the output combinations would appear as shown in the Veitch diagram as shown in Figure 8.8.

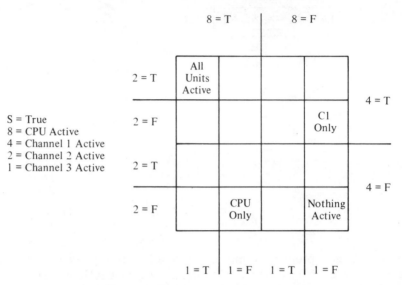

Fig. 8.8   Veitch diagram of CPU, channel activity.

In the general case, the Veitch diagram for the sixteen possible combinations of four events is shown in Figure 8.9. The output in the diagram would be true only if the input to the strobe were true. If the strobe is not true, there would be no true output at all from the decoder.

Although a 4 × 16 decoder has been demonstrated, a decoder of almost any number of input lines can be constructed. The design merely depends on the requirements of the user and the economies of construction.

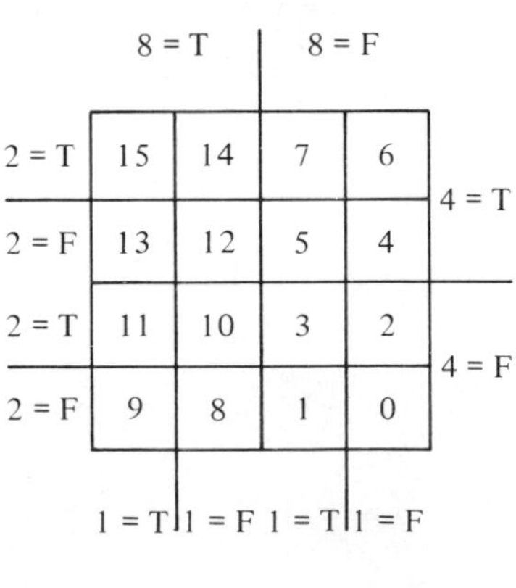

Fig. 8.9   Veitch diagram of four functions.

8.1.3. Comparators

The comparator is a function used by hardware monitors to determine either equality of incoming signals to a preset value or the relationship of the signals to boundary conditions. The comparator is normally used to determine activity within the host system by utilizing the memory addresses generated in the host system. For example, if a routine of interest to the user were always bound by the addresses alpha and beta, a comparator could be used to determine when the CPU is operating within those boundaries and therefore within the routine.

In Figure 8.10, the "equal only" comparator is shown.

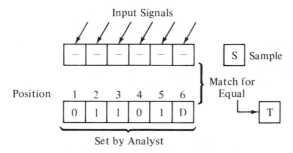

Fig. 8.10 Equal only comparator.

The comparison register is set by the analyst. The most economical method of setting the comparison register is by means of manually set dials or switches. In complex hardware monitors or in some special devices, the comparison register may be set by the host system itself. In Position 6, the letter D indicates that the bit position is in a "doesn't care" condition. In other words, the value of the argument is not taken into consideration when establishing equality of the argument with the comparison setting. In the other positions a zero or a one is used to indicate the desired setting.

Two additional signals are generally associated with a comparator. On the input side, there is usually a sample pulse to determine when the comparator should be active. This signal is used when the input signals are coming from a host system's address register which is used for many different purposes. Typically, the memory address register in most systems will be used for instruction addressing, operand addressing, and I/O activity addressing. If the analyst wants to compare addresses for the instruction addresses only, then a suitable signal which indicates that an instruction address is in the address register is used to strobe the comparator. This separates instruction addresses from all other addresses which may be coming over the signal lines.

The second additional signal associated with the comparator is an output signal to indicate a false output. If the input strobe function is used, then either true or false will be active whenever the strobe is active. If the strobe is false, then neither output will be active.

In the boundary comparator, the input argument is compared to the two boundary registers, called "upper" and "lower," and one of several outputs become active. In Figure 8.11, a set of boundary comparators is shown.

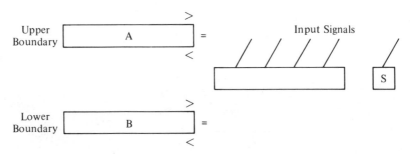

Fig. 8.11   Boundary comparators.

In addition to the input signals, there is the input strobe as well. The action of the comparator depends on the active status of the strobe as in previous examples. The general outputs of the boundary comparison are as follows:

> Greater than A
> Equal to A
> Less than A, but greater than B
> Equal to B
> Less than B

In some comparators, the single output between A and B is replaced by two separate functions: less than A, and greater than B. When this occurs, if the argument is less than B, it is also less than A. Similarly, if the argument is greater than A, it is also greater than B. The "in between" function must then be obtained by ANDing less than A and greater than B.

The reason for the six-output comparator rather than the five-output comparator is to provide more flexibility to the pair of comparison registers. The five-output comparator "joins" the two comparison registers together. The six-output comparator maintains each register as an individual unit which may be joined together at the user's option. In any event, the equal outputs of each register are independently available.

The equal output of the comparator is used to determine when a precise address is encountered. The precise address is generally used to determine when the system has executed either an entry point or an exit point of some routine. Sometimes, the comparison register is set to an address in a routine which is always encountered whenever the routine is entered from one of several entry points (the "common point of entry").

8.1.4.   Sequence Detector

A sequence detection function is used to determine possible actions, depending on a particular sequence of events observed in the host system. In Figure 8.12, the general form of a sequence detector is shown.

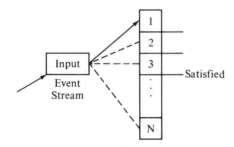

Fig. 8.12   Sequence detector function.

In the general case, the monitor is observing a particular stream of events. When a given pattern of events is observed in a particular sequence, an event of interest is assumed to have occurred. In the three-stage sequence detector, the arguments are continually provided as input to the functions at the first stage. If a match, equivalent to a equal comparison, is found in the first stage, the next argument is provided as input to the second stage. If the second argument does not match the second comparison function, the sequence detector is reset so that arguments are once again fed into the first stage. If the second argument in sequence does match the second stage, the next argument is fed into the third stage. If that argument does not match the third comparison, the sequence detector is again reset so that all arguments are fed into the first stage.

If the third argument in sequence does match the third comparison, the sequence detector provides a true output to indicate that the sequence has been satisfied. Following the emission of the true output for some given amount of time, the sequence detector resets once again, and the argument stream is fed into the first stage.

A consideration in the design of the sequence detector is the speed of the comparison circuits and the input argument rate. In this case, the sequence detector should be fast enough to perform a comparison at two stages between each presentation of an argument. The problem to overcome is that on a comparison subsequent to the first, if an unequal comparison is made, that argument may satisfy a comparison requirement at the first stage. In Figure 8.13, there is shown a list of arguments with a three-stage sequence detector.

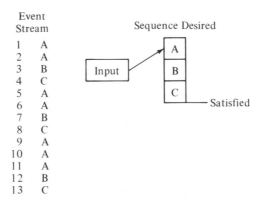

Fig. 8.13   Sequence detection.

In this case, we are trying to detect the sequence A-followed-by-B-followed-by-C. Item 1 satisfies the first stage, so the second argument is fed into the second stage. Item 2 does not satisfy the second stage, so the detector is reset to Stage One. However, we do want to compare Item 2 with Stage One rather than merely stepping to Item 3. Therefore, before the next argument, Item 3, arrives, the detector compares Item 2 with Stage One.

Again, there is a match with Item 2 at Stage One. Item 3 is fed into Stage Two where there is another match. Item 4 is therefore fed into Stage Three where there is again a match. At this point the output of the detector is a true signal of some minimum duration. By repeating this process, the sequence detector will identify sequences of Items 6, 7, and 8; and Items 11, 12, and 13.

In the general case, if we allow identical comparison keys in successive registers, such as identifying the sequence A, A, B, the logic becomes more complex. The detector needs to be able to perform a comparison of each equal argument at each higher stage before the next argument.

In Figure 8.14, we have the same sequence of events as before, but this time the comparison keys are A, A, B. Item 1 satisfies the first stage, so Item 2 is fed into the second stage where it matches. Item 3 satisfies the third stage so that a true pulse is given as output of the detector.

Item 4 fails the first stage so that Item 5 is fed into the first stage. By the same process as above, the sequence 5, 6, and 7 is detected as a true condition.

Item 8 fails the first stage so that Item 9 is fed into the first stage. Item 9 meets the comparison so that Item 10 is fed into the second stage. Item 10 meets the second comparison so that Item 11 is fed into the third stage. Item

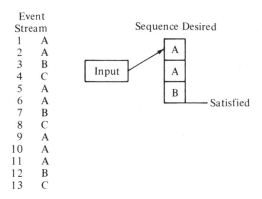

Fig. 8.14   Equal comparison keys.

11, the value A, does not meet the third stage. At this point, the detector needs to move the previous arguments up by one stage to determine whether they have met the comparison requirements of previous stages. In this case, Item 10 meets Stage One, and Item 11 meets Stage Two. Therefore, the detector sets the next argument into Stage Three. If either Stage One or Stage Two had an inequality at this point, the detector would have been reset so that Item 12 would have been fed into Stage One. However, since both previous stages were still satisfied by their new arguments, Item 12 is fed into Stage Three for comparison. Since it matches the key, a true output is given for the detector, and the next input is fed once again into Stage One.

A typical use of a sequence detector would be to determine when a computer system which does not have a wait state is executing a wait loop of instructions. Although such systems may have a single instruction for the CPU to execute while waiting for a channel to complete an I/O operation, the programmer of the system may encode a short sequence of instructions for the CPU to execute while achieving the same function. If this were the case, that sequence of instructions could be set into the comparison key fields of the sequence detector. Any time the detector is satisfied, there has been one pass at the particular sequence. The output of the detector could then be counted. Later on, this could be converted to time by applying the time of the loop to the incidence of the loop.

If concurrency studies were required, the output of the detector could be modified so that both a true and a false signal would be available. If this were done, the true output could be used to set a latch which would in turn cause a timing signal to be emitted. The latch could be reset by the use of the false output which would be available whenever any stage of the sequence detector turned out to be false.

The sequence detector is in somewhat limited use because of two factors. First, the principal application was generally in the area of determining a particular activity by discerning a given sequence of instructions. This was especially the case when that sequence of instructions could occur almost any place in processor storage. Because of the prevalent use of load and control supervision, there are generally other methods of determining the same activity. Secondly, in the general case, the implementation of the sequence detector can be quite expensive. Considering that each stage of the sequence detector is in fact an equal comparator and that the speed of comparison is several times faster than the argument input rate, the resulting equipment can be quite expensive.

Even though the need for a sequence detector has been supplanted by other functions, it still remains a possible solution to activity detection when other methods fail.

8.1.5. Event Distribution Analyzer

A powerful function within a hardware monitor is that of event distribution analysis. Generally, the facility is designed to distribute events by their duration of time.

In Figure 8.15, the general scheme of an event distribution analyzer is

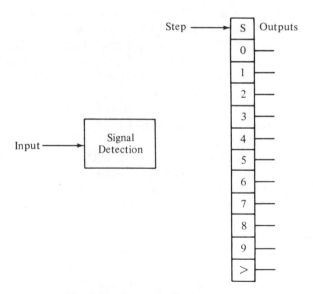

Fig. 8.15   Event distribution analyzer.

shown. In this case, there are eleven possible outputs to the analyzer. There are two signals which are used to control the output of the analyzer. The step rate is to determine at what rate the analyzer steps from stage to stage. For example, if a one megaHertz rate pulse were used as the stepping rate, each output stage would represent one microsecond. If 10 kiloHertz were used, each output stage would represent 100 microseconds.

The signal input is used to both initiate the stepping of the analyzer and the termination of the analyzer. Until a true signal is provided as input, the analyzer does not perform any function even though a stepping rate may be set. Once the input becomes true, the analyzer progressively steps through its stages until the input signal becomes false. At that time, whatever stage is active in the analyzer emits a true pulse as output.

When using an event distribution analyzer quite often a different time base must be used from the normal time base oscillator in the hardware monitor. This is to allow the time base to start at the same time as the input signal. If this were not done, the results could be skewed because of the asynchronous relationship between incoming signals and the timing base of the monitor itself.

A typical use of an event distribution analyzer would be the determination of a distribution of seek times on a particular device. If the minimum seek time of the device was zero milliseconds and the maximum seek time 120 milliseconds, the ideal stepping rate for the analyzer would be 12 milliseconds. However, that particular rate may not be available in the hardware monitor. More typically, one would find a 10 millisecond rate or a 20 millisecond rate. If the 10 millisecond rate were used, all seeks equal to or greater than 100 milliseconds would be counted in the final stage. There would be a reasonably good distribution of all seeks less than 100 milliseconds.

If the 20 millisecond rate were used, all seeks would be contained in the first 7 stages. In this particular example, the 10 millisecond rate would be preferable because more information would be available to the analyst. The stage 5-to-6 at a 20 millisecond rate would be equivalent in count to the stage equal to or greater than 10, for a 10 millisecond rate. Naturally, if the coarser distribution were satisfactory, then it could be used.

The signal representing device seek time is inserted into the analyzer. Any time a signal becomes true, the analyzer starts advancing on its given rate. Whenever the signal becomes false, indicating that the seek is complete, whatever stage is currently active in the analyzer becomes true. This signal can be used to count the incidence of seeks which fall into its time range.

In Figure 8.16, a sequence of seeks is shown with the resulting counts for a 10 millisecond time step.

8.1.6. Miscellaneous Features

In addition to the functions discussed above, hardware monitor features may include other special functions to assist the user in obtaining information. Although there are many additional options, three of interest will be presented here.

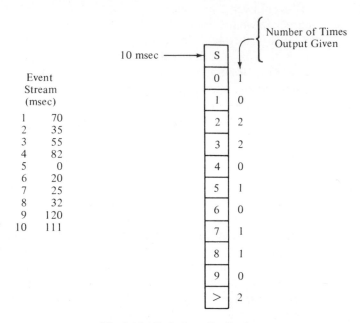

Fig. 8.16   Seek time distribution.

The first additional function would be that of the delay function. In obtaining signals from a host system, there may be events which should be logically combined, but actually occur at a time separation too great for the monitor to use as coincident signals. The delay function is used to delay the earlier signal so that it can be used in conjunction with the later signal. An example of this would be the case where the signal from the host system which identifies the fact that an instruction address is being generated may occur several nanoseconds (or several hundred nanoseconds, depending on the system) before the address itself is available. If the original signal were used to strobe a comparator, the comparator would be active at a time when there would be no input. This may be taken in some devices as an input of zero. By the time the address was actually available from the host system the strobe would no longer be available. Then there would be no output from the comparator. Using a signal delay, the strobe pulse can be delayed until the address is available. The correct function of the comparator would then be performed.

The second function of interest would be the function of the "common" or "gated" AND function. In Figure 8.17, an example of its use is shown.

The common AND is conceptually similar to the co-selector in card processing equipment. There is one common input to switch all possible outputs from a false state to a true state. Whether any particular output

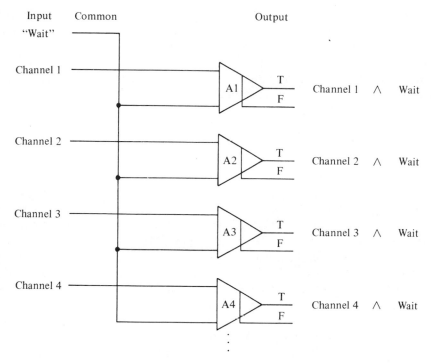

Fig. 8.17   Common AND.

level is true depends on having a true signal as that level's input. This function is used where there is a set of signals which the analyst wishes to individually combine with one common signal. In this case, the item is the wait state of the CPU. Given that state, the user wishes to determine *independently* the status of several other signals in relation to wait state. Here, we have the various channels' activities combined with wait state. Unless the "master" signal, i.e., the common signal, is active, none of the outputs will have a true output. When the common signal is true, then there is the possibility of each level's output being true, but only if its input is true.

In some implementations, the false set of outputs is omitted. This is generally because of considerations such as requirement, cost, and space. If we are accounting for the total activity of, say, Channel 1 separately from any combinatorial logic, given the time that channel is active during wait state, subtraction will provide the time that it is active during a non-wait state.

The third function of interest is the so called "live" register. This register is used to accept signal inputs from the host system for subsequent use over a wide range of possibilities. It may be used to accept information from the host system that identifies information about to be read out onto the device's output media. It may be used in more complex monitors as programmed control on comparator settings. It may be an offset quantity which is used in an arithmetic unit to calculate relative memory addresses. The reason that it is called a live register is that it is generally used to accept live *data* rather than just signals from the host system. Its consequent use depends on the requirements of the hardware monitor.

8.2. STORAGE FEATURES

The storage section of the hardware monitor contains accumulating storage, buffer storage, or both. Accumulating storage is used in devices that count and/or time. Buffer storage is used for the buffering of information for readout purposes. In some dynamic devices, we may have buffer storage without any accumulating storage. This would typically be used in a hardware monitor which is simply performing a trace function.

Accumulating storage, or the counter, is generally the limiting factor of the speed capability of a hardware monitor. If its accumulating storage can operate at a top speed of one megaHertz, then the timing rate is one microsecond and the event counting rate is one megaHertz. If for example, the hardware monitor were attempting to do instruction decoding on a machine instruction rate in excess of 1 MIP, the device would not be able to count each instruction. If the device were trying to time the duration of events less than one microsecond, it clearly would not be able to do so.

A way to overcome the speed limitation of accumulating storage is through the use of "scalars." The scalars are really short length counters which are capable of operating at a higher speed. The overflow out of these scalars may be used as input to the normal accumulating storage. If, for example, we had a set of four bit high speed scalars which operated at a speed of 16 megaHertz, the output of the scalar would be 1 megaHertz.

The second attribute of accumulating storage is the data width of its contents. This attribute, coupled with the basic accumulation rate of the counter, determines the greatest amount of time or greatest number of events that the counter can hold before overflowing its contents. There is a very wide range of maximum time accumulation of the counters. Some are quite small, such as the four binary bit scalar example. Next we find counters that are three decimal positions long. In the general case, we find the range of seven to eleven decimal digits of information in a counter. At one megaHertz, this would represent a range from 10 seconds to over 27 hours. For very short counters, there is usually the facility to couple the output of one counter into another counter. This would then enable sets of counters to be tied together to obtain the desired input rate and data width.

Another attribute of accumulating storage is the ability to set one of a variety of timing rates into any particular counter. This provides more flexibility to the user. This would generally be used for the timing of signals whose minimum durations are far greater than the basic input rate of a counter. For example, if the analyst were timing the duration of reading information from a magnetic tape drive with a start/stop time of 5 milliseconds, a satisfactory timing rate would be 1 millisecond. If greater accuracy were required, a timing rate of 100 microseconds could be used. If extreme accuracy were required, the original timing rate could be used.

A problem facing designers of hardware monitors is how to handle the update of the counters while a readout is taking place. One of two possibilities must be chosen if buffering is not utilized. Either the counters must be stopped while the readout is taking place, or the counters are allowed to continue updating while the readout occurs. If the counters are stopped while readout occurs, then for the duration of the output cycle, data from the host system are lost. The advantage of stopping the counters is that there would be no "skewing" of data on an output record. On the other hand if the counters are allowed to continue updating, lost data is held to a minimum, but the data would be skewed.

In Figure 8.18, Counter 1 represents its own activity up to the time $t(1)$.

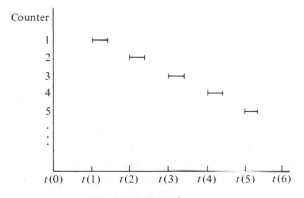

Fig. 8.18   Skewed output.

Counter 2 represents its own activity up to the time $t(2)$. Counter 3 represents its activity up to the time $t(3)$, and so on down the line. If the total time of the readout is small, then skewing does not become a problem. Skewing may not be a problem if all counters were logically different in function. However, if one or more of the counters represented, say, an OR function of two other counters, there may not be closure of results.

A way to overcome the problem of lost data or skewing is to buffer the contents of the counters prior to the readout cycle. Various buffer schemes may be used to achieve the desired result. However the physical implementation is structured, the net result is to hold the lost data content to near zero while eliminating the skew problem. This, of course, means that the storage requirements of the hardware monitor are almost doubled. When the monitor is used to detect activity on very high speed systems, the cost of additional buffer storage may very well be worthwhile.

As mentioned earlier, some hardware monitors utilize only the buffer type storage with no accumulating storage at all. These devices would generally be used to capture a stream or trace of information from the host system. Typical streams would be the instruction counter sequence or the operation code sequence. As each new instruction is brought into the device the instruction, or a special encoding of the instruction, is placed in a buffer register. When all buffer registers are full their contents are again read out to some output media.

It is obvious that a CPU can generate instruction addresses or operation codes at a rate several orders of magnitude faster than electro-mechanical output devices can record the information. Methods to overcome this anomaly have been used. One method is to use the "cyclic" buffer scheme. In this scheme, the device does not wait to initiate output until *all* buffers are filled, but initiates output as soon as the first buffer register is filled. Input from the host system is read into the next buffer as information from the first buffer is being read out. However, this scheme could soon become saturated if the instruction rate is very much faster than the output rate. When that occurs, the device is again limited to the speed of the output media.

Another approach to overcome the differences in speed of the CPU and the output media is to provide a function in which the hardware monitor can force the CPU to temporarily stop the processing of instructions until the buffers are available for more input. This will naturally interfere with the relationship between the CPU and the I/O activity, but in many cases, will not interfere with the acquisition of the required data. If the desired trace were in an application or problem program, such interference may make no difference in the traced output. On the other hand, if the desired trace were concerned with an allocation or scheduling activity in the control program, the forced interference may produce a completely different pattern of activity than that which would have occurred had there been no interference.

A different approach to capturing instruction addresses or operation codes would be to select only a sample of the data. In the case of instruction addresses, it may be possible to get sufficient information from the hardware monitor by merely recording branch or transfer instructions and the next instruction address following the branch. This would be especially true if a storage map were available to determine all other instruction addresses.

In Figure 8.19, there is an example of coding which involves an arithmetic branch and a loop branch. If a full trace of all instructions were made for the number of times each direction was taken, there would be a requirement for

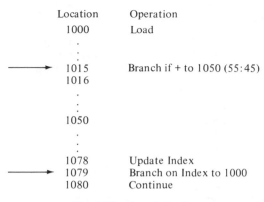

Location	Operation
1000	Load
.	
1015	Branch if + to 1050 (55:45)
1016	
.	
1050	
.	
1078	Update Index
1079	Branch on Index to 1000
1080	Continue

Fig. 8.19 Branch tracing.

the hardware monitor output to have over 6000 entries. (This is calculated, assuming the routine takes the positive branch 55 times out of the 100 times around the loop.)

If only branch addresses and the next address following the branch are recorded, the number of entries on the output media would be reduced to 400 entries. With a storage map of the routine available for the time of measurement, a simple analyzer routine could then calculate all intermediate address locations after the trace was performed. This same routine could also provide a trace of operation codes. Even if such an approach were used, the hardware monitor could still provide for a CPU hold if the buffers were saturated. However, in this case, the chance of that happening is $\frac{1}{15}$th the probability of occurrence in the full trace situation.

8.3. FUNCTIONS OBSERVED

Up to this point, we have been discussing the capability of a hardware monitor observing streams and timing and counting events and some of the methods that are used to achieve that function. Some consideration should now be given to the nature of these events. The events that a hardware monitor observes and records are the physical manifestations of logical activity. The actual interface and connections between the hardware monitor and the host system will be discussed later, in Section 8.7.

The attachment of the hardware monitor is to determine an electronic signal which represents some activity in the host system. In each case, the attachment depends heavily on both the general architecture and the particular design of a system. Although a line of systems may have identical architecture, individual machines in the line would be implemented in different manners. The hardware monitor must be attached in such a way as to recognize the structural differences. For example, a particular CPU in an architectural series may require more than one memory fetch in order to obtain and assemble a complete instruction in its registers. On the other hand, some other CPU in the series may actually obtain more than one instruction in one memory fetch. The attachment and use of the hardware monitor must distinguish between the two implementations.

8.3.1. Device Attributes

Some of the device attributes which are obtained by a hardware monitor are shown by the following examples. These are called device attributes to distinguish them from programming attributes.

In the CPU, the main attribute is whether the CPU is active or not. If the CPU is active, it is processing and executing instructions. If it is not active, it is not processing and executing instructions. Even though this seems like a simple definition, there are times when the electronic definition can become complex. Consider a CPU which has a unique state which is called "wait" state. This state is a mode of operation in which the CPU stops processing instructions, but is capable of starting such action if called upon. At first blush, it seems that wait state would be an ideal definition of CPU active or inactive status. The problem can arise if we consider "not wait" to be the same as CPU active. There can be other conditions which influence the ability of the CPU to be active. For example, if an operator had manually caused the system to halt or stop, it would be possible for the CPU to come to a complete halt without any reversion to wait state. So now we have a more complete definition of CPU active which is "not wait" AND "not stopped."

In many systems, this would be a complete definition of the CPU's being in an active status. But in almost all systems there is the potential of momentarily stopping a CPU because of some I/O activity. In the larger systems, this interference is held to a minimum through the use of separately implemented channels, interleaved processor storage, and the ability of the CPU as such to overlap other memory requests. Occasionally, however, the CPU is delayed because of a conflict of requests with I/O. Even though a hardware monitor is certainly capable of accounting for this time in determining CPU activity, normally no effort is made to do so. This is because such interference is normally well below 1 percent.

Some systems have the implementation of the CPU and channels integrated. The degree of integration can vary, but generally involves the sharing of registers, data paths, and other facilities. In this type of "CPU" (in this case, there are more features in the unit than the usual CPU facilities) a greater amount of CPU interference can occur due to I/O activity. The hardware monitor can and should account for this type of interference. It is not unusual to find such interference on the order of 5 to 10 percent of CPU active time.

Finally, in the determination of CPU active state, the hardware monitor may be used to account for error conditions. Certain errors can occur which stop the CPU without affecting wait, stopped, or channel status. However, when that type of error occurs, there is usually a "master stop" signal which is used to light lights and sound alarms when the condition occurs. The hardware monitor could watch for such a signal, but the user should decide how much logical function in the hardware monitor should be used for such "babysitting" purposes. Of course, if the hardware monitor were being used to determine the number of errors and other incidents in a system, this could well be one of its main input points. In the case of using a hardware monitor to optimize system work capability, such a signal is not normally used. There is generally recourse to manual intervention when an error occurs that shuts down the system.

Other CPU attributes that are observed by hardware monitors are such items as the fetching of instructions and data from processor storage, the decoding of operations, and the generation of various types of addresses. In address generation, we have not only the usual types such as an address for the next instruction or an address for a data operand, but also address generation for such functions as I/O data reference and interval timer update. If the interval timer, or internal timer, is implemented in processor storage, it must be updated for each one of its clock "ticks." The CPU with such a timer automatically interrupts its normal instruction processing long enough to read the timer's current value out of processor storage, update it, and return the new value back into storage. The address generator section of the CPU is normally used to achieve this function. Although the incidence of the function may be relatively rare when compared to the generation of other addresses, the user of the hardware monitor should consciously decide whether or not to account for the activity on any particular system that is being monitored.

For devices other than the CPU, the hardware monitor is generally used to determine the active or inactive status of the device, the number of control and/or data bytes transacted, read or write status, and other information unique to the characteristics of the particular device. In the case of magnetic tape drives, other information of interest may include such items as tape start time, rewind time, skip times, and the number of times various activities occurred.

For direct access devices, items of interest would be seek times, rotational delay times, number of tracks or cylinders traversed, or cylinder addresses, as well as the number of times various events occurred. Card equipment activity would include buffer activity times, card advance times, number of cards, and in some cases, number and length of fields skipped. Printer activity would include number and length of forms skips, number of lines printed, number of pages printed, and in the case of some printers, the number of characters emitted by the printer subsystem itself.

In the case of communications oriented activity, there could be measurements made on the transmission control unit at the central system or measurements at the terminal. Items of general interest would be whether terminals are on-line to the system or not, whether polling is taking place, the number and duration of time-out occurrences, and the utilization of the terminals once they are on-line to the system. At the terminal, response time measurements may be made by latching on to the time from the operator's signal that an entry is complete (usually a carriage return) until there is a signal from the system that the operator can proceed. This return signal can vary depending not only on the type of terminal, but also the control program philosophy of the particular system. In some systems, merely the unlocking of the keyboard is sufficient to allow the operator to proceed. In other systems, the printing of some character such as an underscore or a question mark would indicate that the operator may proceed. In still others, a line number or key phrase such as "next" may be printed. The hardware monitor must be able to react to a variety of responses as determined by the user. Sometimes it is desirable to obtain either control characters or complete messages transmitted to and from the terminal. A special case of general terminal function would be the operator's console on the system. It may be desirable to capture the message stream over the console to later allow for job identification or other pertinent information.

Again, in the general area of terminals and consoles there would be the graphic or cathode ray tube devices. Here, special information of interest could be regeneration characteristics, utilization of buffer storage, if applicable, use of light pen operations, and perhaps special coding signals if overlaid keyboard techniques are used.

Other devices that may be monitored include the channels of the system in whatever implementation they may exist. Special items of interest could include the particular activity of the channel, whether it is transmitting data, fetching control words, chaining data or commands, sensing, searching, or looping. At this level, interdevice activity could also be determined. Again, it should be emphasized that the functions of interest will depend on the architecture and particular implementation of the system. The preceding notes merely indicate some of the device functions of general interest to the user of the hardware monitor. They are by no means all-inclusive or even exhaustive. As the analyst designs his measurement experiment, he will determine new and useful device functions which will aid him in the measurement of the system.

8.3.2. Programming Attributes

A programming attribute is one which reflects the intent or logic of a particular program or section of program within the attributes of a device. Normally, program attributes are measured within the scope of signals obtained from the CPU. The intention is to obtain signals from the CPU which represent unique program actions. At the broadest level, we may wish to distinguish between the control program activity and all other activity. If all control program coding were contained in a contiguous area of processor storage, address comparators could be used to determine when the CPU was executing instructions from that area. It is common practice for such coding to start in "low core," i.e., starting with location zero and moving upward. If this is the case, one comparator could be set to the high boundary of storage. Any time the CPU instruction address was in that area, the comparator would provide a low or equal output. As a matter of interest, if the address comparator were set to one location higher than the high boundary of control program storage, the low output alone could be utilized.

In some systems, a memory protection scheme is used. Again, it is common practice to use one or more unique patterns of memory protect key for the control program, usually zero at least. If this is the case, the hardware monitor can be used to decode the memory protect key while the CPU is active to determine the duration of control program activity.

For determining the extent of activity between various problem programs operating concurrently within a CPU, either the address comparison or memory protect decode scheme can be used. In those systems which dynamically assign processor storage, there is usually some type of memory protect scheme. When processor storage is dynamically assigned, the use of a manually set address comparator becomes so unwieldy as to be impossible to use. This is because the CPU has the capability to change address assignments several orders of magnitude faster than any operator could hope to set dials and switches. If the hardware monitor has the capability to have its comparison limits set by a live register under program control of the host system, then it could be used to distinguish activities by address in a dynamic environment.

Even the use of memory protect bits can pose a problem. Since there is generally a limited set of memory protect options, the control program would reassign a particular code to new programs as they progress through the system. A summary type device may not be able to distinguish between various problem programs because the memory protect key assignment may change many times during an observation. A dynamic hardware monitor could keep up with the rate of change of memory protect key assignment. If nothing else, an excellent approximation may be obtained by combining the dynamic observations of a hardware monitor with a job log obtained from the host system. The job log would be expected to provide not only the various job identifications but also the assigned memory protect key and the times of day that the job possessed that key.

To identify particular functions within a program, address comparison may be used in some instances. If the address which represents the exit and/or entry point is static, normal equal-only comparators may be used to detect entries into the routine of interest. If the comparators can be dynamically set in themselves, then they can be used on dynamic storage systems. Since the dynamic comparator is considerably more expensive, it may not be generally available for this type of analysis. Therefore, a different approach must be used.

In the control program, certain facilities may be entered through the use of an interrupt mechanism to a unique location through hardware assignment. Although here we have the perfect circumstance to use an equal-only comparator, there may be a simpler way to determine the entry. When the hardware of the system forces the address of the interrupt location, it is normally done through a peculiar combination of circuits within the CPU. There is generally a single, unique signal which represents the interrupt. In this case, rather than using a comparator requiring 16 to 24 bits of input information, the monitor can detect the same action by one signal.

In some systems, an entire class of interrupt may be forced into a unique address by a unique signal. There is generally within the architecture of the system further information which identifies the specific nature of the interrupt. For example, there may be a particular instruction in the architecture that is used by the problem programs to call upon the services of the control program. This instruction could have an identification field which is used to identify the particular service required by the requesting program. If this were the case, the hardware monitor could be set up to look for this additional field whenever this particular instruction was decoded. The monitor could then decode or simply record this field to determine the particular section of control programming that was entered.

When determining particular routines of interest within problem programs, such special instructions may not be available, such as in the case for calling on control program services. However, a similar solution can be utilized. Some particular instruction can be used in a particular way to indicate to a hardware monitor that a particular routine has just been entered. This instruction may be an unused instruction in the CPU's repertoire which is normally considered an invalid instruction. Assuming that the use of such an instruction does not bring the system to a grinding halt, it could be used by the problem program.

The ideal case in CPU design is to have in the CPU's repertoire a special instruction which would be utilized to pass information to a hardware monitor. The characteristics of the instruction could be used to control various activities within the monitor as well as provide individual program routine identification. If this facility is not available, yet another alternative would be the use of normally valid instructions in an unusual manner. A no-operation (NO-OP) instruction could have its unused fields specially coded to represent information of interest to the monitor. The danger here is that someone else may have had the same idea for some entirely different reason. In this case, the conflicting use of conventions could cause erroneous results in the hardware monitor.

If unique facilities are not available by design, the user of the hardware monitor uses an opportunist approach to define either special instructions or unusual uses of instructions to provide the information that is required by the monitor. This approach requires a knowledge of not only the program routines of interest, but also of the particular design implementation of the system under study. If, within a single installation, a convention of use can be established, the problem of assigning special usage to instructions can be minimized.

In addition to determining particular program activities by examining special situations in the CPU, certain program activities may be determined by examining special conditions in the I/O area. For example, particular control program services may be held on a particular track on a particular direct access device. If the hardware monitor observes that device going to that particular track, it may be inferred that that particular routine is being fetched. There may be a particular language compiler housed in a certain area. Any time the system reads information from that area, it may similarly be inferred that that language compiler is being used. Similar inferences may be made to other areas of the direct access subsystem.

8.4. SUMMARY DEVICES

Before describing some of the early summary type devices, it is worth-while to consider the nature of a summary counter. Normally, through some amount of signal detection and logic wiring, an individual counter will be able to either count pulses or time a continuous signal. The signal may be a direct signal from the host system or it may be the output from a local latch which is set and reset by signals or pulses from the host system. The following devices had one or more of these attributes.

Furthermore, the intent of this section is to provide historical reference. There are many monitors available today which are not covered here. All of the following were developed by IBM.

8.4.1. 7090 Machine Usage Recorder

Earlier, there was described a particular application of a hardware monitor by IBM in 1961. The 7090 Machine Usage Recorder was created to obtain basic system profiles to provide guide lines of performance improvement.

The device was about the size of a large magnetic tape unit and contained six counter groups. A counter group consisted of six electronic decade counters which would overflow into mechanical counters of four positions. The device was constructed in vacuum tube logic. The electronic counters counted pulses of machine cycles, each cycle being 2.18 microseconds. The following functions were assigned to the counters:

Total cycles from start to stop

Cycles of Channel A operating.

Cycles of Channel B operating.

Cycles of CPU operating alone.

Cycles of either channel operating alone.

Cycles of unit record equipment operating alone.

The data were transcribed manually from the visual display of the counters. Subsequently, the information was transcribed onto punched cards for processing by a data reduction program. The data reduction program converted cycle counts to time and also performed the necessary calculation to complete the basic system profile.

All combinational logic was "pre-wired" into the unit. The only way a modification to the combining logic could be made was to perform a small redesign of the hardware monitor.

On this particular system, if any device was in operation, either magnetic tape or unit record equipment, the channel was in operation. Since the unit record equipment operated in a mutually exclusive manner with the tape on Channel A, the cycles of operation for unit record were not counted in "Channel A operating." There was also prior knowledge that the CPU waited in a program loop any time the unit record equipment was in operation. This allowed the simple detection of the unit record equipment operating alone.

The method of attachment involved building additional logic onto the main frame of the 7090 system. Most of the logic was to detect one of many possible wait loops which occurred in the various programming systems which could have been present on the host system. The unit was first installed in the Poughkeepsie Laboratory. In October, 1961, it was installed in the Western Data Processing Center of the University of California, Los Angeles. A second unit was installed shortly thereafter in the IBM Datacenter in New York City. They remained in operation for about one year.

8.4.2.   7090 Portable Hardware Monitor

Following the primary use of the original 7090 monitor, it was determined that the monitoring techniques would be invaluable in determining ways to optimize systems to obtain better performance. Since it was not feasible to transport around the original monitor, it was decided to create a portable hardware monitor. This monitor was about the size of the well known footlocker so it was not surprising that "Footlocker" became one of its popular names. It was also popularly known as the "channel analyzer," because it did in essence perform the function of relating channel utilization to the CPU processing activity. Again, the purpose was to obtain a basic system profile, but rather than doing it on only the work that could be brought to some center, profiles could be collected on every job processed for days at a time. To individual users, this had much more meaning than the results of just one or two sample jobs.

The monitor consisted of five counter groups plus an elapsed time clock. (In some of the earlier models, the elapsed time clock was not there. In some cases a kitchen clock was used to obtain elapsed time.) Each counter group consisted of 16 binary positions of electronic counters and six positions of a mechanical counter. The unit was built in solid state logic and first used in October, 1962. The counters were originally constructed to count in machine cycles, but later they were changed to time signals in one of two switchable frequencies provided by the unit's own oscillator, 500 kiloHertz or 1 megaHertz.

The data were again manually transcribed for subsequent keypunching. This was the normal manner of recording the data. However, an interesting variation to obtaining data was also utilized. Since all of the counters were visible at the same time, an automatic camera was used to record the data. Given an impulse, the camera would take a picture of the counters and then advance to the next frame. To provide the pulse to the camera, one of the instructions in the 7090's repertoire was used in an unusual manner. This instruction was inserted into the control program so that it was encountered every time a new job was read into the CPU for processing. A special signal detection attachment was made to the logic of the 7090 so that the pulse for the camera was activated whenever the control program executed the modified instruction. In this way, the program was able to exercise control over the recording process of the hardware monitor.

Although this was not a true buffering arrangement, information was obtained from the device without stopping the counters, and with very little lost data. The data loss was in fact the information contained in the binary lights. The mechanical counters were normally used as the primary data source in any event. Later on, the prints of the film were used for the data transcription process.

The attachment to the host system was the same as the original hardware monitor. The information obtained by the counters was also the same as the original. It was possible to make slight variations on the information content of the counters, but this involved rewiring the logic of the unit. The primary reason for not changing the setup of the unit was the need to rewire the logic on the main frame of the host system.

8.4.3. Assignable Functions

With the application of the 7090 monitors proving the need for measurement to optimize computer system performance, it was only natural that a similar facility be provided for other computer systems. The intention was to provide basic systems profiles, but with the recognition that additional information may be required. The best way to indicate the information is to outline the functions assignable to the counters. The application of the information was similar to the 7090. Attachment to the host system was achieved by adding logic to the main frame of the host system. An example of a system monitor with variable function is the 1410/7010 monitor. The 1410/7010 monitors were built in solid state technology packaged in one "cube" in 1963. There were seven counters with most of the required combinatorial logic built into the monitor rather than onto the system. The time interval was 1.5 microseconds. With the 18 binary electronic positions and the six decimal mechanical overflow positions, the recording span was 109.2 hours. Four of the counters had switched input controlled by a rotary switch on the monitor panel. The information obtained was organized as follows:

Ctr A   Total Enable Time

Ctr B   CPU Only

Ctr C   Channel 1

Ctr D   Switched

    1. Off
    2. Channel 2
    3. Internal Data Moves (Counted)
    4. Typewriter
    5. 7750 in Operation

Ctr E   Switched

    1. Off
    2. Wait for Any Tape
    3. Internal Data Moves
    4. Typewriter
    5. 7750 in Operation

Ctr F   Switched

    1. Off
    2. Waiting for Any Disk
    3. Internal Data Moves

4. Typewriter

5. 7750 in Operation

Ctr G   Switched

1. Off

2. Waiting for Unit Record

3. Internal Data Moves

4. Typewriter

5. 7750 in Operation

As seen from the above functions, variability was achieved by providing pre-packaged functions which could be selected by the user/operator. Any further variation would be achieved by rewiring the unit itself.

The determination of waiting in the CPU was again through the use of wait loop detection. A data reduction program was also available to convert the time base and to produce basic system profiles.

Notice that some functions are repeated in more than one counter position. This technique can be used to obtain the greatest flexibility in use. Since the functions themselves were generated within the monitor whether used as counter input or not, it was a relatively simple matter to allow for their input to any number of counters on an option basis.

To get all available information, multiple runs were made of a single program. When making multiple runs of a single program, the user must take care that there is closure between the two runs. It is the nature of a computing system that there will be different job times when running the same program in the same environment more than one time.

As another example of an implementation for assignable functions, let us consider the 7030 System Monitor developed in 1963. In addition to the component actions as determined by the previous monitors, it was designed to obtain information on the use of instructions available in the system. Naturally, the floating point set was of great importance.

The 7030 System Monitor was built in solid state logic and was packaged in a specially built systems console. There were logic changes to the 7030 to allow signal lines to be brought out to the monitor circuitry. The monitor circuitry contained combinatorial logic which produced specific functions available as hubs on a patch panel. There were four, five-counter units housed in the console. The five-counter units were the same design as the 7090 Portable Hardware Monitor.

An extensive list of functions was presented to the hubs on the patch panel. A sample of the functions are as follows:

1. Total Job Time

2. Total CPU Time

3. Total Number of Instructions

4. Total Floating Point (F.P.) Instruction Count

5. F.P. Loads

6. F.P. Stores

7. F.P. Adds

8. F.P. Multiplies

9. Disk Read/Write Overlapped with CPU

10. Disk Read/Write Non Overlapped

11. Disk Locate Time Overlapped

12. Disk Locate Non Overlapped

13. Any Tape Chan. Overlapped

14. Any Tape Chan. Non Overlapped

15. Unit Record Overlapped

16. Unit Record Non Overlapped

17. Operator Console Overlapped

18. Operator Console Non Overlapped

19. Disk/I-O Overlapped with CPU

20. Disk/I-O Non Overlapped

21. F.P. Multiply/Add

22. F.P. Divide

23. F.P. Double Divide

24. Square Root

25. I Box Stores

26. Variable Field Length Stores

27. LX, LV, V+

28. E-Box Cond. Branches: Successful

29. E-Box Cond. Branches: Unsuccessful

30. I-Box Cond. Branches: Successful

31. I-Box Cond. Branches: Unsuccessful

32. Branch on Accumulator: Recovery

33. Branch on Accumulator: No Recovery

34. CB, CBR: Successful

35. CB, CBR: Unsuccessful

36. Unconditional Branch

37. Time in Master Control Program

In this case, a small patch panel was used as the primary method of function selection. Any function could be directed to any counter. Timed functions were presented to the counter as a string of 1 megaHertz pulses for the duration of the signal. Counted information was presented to the counters as single pulses. Although later models of the monitor reverted to alteration switch control of functional assignment to the counters, the patch panel version was used to determine optimum mixtures of functions.

To get complete information, two runs of a single program had to be made. The problems of closure were again with the user. In this case, not only total time but total instruction count was also used as a control for closure. Since total instruction count included the instructions executed while in a wait loop, an adjustment was made by considering the length of the loop and the amount of time detected. The adjusted total instruction counts were then used for control of closure.

To obtain time in Master Control Program, one of the normal instructions was used to set an unused bit in one of the registers. The Master Control Program was modified so that every time an entry to the program was made, it would immediately execute that instruction, setting the bit "on." On each exit from the program, a similar instruction was executed to turn the bit "off." In this way the monitor was able to detect the amount of time in the control program.

Although providing much more information, the results were still in summary form. Dynamic instruction information was still obtained by the use of programmed techniques.

8.5. DYNAMIC MONITORING

Having used the early summary devices, there developed a requirement to have not only summary form information on a wide variety of applications, but also a more dynamic profile of input-output activity and instruction processing. Information was required for input to various simulation programs whose accuracy depended on the actual and projected distributions of I/O activity. Programmed routines such as the "Select Trap Trace" had been used in a number of installations, but again there was the problem of tailoring the program to operate under a wide variety of operating systems. To overcome the general problem of implementing trace routines into a number of operating systems, devices were created to obtain the information.

The devices from that time onward were generally classified in one of three categories: recording devices, display devices, or a combination of both.

The recording type device is generally used so that the information obtained from the host system is in machine readable form for later processing by data analysis programs. The display device has the advantage that the user can see the results of the measurement in a relatively short time. A device which has both recording capability and display capability would naturally provide the best features of both worlds, but would be more expensive. As the cost of technology reduces, devices with multiple functions become economically attractive.

The following devices were also developed by IBM.

8.5.1. Dynamic Recording Devices

In 1963, a device was developed to specifically replace the Select Trap Trace routine. This device, called the Program Operation External Monitor (POEM) was a follow-on to the 7090 channel analyzer in that it utilized the same attachment to the mainframe of the CPU. Externally it was quite different in that it included a built-in incremental tape unit and no counters. Instead of counting, during operation POEM would, at 256 microsecond intervals, sample the system and write on the incremental tape coded list patterns representing a picture of the 7090's activity. Recorded were channel(s) in operation, CPU in operation, or CPU waiting. When a channel initiated operation, the unit was noted. This created a dynamic profile of an actual job being executed.

In Figure 8.20, we see the type of information available on the recording.

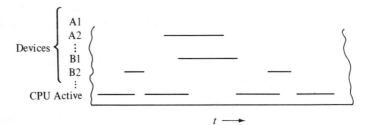

Fig. 8.20   POEM output.

This is translated in that it is not in the precise format that would be found on the tape. Since there was a one-to-one relationship between a device in operation and the channel in operation, it was sufficient to obtain the device address when the channel was first initiated. Additional logic and signal lines were used to obtain this information. The information obtained from the device was processed by a variety of data reduction and analysis programs to provide information to the analysts. It was also used as input to simulation programs to project the effects of various system modifications.

The sample rate of 256 microseconds was generally satisfactory because the cogent information was concerned with the pattern of channel activity and its relationship to CPU activity. The shortest activity on the channel was on the order of milliseconds, usually a minimum of five milliseconds. The greatest error in the sample would be to miss CPU activity at the beginning and ending of wait loops. This would be a maximum error on the order of 512 microseconds. Normally, we would expect the error to be on the order of 128 microseconds.

The Program Monitor, on the other hand, was designed to obtain not only the dynamic characteristics of input/output, but also a dynamic indication of the activity of the central processing unit. Briefly, the Program Monitor consisted of two units, a monitor and a magnetic tape unit. The monitor portion was capable of recording any selected 24 bits of information from the host system. The most frequent usage was the recording of instruction counter information as well as channel activity. Subsequent analysis of the information recorded on tape allowed a resolution of about 45 microseconds.

Special encoding schemes were utilized to obtain an effective resolution of 20 microseconds. The device also used data selection techniques (e.g., recording branch points) so that with its buffered storage the device could just about keep up with a 0.125 MIP CPU. If the buffers overflowed, "lost data" signals could be placed on the tape and/or the hardware monitor could cause the host CPU to pause. This analysis allowed an investigation into not only the I/O activity, but on a sample basis, the type of activity of the CPU. Dynamic instruction location tracings were correlated with memory mappings to determine the particular activity of the CPU. The connection to the host system was through a specially designed interface which sensed relevant data from the host system and then sent the signal information to the program monitor. One of the data reduction routines allowed the display of the reduced information on a graphic console. The analyst could then examine the performance of the host system in some multiples of real time.

8.5.2. Dynamic Display Devices

In many cases the analyst required information about the flow of a program in terms of the sequence of I/O activity and relationships rather than the detailed flow of instructions. It was desired to have this information on an immediate basis. When information was obtained from a recording device, the data had to be passed through one or more formatting and data reduction programs in order for the analyst to see the traced information. This took some amount of time, not the least of which was getting time on some system to execute the analysis programs.

To allow for this capability, in 1964 a series of devices was developed to provide immediate information to the analyst concerning the dynamic flow of the program under observation.

The Execution Plotter was a device designed to produce directly a graphic display of the activity of the host computer. Examples of the activities displayed were the activity of the channels, and a distribution of the memory addresses for instruction fetches, data fetches, and/or channel access fetches to memory. The output of the Execution Plotter was presented to a cathode ray tube. This output could be either observed by the analyst (!), or recorded on either Polaroid or 35 mm film. This recording could be used for subsequent examination. The method of connection was essentially the same as the Program Monitor.

The direct observation facility was normally used only during the set-up of the experiment. The camera was the normal observation method. Controls were supplied to determine the time sweep across each frame of film, the shutter control, and in the case of the 35 mm camera, the automatic frame advance.

The Polaroid camera offered immediate output to the analyst, but was naturally limited in the rate of observation. So that a picture was made at the correct point in the program activity, an equal-only comparator was provided as another means of initiating recording operations. The 35 mm camera provided a satisfactory observation rate, but had the disadvantage of the time required to develop and process the film.

The distribution of memory address was obtained by decoding within the device. It was possible to select various parallax and scale factors of the display of memory activity.

In Figure 8.21 is a diagram of the type of information obtained from a frame of film. Here we see that at time zero, the CPU is operating in a storage area with an address of about 24K. Channel A is in operation at this time also. At 25 milliseconds, the CPU operates for a short time in the area of 20K. At 35 milliseconds Channel B is initiated. At this time, the CPU is operating in the area of 8K. Given a storage map of the program currently in process,

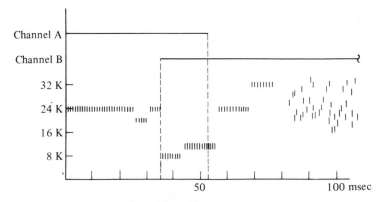

Fig. 8.21 Execution plotter output.

the analyst could determine the functions at the various address areas. For example, the code at 8K could well be the IOCS routine for the system.

If a program were skipping around the various areas at a high rate of change, the resulting plot would appear as a scattergram as shown at the time 80 milliseconds. In this case, the information would be almost indistinguishable from either noise on the cathode ray tube or granularity in the film.

To overcome by compromise the delay in processing film or the lack of frame rate, an electrostatic recorder was adapted to provide the functions of an Execution Plotter. A multiple "pen" recorder was used to produce immediate hard copy for the analyst. The compromise was in the basic sample rate of the device. However, when obtaining information on channel activity and the wait state of the host system, satisfactory results were obtained. (There was some problem in the amount of paper obtained during the measurement process and the wall area necessary to mount it for examination.) In most cases, the sample rate was satisfactory to determine which of several major blocks of coding were being executed by the CPU. Analysts soon developed the capability to recognize program functions such as a particular compiler by simply observing the pattern of the dynamic profile.

The concept of plotted output can be adapted to operate in conjunction with most hardware monitors, whether the device is a summary type or dynamic device. This is because the plotted output is obtained from the input signals to the device.

In the general area of displayed information, we should also include the simple galvanometer used as an "utilization meter." Such a facility utilizes the inherent time delay of the meter plus any other time delay developed by circuitry to integrate an input signal representing some activity over a period of time. Since device utilization is in fact a bi-stable activity, either active or inactive at any given time, if the meter were highly responsive it would alternate between zero and full scale. Time delay integration tends to slow down the movement of the needle and therefore allow visual observation. Depending on the input and the wiring of the meter, the scale could represent percentage utilization or an activity rate such as instruction processing. The use of such a facility would probably be limited to casual observation rather than being a primary measurement technique. If the facility were on a hardware monitor, it could be used during the set-up phase so that the analyst could determine that he is getting the expected signals in the correct combinations. However, simple display lights could provide the same information.

8.5.3. Combination of Monitoring Activities

The previous hardware monitors had either the characteristic of being a summary device or a dynamic device which had a regular time based sample rate. In addition to these facilities, there was a critical requirement for the analyst to be able to exercise more control over the way in which the data were being gathered. Since 1963, monitors have generally been designed to be more general in purpose. They combine many facilities found in the simpler devices. For example, in 1964 the Program Event Counter was developed to provide in one unit many options. The Program Event Counter consisted of a monitoring device and one or two magnetic tape units for output recording. The data accumulation portion of the device consisted of 24 three-digit electronic counters and 12 six-digit mechanical counters. The contents of electronic counters could be written onto the magnetic tape. The mechanical counters were displayed for either manual transcription or for recording by camera.

Other functions which were available to the analyst for the control of the measurement included sequence detectors, comparators, combinatorial logic, clocking circuits, counter coupling, and other control functions. All of the functions as well as the signal input from the host computer and data paths and control for output were available at a removable plug board to allow fast set-up for various users. It was also possible to couple a strip chart recorder to the device so that the analyst could obtain immediate, but gross, data. The connection to the host computer was through a specially designed interface similar to the one for the Program Monitor, but with more functions. Typical of the stream of information sent over the interface was information on the contents of the instruction counter, operation codes, operand addresses, and operand data, as well as information on channel and device activity.

Since 1964 many different monitors have been developed to solve particular measurement problems. As technology improves in cost and performance, the hardware monitor provides more functions to the analyst.

8.6. THE COMPUTER AS A HARDWARE MONITOR

In the preceding sections the hardware monitors were all specially constructed devices to perform particular functions, however general in nature the functions may have been. As the variety of function and complexity of individual devices increases, the question that comes to mind is: why not use a computer as a hardware monitor? The response: why not, indeed! The only thing that would stand in the way of using a computer of any size, description, or architecture would be the cost of such a facility. However, as hardware monitors become more complex, the cost approaches that of a general purpose computer. There has been and probably will be a declining cost for computers. Small, high-speed computers are common-place. If such a computer provides the required speed for monitoring functions at an attractive cost, the designer may well incorporate a computer in some form or another. It should be noted that by 1967 (or even earlier in some applications), the small, high-speed, binary computer was in general use as a control unit or controlling element in a wide variety of applications.

In one sense, the instrumentation and measurement of an electronic computer is essentially the same application as the instrumentation and measurement of an oil well. The differences should be obvious. The similarities are that signals must be obtained from the system under study which represent certain functions. These signals must be transmitted to the observing device. Given the signals, the device performs certain calculations to present cogent information to the analyst, operator, or user. There is also the capability for the observing device to exercise some element of control over the observed system.

An early example of using a computer as a hardware monitor was in the use of a "Direct Couple" system. The Direct Couple system was an operating environment which utilized a 7040 as a data management subsystem for a 7090 type computer. Inherent in the design of the system was the ability of the 7040 to cause the 7090 to pause in its instruction processing whenever the 7090 encountered an I/O instruction. This mode of operation was called "Halt on I/O and Proceed (HIP)." A modification was made to the system which caused a mode of operation called "Halt on All instructions and Proceed (HAP)." As each instruction was processed in the 7090, the CPU would pause before obtaining the next instruction and signal the 7040 that such an event had occurred. The 7040 had the ability to obtain information from various storage and register locations in the 7090. After the 7040 had obtained whatever information it required, it would then signal the 7090 to proceed.

In the HIP mode, the 7040 could perform an I/O trace of the 7090's activity. In HAP mode, the 7040 could perform a full trace of each instruction in the 7090. The delay in the 7090's instruction processing varied, depending on the amount of information the 7040 extracted. Various techniques and levels of information were used to minimize the delay in the 7090.

Whether performing a special trace or not, there was capability in the control program of the 7040 to perform an I/O trace of the 7090 when operating in direct coupled mode. This information could be logged out of the system along with pertinent job identification and other information. Since that time, other research and development has been performed on the general subject of using a computer as a hardware monitor.

Having used an independent computer of some type to perform the function of a hardware monitor, it is natural to examine whether equipment can be added to the host system, itself, to perform certain functions. With technologies such as read-only control storage and "writable" control storage available, there is more opportunity to add monitoring facilities to the host system. For example, assume that a particular system had 100 different operation codes in its repertoire. If 100 locations of storage could be set aside, the CPU could be designed to create a frequency distribution of operations by simply adding "one" to a storage location depending on which particular operation was decoded. Since most of the work of decoding is necessary within the CPU in order for it to perform its intended function, the additional logic to provide a frequency distribution may be very small.

Given such function in a system, there would be a desire to have some of the functions under program control. Certainly all results from monitoring functions should be at least readable by a program. As soon as we discuss program controlled monitoring features, we complete the loop back to hardware assistance to measurement techniques. Rather than having only the facility of an interval timer, we can consider many functions of the hardware monitor to be available to assist the measurement routine in performing its job.

The fact that a facility is available for program control and data reading does not necessarily imply that the monitor function is physically integrated into the frame of the CPU. There may be many reasons why some of the monitor facilities would be packaged as a separate unit. For example, there may be requirements to account for activities such as terminal action which require a relatively low speed counter facility. If this facility were implemented within the frame of the CPU, the design of the counters may be forced into using very high speed circuitry. On the other hand, if the counters were packaged in a separate unit, the cost of adding a power supply may be more expensive than if they had been integrated into the main frame. Given the requirement for a facility, the systems designers must determine the best method to implement the feature.

8.7. MEASUREMENT CONNECTIONS

One of the most critical considerations in the application of hardware monitors is the design of the interface. In most of the cases listed above, the functional capability of the monitor was based, in part, on the type of information that could be obtained from the host system. When used in a laboratory environment, the interface could be more sophisticated than when applied to a large number of systems. The general characteristic of the interface is that signals in the host system are either sensed or derived by combinatorial logic within the system itself and then driven down an appropriate signal cable for termination in the measurement device. The circuitry necessary to sense as well as amplify for transmission is constructed in circuit locations of the host system. Even for a simple path, this can be quite time consuming and costly. There is also the problem of finding space available on the circuit boards of the system. When considering the various functions that the hardware monitors can perform, it would not be unusual to find interface requirements of over 200 signal lines. This is especially the case if the memory address generation is distributed over several functional areas.

To overcome the problem of essentially rewiring the host system for the purpose of supplying an interface, the "measurement probe" was designed. This probe may be compared with the attachment of an oscilloscope probe in that it does not interfere with the performance of the circuit that it is sensing. Very short leads are attached to pin connections for signal and reference voltages. These in turn are amplified in the probe itself for transmission to the measurement device. Power for the amplification is supplied by the monitor. This allows for a very quick connection to a host system, with no change in the original wiring of the system. The functions observed by the monitors are then variable, depending almost only upon the imagination of the analyst.

PROBLEMS

1. For four inputs, construct Boolean truth tables for
   (a) the AND function.
   (b) the OR function.

2. Given three channels and a CPU, structure by equation or block diagram the function: "Any channel operating while the CPU is active."

3. Use two equal-only comparators and a latch to time a routine which has an entry point at alpha and an exit point at beta. Assume that there are no interruptions to the routine.

4. Block diagram the logic necessary to determine the total time and incidence of use of the routine in Problem 3 during the time it is being used by a program whose memory protect key is 1011. Assume that alpha and beta are invariant and that the routine is assigned the memory protect key of the using program. (This is typical of re-entrant routines.)

5. Block out the functions of an event distribution analyzer that will distribute the occurrences of printer skipping by the number of lines skipped. Assume that a pulse is available for each line skipped as well as any other necessary control pulses. The maximum number of lines skipped is 60. (In a classroom environment, discuss the variety of assumptions and approaches.)

6. What would be the setting for an equal-only comparator (trivalue with 20 positions) to determine activity in a control program which uses storage from location zero to location 32,767.

7. Structure a computing outline to calculate the data obtained from the monitor in Section 8.4.1 to complete a basic system profile including channel to channel overlap.

8. Block diagram the functions of a dynamic monitor which would be necessary

to obtain event information for input to the simulation program of Problem 9, Chapter 5 (i.e., Section 5.3).

Note: The following problems are optional, depending on facilities available.

9. Set up and perform an experiment to determine timing error curve based on an asynchronous string of pulses of a set length. Let the variable be the pulse length. Calculate the error for at least the range of variables of one-quarter to four times the basic cycle time of the monitor. (E.g., if the basic cycle time were 1 microsecond, the range should be 250 nanoseconds to 4 microseconds.)

10. Assuming that there is a NO-OP instruction or other special instruction which could be used to uniquely provide special information to a hardware monitor, set up and perform an experiment to determine whether any of the desired fields is currently in use. (E.g., if within the normal NO-OP definition there were an unused address field which could be used for monitoring purposes, use a hardware monitor to determine whether that field is in current use.)

11. Assuming the presence of a CPU which has various states similar to the CPU states in Section 8.3.1, design and implement an experiment to determine percentage differences in defining "CPU active."

9 PRESENTATION OF DATA

There are many options available to the analyst in performing evaluation and measurement of computing systems. Having progressed through various approaches and techniques, we should not let the mass of methodology hide the intended purpose. In the final analysis, the purpose of performing a measurement or an evaluation is to provide guidance in making a decision. Whether the decision is an installation manager's concerning acquisition of equipment or a designer's concerning choice of technology, results must provide guidance. In structuring a measurement or an evaluation, the analyst should prepare an outline. Elements of the outline should include the following:

What decision is being made?

How should the results be interpreted?

What presentation of data should be used?

What sensitive elements should be examined?

What technique should be used to process the data?

What input is required for the technique?

How can the input data be acquired?

The preparation of an outline can sometimes be more difficult to perform than an evaluation or measurement. It can, however, overcome one of the more perplexing problems that the analyst may have, namely, the execution of an experiment only to find that the results are irrelevant to the problem being addressed. This can easily happen if the recipient of the information cannot comprehend the information, or if the analyst produces results which the recipient can not consider as being germane to the decision.

9.1. PROCESSING MEASURED DATA

Whether measured data are obtained by manual transcription or a magnetic media, there is normally some amount of processing to present the data in the most meaningful form. In computer systems, the most popular forms of expression of the data are percentage utilization or event rate. Although the direct output of the monitor or trace program provides meaningful data, conversion may make the data more understandable. For example, we might have a result that "the CPU was used for 400 seconds over the last half hour." Would that be as meaningful as "the CPU utilization was 22% over the last half hour"? Similarly, we could replace the phrase "the tape drive transmitted 18,000,000 bytes in the last half hour" with "the tape drive averaged 10kb in the last half hour." If, in this case, the drive were rated at 15kb, some idea of its attaining peak performance would be given. There could be many reasons why the tape drive performed the way it did, and the CPU performed the way it did. If the results were disturbing, the analyst could investigate the reasons more thoroughly.

In Chapter 4, the information to establish a basic system profile was presented in graphical form as shown in Figure 9.1. An alternative would be the same information as a normal bar chart as shown in Figure 9.2.

For those unaccustomed to the form of the original profile, the bar chart may provide a better diagram. In the bar chart, there is no implication of ordinal event activity as might be inferred from the profile chart. The profile

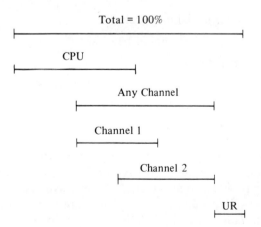

Fig. 9.1   Basic system profile.

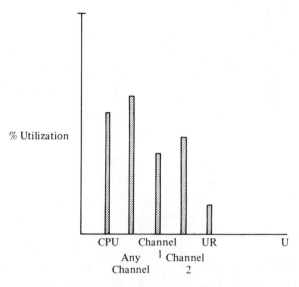

Fig. 9.2   Bar chart of basic system profile.

chart is utilized as both a presentation vehicle and as a basis for the technique of profile conversion.

On many occasions, a double variable plot is used to present measured results. This is especially true when time is taken into consideration as one of the factors.

In Figure 9.3, we see a plot of CPU utilization versus time of day. This is shown as a point plot. If the same information were presented as a point-to-point curve, it would appear as shown in Figure 9.4. Yet another approach would be to present the same information as a histogram as shown in Figure 9.5.

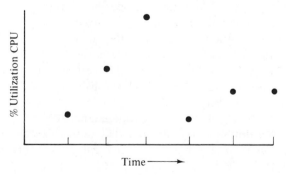

Fig. 9.3   Point plot.

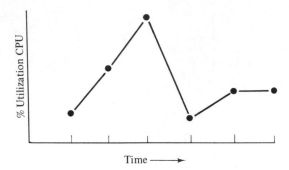

Fig. 9.4   Point to point curve.

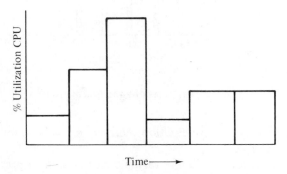

Fig. 9.5   Histogram.

When presenting utilization information for various components in the system, multiple sets of information may be presented on the same graph. In Figure 9.6, we have two variables, CPU and ANY Channel, plotted as point plots, point-to-point curves, and bar charts.

Multiple plots are not restricted to the same scale. For example, in Figure 9.7, there is a plot of CPU utilization versus time of day with the super-imposed plot of message rate (messages per hour) versus time of day. Presentation in this manner allows some visual correlation on the two activities.

Frequency distribution curves are often used to get a picture of the variation of a variable. In Figure 9.8, a frequency distribution chart for disk seek time is shown. In Figure 9.9, there is a frequency distribution of record length. These types of charts are used to establish modal information.

Information can be very useful in tabular form. In Figure 9.10, there is shown a distribution of job activity by source language and size of program. Here, we have a double entry table in that both the absolute number of jobs in each category is shown as well as that entry's percentage of the entire volume of jobs.

In Figure 9.11, again a double entry table is used, but this time there are

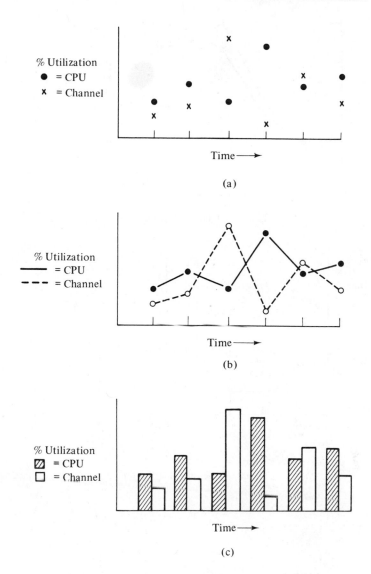

Fig. 9.6 Multiple variables (a) point plot, (b) curve, (c) bar chart.

shown an entry as a percentage of total number of jobs and an entry as a percentage of total amount of computing time.

Another type of tabular approach which can be used is an ordinal distribution table. Such a table is shown in Figure 9.12. Here, we are determining the relationship of various data sets, specifically, the number of times any particular data set was used after reference to a preceding data set. We see

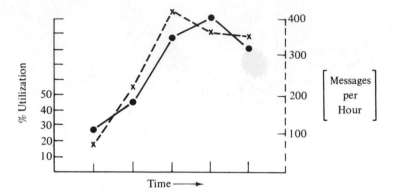

Fig. 9.7   Combination scales.

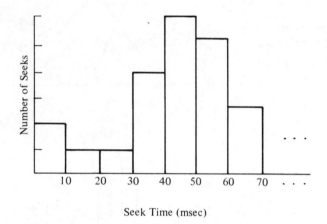

Seek Time (msec)

Fig. 9.8   Seek time distribution.

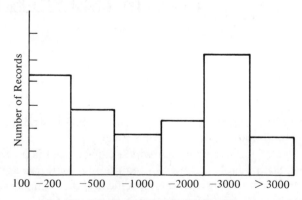

Fig. 9.9   Record length distribution.

Language	Program Size (Source)											
	< 200		200 − 399		400 − 599		600 − 999		1000−1999		2000+	
	I	%	I	%	I	%	I	%	I	%	I	%
Assembler			22	2								
Compiler A			38	4								
Compiler B			115	11								
Compiler C			9	1								
⋮												

Fig. 9.10 Job activity distribution.

Language	Program Size (Source)				
	200	200 − 399		400 − 599	
		%V	%T		
Assembler		2	1		
Compiler A		4	2		
Compiler B		11	15		
Compiler C		1	5		

Fig. 9.11 Job distribution percentage volume and time.

Data Set	Followed By				
	A1	A2	A3	A4	· · ·
A1	1529	628	0	22	
A2	200	0	628	0	
A3	0	0	19	840	
A4		· · ·			
⋮					

Fig. 9.12 Distribution of ordinal relationship.

that a reference to data set A2 was followed by a reference to A1, 200 times; A2 (itself), not at all; A3, 628 times; and A4, zero. Such a table would be used to determine conflicts between data sets for allocation across common devices.

So for measured data there are many methods of processing the information to provide guidance in making a decision. Data conversion, reduction, analysis, and statistical routines can be used. Various projective techniques such as profile conversion, synthetic routines, or simulation programs may be used to project various effects of change. Consider the following as guidelines to the analysis of measured data.

(a) *Eyeball*

Don't let the magnitude of computer systems and the measurement and evaluation of such systems overwhelm the user. Although this is presented in a half-serious vein, one should not overlook the fact that much information and many decisions may be made with a simple examination of the data.

(b) *Graphical*

Simple graphs of the measurements may indicate the type of action which should be taken. Plotting variables against one another or against time may indicate patterns and trends which will assist the analyst. In using graphical techniques, one may discover that the shape of the curve will tell a more significant story than the determination of particular points on the curve.

(c) *Synthetic Routines*

To determine the results of projecting proposed courses of action, the synthetic routine should be examined for adequacy. Even in the cases of projecting improvements in a dynamic environment, one can establish envelopes of performance by arbitrarily holding many variables fixed, even though it would not be realistic to do so.

(d) *Simulation Routines*

In this day and age, many of the system environments are such that simulative techniques must be employed in order to do any projection of proposed courses of action. Before going into a simulation project, one should progress through the three prior approaches. This is because a simulation project can be lengthy and expensive to perform. Even so, where the previous techniques prove inadequate, simulation may be the only recourse. If this is the case, there should be careful consideration that the input to the simulation can be obtained either by measurement or derived from some other source. In fact, an iterative approach should probably be assumed between the modeling and the measurement. This assumes that the requirements of the model are spelled out before the measurement effort is initiated.

9.2. INTERPRETING PROJECTED RESULTS

Many of the preceding examples implied the use of a single number as an expression of a system's merit. The next question is how can the single number result be applied to some other environment or application. To change an environmental or application characteristic could require a new complete calculation. When considering the almost infinite number of combinations of environments and applications, one could foresee a never-ending regimen of calculation. To overcome this problem, many approaches have been taken. Two approaches are more popular than the others, namely, "standard" environments, and "average" environments.

In considering the use of these two approaches, we can draw a parallel with the Stock Market. The "Dow Jones Average" is a "standard" along with subsidiary standards of "Transportation" and "Utilities." It is a weighted average of a selected set of stocks which have been chosen to represent the direction of the marketplace as a whole. Statistically, it is considered to be a reasonable measure of market activity. On the other hand the New York Stock Exchange Index does actually average all transactions which took place that day. It is truly an "average." We all realize, however, that neither of these excellent indicators will let us know what happened to any particular portfolio. Furthermore, because of the difference in approach, it is possible to have one technique indicating that the market is up and another indicating the market is down. This does not mean that one is right and the other is wrong. It simply means that while there is general correlation for the complete market over a period of time, there will be instances where there is divergence of results, depending on one's point of view.

We have the same situation with regard to performance data. Although one may establish standard environments, it is always possible that some average environment will produce results that vary. Neither calculation may necessarily produce a result that is applicable to a particular configuration in a particular environment. In many cases, it may be more desirable to calculate a range of variables for graphical display. If a major attribute of interest can be isolated, then it can be used as an independent variable for the projection of system performance. Consider an example in which a proposed change to the system has an influence on relative system throughput depending regularly on the percentage of execution time (e.g., percentage of time of non-compile work compared with total work performed) on the base system. This information can be plotted as RST versus percent of execution time as indicated in Figure 9.13. Given such a plot, an analyst can then determine the probable system improvement for any particular environment by applying the execution percentage established for that environment.

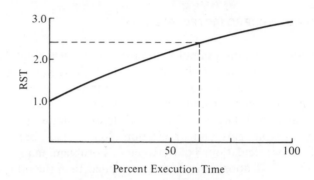

Fig. 9.13   RST versus execution percentage.

Assuming that the analyst wished to establish relative system throughput for an installation that operated with 60% execution (i.e., 40% of the time is spent in compilation and allied activities), the above graph indicates that he can expect a relative system throughput improvement of 2.4. If this percentage activity represented 100 hours of computer time on the present system, he could plan on about forty-two hours of computer time for the projected system. Naturally, some adjustment to these figures would be necessary to convert from computer hours to scheduled hours.

Many times, the shape of the curve itself may be more important than any particular point. If the region of interest is in the flat area of the curve, coarse information may be applied. If the region is in the steep portion of the curve, then the probability of error and resulting deviation range of the answer is

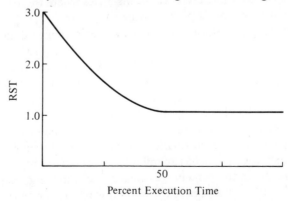

Fig. 9.14   Sensitivity of function.

greater. Consider a curve as given in Figure 9.14, which again is a plot of relative system throughput versus percentage execution.

This example indicates that if the work load of interest had a percentage of execution time greater than 50%, then little or no improvement would result by changing the facility in question. This knowledge would eliminate the necessity to determine a closer approximation in *that* region. If the work load of interest had a percentage of about 25%, then one would want to make a closer examination of the installation. The closer examination would not necessarily be with the intent of finding a more precise percentage, such as 22.5%, but to determine the variation about a percentage. For example, if the range of activity were narrowed down to something like 20 to 25 percent, then a range of expectation can be established.

9.3. MIGRATION OF SYSTEMS

One of the biggest problems facing an analyst is the fact that systems migrate (or perhaps wander might be a better description). The problem is not so much in the area of obtaining data, but in the fact that a computer system is used for a wide variety of applications within a single installation. As time goes on, the application set changes not only by restructuring given applications, but also by dropping old ones and adding new ones. Observation of an installation for a given period of time such as a week or a month will provide information for an analysis. Repeating an observation over time, however, will also provide "migration" data. In this way, one can hopefully determine trends.

Without such migration data, whether obtained by special measurement or merely by an examination of normal computing center records, one may be faced with an old adage in the computing industry. An installation requests bids or proposals assuming one environment, selects a vendor on another environment, checks out acceptance or benchmark tests on a third, installs on a fourth, and operates "with a fifth" (Drummond's Law, circa 1961). With migration data, the analyst may be able to project the operational stage early in the acquisition cycle.

PROBLEMS

Note: All problems are optional, depending on facilities available.

1. Given the following basic system profile, structure a plot of RST versus record length (see diagram at top of page 292).
Assume that the observed magnetic tape unit had characteristics of 7 millisecond start time and a 60 kb rate, and that the projected unit has characteristics of 5 milliseconds start time and a 90 kb rate.

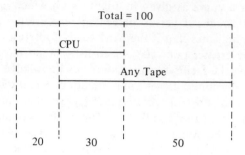

2. From data obtained from your own installation construct a bar chart of the basic system profile information.

3. Assuming a trace tape from either a programmed measurement routine or a measurement device, write a data reduction program to provide a general purpose frequency distribution function. Assume a maximum grid size of 100 subdivisions.

4. Modify, if necessary, previously written programmed measurement routines to provide either data set identification or unit identification. Write a data analysis routine to provide ordinal distribution information as outlined in Figure 9.12.

10 APPLICATION NOTES

In this chapter some approaches to solving some of the more general problems will be addressed. Because a particular approach may be used this is no indication that it is the only approach which should be used. For any particular problem, there can be many ways of applying measurement and evaluation techniques to obtain sufficient information for guidance. The techniques used here will have been previously discussed.

In general, the analyst is faced with one of two categories of measuring systems and projecting the effect of change. The first, and simplest, is that of unit replacement with no change in job or application structure. Even though this type of change is commonplace in installations, it is by no means the more flexible type. The type of component replacement which can be projected with the simple unit replacement philosophy would be change in CPU, serial devices such as magnetic tape, card or paper tape equipment, printers, and programming components such as language compilers. Even in this case, the simplicity is based more on replacing units with like units rather than changing the number of units involved. If a direct access device replaces a unit such as a magnetic tape unit, simple techniques may be used if the direct access device is used in a sequential environment.

The second category of change involves restructuring of jobs or applications. In this category we find the problems of projecting the effects of changing number of devices, changing access methods, which involves restructuring jobs, changing size of memory, and changing scheduling and allocation algorithms in multiprogramming or interactive systems. When an application structure is changed, whether for an internal structure of a single application or an external structure such as the method of dispatching a stream of applications, interactive effects should be taken into consideration. This generally implies the use of simulative techniques. The input to such techniques would necessarily be more detailed than input to the simpler techniques.

Wherever the requirements of the problem lead the analyst, an initial investigation of the work load being performed would be in order. One or two measurement techniques are recommended for initial studies. The techniques would be used to provide information to perform a job stream analysis and a basic system profile analysis. These two analyses would provide limit information, or boundary conditions, for further projections.

An investigation of the job stream would provide information concerning the source languages used, the relationship between compile activity and execution activity, a distribution of job times (classically, many short jobs or a few long jobs), and the general data set allocation requirements of the jobs.

Basic system profiles would provide information on the utilization of various systems components within the system. If, for example, the profiles consistently indicated that almost all CPU and channel activities were overlapped with one another the conclusion could be that the system is balanced with regard to its work load. Any system change would therefore involve an improvement in all active components. Conversely, if one of the components were seriously out of balance, then investigations for improvement would be directed at that area.

Ideally, the two analyses should be performed in such a way as to allow some correlation between the job stream and the system profile. Usually either profile conversion or a synthetic technique can be used to assess the effect of a component replacement in a sequential environment. Job timers and formula evaluations can also be used in these environments. When these same techniques can be used in the more complex environments, they will be addressed in later sections. The general questions which can be addressed by the simple techniques are given in the following parts of this chapter.

10.1. CPU PROJECTION

One of the simpler questions to address is the effect of changing CPUs and their associated speed of processor storage. The question is generally asked with an implied assumption that all other attributes of the environment including system options, configuration, and application structure are held constant. It should be noted that although the question may be well considered, it may not be realistic. When a component such as the CPU is changed, we generally find that all other attributes will *not* remain constant. (As a matter of fact, even if the CPU were not replaced, the other activities would not remain constant.) Unless migration data are available, the simple question will have to suffice.

The two primary factors in assessing the change of CPU speed would be the CPU improvement factor as compared to the observed system and the amount of nonoverlapped CPU time on the observed system. In applying these factors, either averages over sets of jobs or individual factors averaged over an individual job may be used. (In a multiprocessing or real time environment, averages over sets of activities are normally used.)

In either event, the profile conversion technique will provide a reasonably good approximation to the effect of change. The technique of converting basic system profiles for either individual jobs or sets of jobs would be performed by the same basic calculation procedure. Of course, if many different profiles are converted, the analyst's calculation load would increase. This would be due not only to the number of individual profiles, but also because of the use of some combining algorithm.

The determination of CPU improvement factor could be one or a combination of three techniques. If the projected CPU is architecturally the same as the original CPU, then simple instruction mixes would probably suffice. The instruction mix technique may not be applicable if the projected CPU has a parallel or pipelined structure. In this case, instruction tracing may be in order to determine the net effect of CPU improvement factor for the replacing CPU.

If the projected CPU is architecturally different from the original CPU, either kernel analysis or functional mix calculation may be in order. It should be noted at this point that if the replacing CPU involves a different structure to the problem solution, techniques for problem restructuring, such as job timers, should be utilized in the evaluation.

In Figure 10.1, we see the various relationships between the original CPU and the projected CPU which would indicate the use of various techniques.

Taking the approaches one at a time, let us examine the possible measurement techniques which could be used to obtain the data necessary for the approach.

The instruction mix which we should obtain for the calculation would be the dynamic instruction mix. There are two primary sources for obtaining this mix. If sufficient loop control and branch direction information were available, the mix could be determined from a static listing of the instruction coding. The problem in this type of analysis would be in the data dependent portions of loop control and branch directions. Analysis time required to obtain the data dependency information could be almost as much as the time to obtain data on the dynamic instruction processing during execution.

A simple technique to determine the sufficiency of obtaining information from static coding would be to simply take the "shortest" and "longest" paths for any data dependent operations. If the results from these two paths are sufficiently close together, then a simple average from the two results would probably suffice for the determination of the CPU improvement factor.

If a dynamic instruction mix must be obtained, a summarizing facility must be used while the program is in the process of execution. To obtain this type of information, the hardware monitor approach would probably be preferable to the programmed technique. The use of a hardware monitor in this case is not clear cut. It really depends on the level to which an instruc-

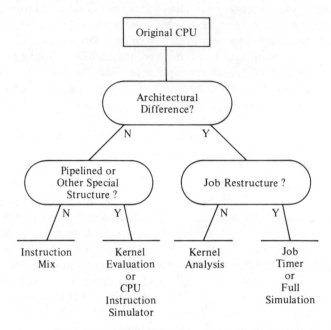

Fig. 10.1   CPU relationships and techniques.

tion mix must be obtained. Assuming that the original CPU has a repertoire of about 200 instructions, an instruction mix can be developed for each individual instruction, or it may be developed for a much smaller number of instruction classes. Depending on the variation of instruction times between the original CPU and the projected CPU, it may be possible to summarize an instruction mix to 16 classes or smaller.

Since a hardware monitor does require an individual count capability for each instruction or instruction type summarized (plus one for total instructions counted), it may be more economical to use a programmed routine to obtain the frequency of instructions used. To obtain an instruction frequency for almost every instruction requires either a full trace routine with its attendant explosion of computing time, or the use of a module trace with subsequent correlation to a static map of the instruction coding in the system at the time of execution.

If a module trace is used, there must be some provision to determine data dependent branching within the module which a normal module trace would not intercept. This, of course, requires additional intercept points with an expansion of processor storage requirements. The additional storage requirement would be for either additional problem program space to allow for the intercepts or for additional instruction replacement space in the measurement routine itself.

If the method to use is not obvious from the relationships between the original CPU and the projected CPU, some tests may be performed to determine the adequacy of simpler methods. Assuming that a job profile analysis has been performed, a small set of jobs can be selected from the entire set of jobs performed. The selection criterion would be for those jobs which require the greatest amount of system time for their execution. Let's take one of the "criteria" jobs and analyze it both ways.

Using one of the criteria jobs, obtain a dynamic instruction mix utilizing a hardware monitor for a small class of instructions, say 8 or 16. (If counter capacity is available, both 8 and 16 may be taken at the same time.) Following the run which provided the hardware monitor information, repeat the run using a programmed trace routine to obtain a frequency distribution for each individual instruction executed. These two runs would produce the extremes of dynamic instruction counting. Given both sets of information, use average instruction times of the original and projected CPU's to calculate two different CPU improvement factors. If the results of these two calculations are too divergent for the analyst to have confidence in using the simpler method, then the exercise should be repeated with the same job. Increasing the lower boundary may soon cause the analyst to exceed the capacity of the summarizing hardware monitor. At this point, the analyst is forced into one of three directions: either a programmed trace routine, or the utilization of a dynamic hardware monitor to obtain a full trace of all instructions executed, or a sample trace technique. Again, the sample trace routine can be implemented in either a hardware device or a programmed sample routine.

At this point, we have involved at least two types of hardware monitor and three types of programmed trace technique. The two types of hardware monitor were the summary type device and the dynamic type device. The dynamic device could be used as a full trace technique if its capability and media rate allowed; or if its capability were limited, as a sampling device. The three programmed techniques were the full instruction trace, the module trace, and the sample routine. There are variations in the sample rates of both the programmed routine and the hardware monitor. Within each technique's capability, the analyst may vary the sampling rate to determine sufficiency of data.

Whichever techniques are used, the analyst will be able to reach a point of convergence between the various techniques which will give him confidence in the use of a particular technique. If, on the original comparison, the classification results from the hardware monitor and the complete execution frequency of each instruction from the full program trace were satisfactorily close, at that point the analyst could select the simpler technique to use. If this detailed study of one job were not sufficient to provide satisfactory confidence limits, then the exercise could be repeated for the next job, and the next, and so on, until sufficient confidence could be obtained. The progression of these techniques is shown in Figure 10.2.

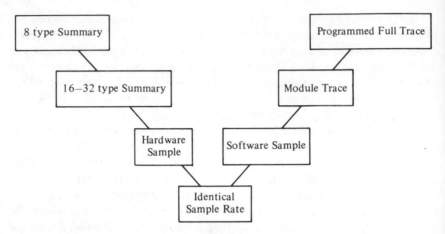

Fig. 10.2   Closure sequence.

In the above techniques, it should be noted that some of the techniques could cause some interference between the relationship of CPU execution with the I/O activity. The reason for separating the determination of CPU improvement factor from basic system profile studies is to allow the use of such techniques. When determining instruction frequencies in the simpler environments, the disruption of the CPU and I/O relationship should not perturb the determination of CPU improvement factor. This can be a critical problem in multiprogramming and real time systems.

Assuming that closure of a satisfactory confidence level has been obtained for the determination of a CPU improvement factor, this technique would be used across individual jobs or sets of jobs as required.

The job profile analysis will also provide guidance as to how many different profiles will be required for conversion. If there were a limited number of jobs which accounted for a large portion of the computing system's time with the residue of time taken by many small jobs, individual profiles and CPU improvement factors could be established for the major jobs and profiles and CPU improvement factors could be established for all of the remaining jobs as a single set. Consider that such an analysis indicated job information as shown in Figure 10.3.

Here, we see that the first five jobs account for 50% of the computing time. The other 45 jobs account for the remaining time with no particular job accounting for any appreciable period.

The approach to obtaining instruction frequency information is to take a special reading whenever one of the five major jobs is executed. All other instruction frequency information is taken for the remaining jobs as a set. Assume that the result of CPU improvement factor determination is shown in Figure 10.4.

If the acquisition of instruction frequency information does not perturb

Job	Percent Time
1	15
2	10
3	10
4	10
5	5
6	0.5
7	. . .
.	
.	
.	
50	. . .
50	100%

Fig. 10.3   Job time information.

Job	CPU IF
1	1.5
2	1.8
3	1.4
4	1.5
5	2.0
Others	1.7

Fig. 10.4   CPU improvement factors.

the relationship of CPU activity with I/O activity, basic system profiles may be taken at the same time. If the relationship is perturbed, profile information must be obtained separately from instruction frequency information.

Assume that the unperturbed profile information is shown in Figure 10.5. Here we see individual profiles for the 5 major jobs and a composite profile for the remaining 45 jobs. The profiles are shown in tabular form rather than graphic form. For reference, the profile of job one is shown in graphic form in Figure 10.6. In Figure 10.7, we see the profile conversion table for each profile and its associated CPU improvement factor (IF).

Job	CPU Only	Other
1	20	80
2	25	75
3	10	90
4	30	70
5	40	60
Others	30	70

Fig. 10.5   Job profile information.

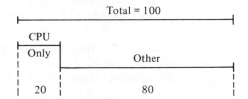

Fig. 10.6   Profile of job 1.

Job	CPU Only	Other	CPU IF
1	20	80	1.5
2	25	75	1.8
3	10	90	1.4
4	30	70	1.5
5	40	60	2.0
Others	30	70	1.7

Fig. 10.7   Job profile and CPU improvement.

In Figure 10.8, the resulting time profile is shown with the job execution frequencies which were obtained from the job profile analysis. In this calculation, the new total machine hours required to perform the workload on the projected CPU is produced. The calculation for a multiprogramming or interactive environment will be shown in later sections.

| Job | Observed | | | Projected | | | |
	CPU Only	Other	CPU IF	CPU Only	Other	Total	Percent Time
1	20	80	1.5	13	80	93	15
2	25	75	1.8	14	75	89	10
3	10	90	1.4	7	90	97	10
4	30	70	1.5	20	70	90	10
5	40	60	2.0	20	60	80	5
Others	30	70	1.7	18	70	88	50
Total	100 hrs					90 hrs	

Fig. 10.8   Resulting job profile.

To determine scheduled hours for the projected CPU, we again return to the job profile analysis to determine the utilization of scheduled hours to utilized hours. In the job profile analysis, the number of scheduled hours must be obtained from one of two sources. The sources are either the total elapsed time from entry of the first job to completion of the last job, or by the interview method with installation management. Using the first technique, there is an implicit assumption that all time between the first job and the last job is scheduled. The truth of this assumption can be determined by the analyst by simply checking with the installation management. If the assumption is false, they will probably provide the characteristics of scheduling the system in short order.

Since the primary assumption of this section is that there was no change in other activities, scheduled hours can be constructed from the same expansion factor as observed on the original system. Unfortunately, this particular calculation may attenuate seriously the effects of changing to some projected CPU, but would provide a rather realistic approximation of the effect of change to installation management.

10.2. MAGNETIC TAPE PROJECTION

When we think of projecting magnetic tape effects, we normally think in terms of start/stop time and transmission rate characteristics.

As shown in Figure 10.9, there are many more characteristics which should be taken into account when executing a general performance evaluation.

The simplest projection involves the use of a basic system profile and a tape improvement factor. The projection algorithm will decrease the amount of "tape only" time by the improvement factor. The residual time will then be the new job time. Just as in the case of CPU projection, individual profiles and individual tape improvement factors may be used for each job, or averages may be used across sets of jobs.

Start/Stop Time
Transmission Rate
Rewind Time
Reel Capacity
Reel Change Time
Backspace Time
Read Backwards Time
Reselect Time
Frame Width (Packing)   **Fig. 10.9**   Magnetic tape characteristics.

To obtain the tape improvement factor, we need either average record length of the total number of records transmitted or record length on each individual tape drive. If total number of records is the information available, then the profile should provide information on individual channel activity (or device activity, depending on the architecture). This profile is shown in Figure 10.10. The reason that the profile should give individual channel activity is that the calculation of average record length must be based on total channel activity, not just the time that any one or more channels are in operation.

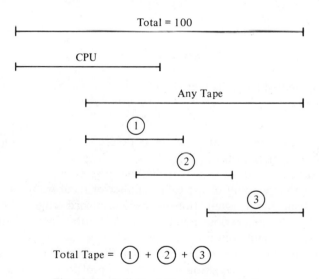

Fig. 10.10   Individual tape channel activity.

Because individual channel or device operations may be shown in the profile, a more accurate estimate of average record length may be obtained by accounting for number of records by each device and channel. Although this information may not be necessary for a simple profile conversion, it may be used in more complex routines.

If total channel time and number of records transmitted are available, average record length is calculated by first dividing total channel time by total number of records. This result is the average record time. Subtracting the start time of the observed device, the transmission time of data is established. Dividing this by the transmission rate of the observed device, the result is the average record length. In equation form we have the following:

Let $T =$ total channel time (sum of individual channels)

$N =$ total number of records transmitted

$t(r) =$ average time of individual record

$t(d) =$ average transmission time of individual record

$S =$ start time of observed device

$L =$ average record length

$R =$ transmission rate of observed device.

From the above information, average individual record time is

$$t(r) = T/N.$$

The average data transmission time is

$$t(d) = t(r) - S.$$

The average record length is then

$$L = t(d)/R.$$

This final result would then be used to determine the unit improvement factor of the projected device.

Many times, the measurement technique may provide a total character count rather than a count of the total number of records. When this information is given, the determination of average record length is as follows.

In addition to the previous notation, let $C =$ total count of the number of characters transmitted.

The determination of average record length comes from the solution of two equations. The first equation is the make-up of total channel time,

$$T = N*(S + L*R)$$

Here we see that the total channel time is accounted for by taking the average time of each record, here expressed as $S + L*R$, times the total number of records, N. Expanding this formula in preparation for the next step, we have

$$T = N*S + N*L*R.$$

The second item of information that we have is the total number of characters transmitted, C. Another way of expressing this is

$$C = N*L.$$

In other words the total number of characters transmitted is equal to the average number of characters per record times the total number of records. Substituting C for the factor $N*L$, the total time equation is

$$T = N*S + C*R.$$

The only unknown in this equation is the total number of records, N. Solving for N, we have

$$N = (T - C*R)/S.$$

Having obtained a value for N, we can calculate the average record length by the formula

$$L = C/N.$$

Again, this result would be used to determine projected unit improvement factor.

From the above set of equations, it should be obvious that the more desirable measurement to make would be both total number of records as well as total number of characters transmitted. If these two items of information were measured, the determination of average record length would be simply

$$L = C/N.$$

Having arrived at average record length, the next step is to determine the magnetic tape's unit improvement factor. This is obtained by developing a ratio of the average record time for the observed device to the projected device. The additional subscript "o" shall indicate the observed device, and the subscript "p" will indicate the projected device.

$$t(r_o) = S_o + L*R_o,$$

and

$$t(r_p) = S_p + L*R_p.$$

The unit improvement factor M, would then be

$$M = t(r_o)/t(r_p).$$

This factor would then be applied to the tape-only portion of the system profile to obtain a new job time. Assuming that we have the same jobs as in the previous example, Figure 10.11 shows in tabular form the profile information for the 5 major jobs and a composite profile for the remaining 45 jobs.

Job	Tape Only	Other	Tape		
			C1	C2	Total
1	60	40	50	50	100
2	50	50	40	35	75
3	80	20	60	70	130
4	50	50	20	40	60
5	40	60	35	30	65
Others	50	50	40	40	80

Fig. 10.11   Job profile information.

It is assumed that there is also available the total number of records and total number of characters observed during execution. For reference, the profile of job 1 is shown in graphic form in Figure 10.12.

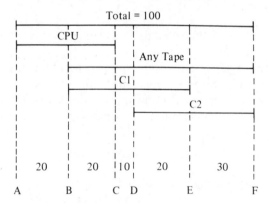

Fig. 10.12   Job 1 profile.

Total channel time is given by the region B to E, *plus* the region D to F. In Figure 10.13, the resulting time profile for each of the entries is shown with the job execution frequencies obtained from a job profile analysis. Again, the conversion from machine hours to scheduled hours would be the same type of calculation as shown in the previous section.

The next characteristic in Figure 10.9 was the rewind characteristic. Again, a simple approach to projecting the effect of rewind characteristics would be the utilization of profile conversion. In this case, we would need to isolate the amount of time where tape rewinds are the governing operations contributing to job time. To this time, the rewind improvement factor would be applied. Most rewind characteristics are expressed as either an

	Observed						Projected			
			Tape							
Job	Tape Only	Other	C1	C2	Total	Tape IF	Tape Only	Other	Total	Percent Time
1	60	40	50	50	100	1.5	40	40	80	15
2	50	50	40	35	75	1.5	33	50	83	10
3	80	20	60	70	130	1.6	50	20	70	10
4	50	50	20	40	60	1.3	38	50	88	10
5	40	60	35	30	65	1.2	33	60	93	5
Others	50	50	40	40	80	1.3	38	50	88	50
Total	100 hrs							85 hrs		

Fig. 10.13 Resulting profile.

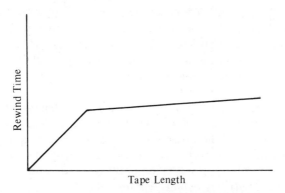

Tape Length

Fig. 10.14 Rewind characteristic.

equation or table entries based on length of tape to be rewound. A typical form of curve is shown in Figure 10.14.

The measurement technique should supply sufficient information to allow a calculation of tape length of total rewinds. If by some method or another we can obtain average record length and number of records for each rewind, using density information and physical spacing of gaps, the length of tape to be rewound can be calculated. The calculation of rewind performance information is especially important for applications which involve inter-mediate data sets on magnetic tape. When such data sets are present, it is common practice to wait until the end of a phase of a job or job step to rewind the tapes. Such practice can easily result in the tape rewind time being the major contributor to job time.

A profile including rewind time is shown in Figure 10.15. Notice that it is possible to have tape rewind operation overlapped with tape transmission activities. This is because the program could simply have initiated a tape re-

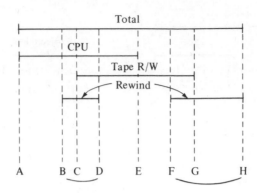

Fig. 10.15   Rewind profile.

wind on a particular unit as soon as the program had determined that such an action could have taken place. Regions B to D and F to H of the profile should be summed for the determination of total rewind time. (Again, the discontinuity in the profile is due to the summarizing effect of the information rather than any ordinal implication.) The determination of improvement factor to project the effects of rewind capability is similar to projecting tape transmission improvement factors. Average tape lengths for either the summary or individual devices are determined. These lengths are then used to find rewind times on the observed and projected devices using character- istics as shown in Figure 10.14. The times are then used to produce an im- provement factor. This factor is then applied to the portion of the profile governed (dominated) by rewind activity.

The determination of reel changes is a compound problem. The *incidence* of reel change can be objectively determined from observed data. The *dura- tion* of reel change is subjective and is normally determined by human factors studies. The duration of reel change depends on the presence, attention, and competence of individual operators in individual installations. Since human factors studies and application of those techniques is beyond the scope of this text, it is recommended that the system analyst restrict himself to the determination of incidence only.

Measurement routines can provide information regarding the number of reel changes required on the observed system. The only reason to project a different number of reel changes for a projected device would be a change in reel capacity. Even if there were capacity differences, the analyst should first determine whether the observed system was utilizing full reels or not. There would be two reasons for having to change a reel in a multi-reel file operation. The first, and obvious, reason would be that the capacity of single reels was being exceeded for the application being processed. In this case, a new projection of reel changes based on capacity considerations would be in order. On the other hand, the second reason for reel changes would be that the individual reels of a multi-reel file had different origins in either time or location. The implication here is that those reels may not necessarily be full. The reason for using multiple reels would not be based on capacity considerations, but on reasons of convenience. In this case, there would be no rationale for attempting to convert the number of reel changes.

A suggested technique would be to measure the amount of time on the observed system where the governing factor was reel change time. The observed total run time of the application could then be reduced by this amount of time for processing by the other techniques and conversion factors. In a separate column or separate entry, indicate that a certain amount of time was involved for a given number of reel changes. On the projected profile, maintain separate entries simply stating that in addition to the converted profile and job time, a certain number of reel changes must be performed. In any given installation, the management of the installation can provide the best estimates for the time to change a reel. If various forms of reel change are considered, e.g., spindle knob versus "quick release" latch, the supervisors or senior operators can again provide the best estimate of the *duration* of a reel change.

The next item in Figure 10.9 was the backspace characteristic. Although the calculation of improvement in backspace characteristics may be objective the incidence can be random in nature. Backspace occurs under two conditions. The first condition is when a normal processing program causes a backspace of a record to achieve some logical processing. With larger memory capacities, the incidence of such program logic is very rare. It would normally be used to ensure correct positioning of tapes which have labeled files. This would normally occur only at the initiation of a job.

If a large number of backspaces occur, it is probably because an error routine has been called into the system to recover information from a drive which has given an error indication. It is not unusual to invoke error routines which try to re-read an erroneous record a large number of times. Up to 100 times is not unusual. The reason for such a large number of re-tries is the assumption that most of the tape errors are transient in nature, caused by either dust, oxide buildup, or other foreign matter temporarily deposited on the tape or the reading heads. Since it is commonplace to have tape drives that actually read back information from the tape itself after writing information on them (dual gap heads), such an assumption is reasonable.

Therefore, the analyst finds that this characteristic would normally be taken into consideration during reliability calculations rather than work capability calculations. There is one major exception to this statement; that is when a programmer has determined that his application operates faster by using a sequence of backspace, backspace, read rather than executing a rewind followed by a series of normal reads. For some magnetic tape drives, such activity does speed up the application processing time. When such an application is encountered, the analyst should examine the application for possible restructuring in light of the characteristics of the projected device.

A natural technique to replace the above sequence of two backspaces and a read would be the provision of a read backward capability as shown in the characteristics chart of Figure 10.9. If the observed system was performing a rewind followed by a normal sequence of reads, the incorporation of this feature implies a change in program structure. If the analyst can obtain information about the program structure to ascertain that the program could perform its intended function by utilizing read backwards without a major restructure of the program, the analyst can assess the effect of this feature by eliminating all time required for rewinds from the observed profile. If there are differences in timing formulae for reading forward and reading backward, a first approximation can be made by using a simple average of the two timing formulae. If this approximation does not provide satisfactory confidence due to the differences in the two times, the analyst must separate the application activity by phases. Separating basic system profiles within a job by phases would provide a profile as shown in Figure 10.16.

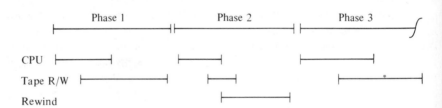

Fig. 10.16   Profile by phases.

Between phase two and phase three, a nonoverlapped rewind takes place. With a read backward capability and the assumption that the application did not have a major restructure, the analyst can simply reduce this rewind time to zero.

When the analyst is assessing the effect of read backward on a program which was originally using the sequence of two backspaces and a read, the projective technique approaches that of a normal unit replacement. However, the measurement technique should isolate that part of the activity which is utilizing this particular reading sequence. The profile for such an activity would appear as shown in Figure 10.17. Here we see the timing of this particular sequence isolated from the other tape activity. The variables involved are as follows. (Other variables were previously defined.)

Let $T(b)$ = Total time in backspace-read sequence

      $N(b)$ = Total number of records in backspace-read sequence

      B = Backspace reversal time.

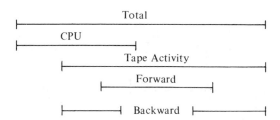

Fig. 10.17 Isolation of backspace—read sequence.

Before going into the formulae, it is assumed that the backspace reversal time is added to the time of the normal gap passing time, i.e., the value S (start time). In this particular sequence, two reversals take place. The first is at the beginning of the backspace sequence, and the second is before the read (or write) operation is performed. Therefore, the general formula in expanded form is as follows.

$$T(b) = N(b)*(B + (S + L*R) + (S + L*R) + B + S + L*R)$$

The first reversal is B. Given the reversal time, the drive spaces over the first record in the time $S + L*R$. It then continues over the second record in the same time. At that point, another reversal, B, occurs, and then the latter record is read in the time $S + L*R$.

This formula can be combined, and as in previous techniques, the average record length and/or number of records may be either calculated or provided by the measurement technique.

The average record time for the observed device may be calculated by the formula

$$t(r_o) = 2*B + 3*(S + L*R).$$

The average record time of the projected device would be calculated by using its normal read backward timing formula. From this point, a unit improvement factor would be calculated to attenuate the amount of time in the profile which would be the "read backward only" time.

The next item in Figure 10.9 is the characteristic of reselect time. Reselect time for a magnetic tape is the characteristic which determines how the motion of a magnetic tape is controlled between the time it has finished the transmission of a record and the next record is initiated. A typical timing chart for reselection is shown in Figure 10.18.

In this figure, we have what might be called a "constant start time" reselect characteristic. This is because whether the tape is initiated from a stopped state, or reselected at any time during the deceleration period, the start time of the operation in constant. In Figure 10.19 there is a timing chart of a tape drive which has a prescribed period of reselection.

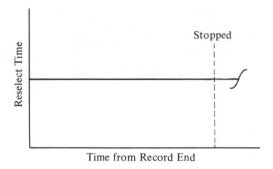

Fig. 10.18   Constant reselect time.

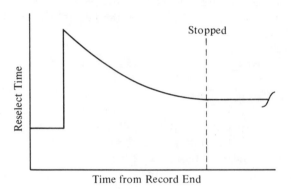

Fig. 10.19   Prescribed tape reselection time.

In this case, if no reselection of the unit occurs within the reselect period of the tape drive operation, the drive will decelerate to a full stop and then initiate the acceleration time, or start time. Naturally, the constant start time tape drive is more flexible than the drive with a prescribed reselect time. If the computing system were to miss the reselect time by only a matter of a few microseconds in the latter case, a full recycle of stopping and then restarting would be necessary.

To illustrate this effect, consider two tape drives, one of which has a constant gap time of 5 milliseconds, and the other with a more complex gap time as follows. From a standing stop, the gap time is 4 milliseconds. Once the tape is in motion, the gap time is 3 milliseconds, providing the reselect occurs within 500 microseconds of the previous end of record. If a reselect does not occur within 500 microseconds, the tape starts a deceleration period of 4 milliseconds, and must come to a complete stop before accelerating once again. This type of start/stop condition could well be expected using certain types of motors and drive assemblies.

If the system under study had a constant gap time tape drive complement, whenever the reselect occurred, or initial select as well, the start time
would be 5 milliseconds. If the system under study had the variable gap time
tape complement, the gap time could be 4 milliseconds if from a stopped
condition, 3 milliseconds if reselected within the first 500 microseconds, or
8 milliseconds if reselected just after the 500 microsecond criterion. In Figure
10.20 the reselect timing chart for the variable gap time device is shown.

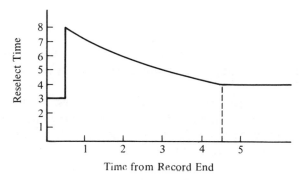

Fig. 10.20   Variable reselect.

Notice that any reselect time occurring more than 4.5 milliseconds from
the end of the previous record would have a constant start time of 4 milliseconds.

This variable gap time not only affects the system performance, but
puts an added requirement on the analyst. If such devices are in either the
observed system or the projected system, reselect time must be taken into
account. When determining reselect time, it is better to obtain a flow trace of
reselect times rather than merely obtaining an average reselect time. The
reason for this is the large discontinuity as exemplified by the step function
at 500 microseconds shown in Figure 10.20.

If the flow trace of reselect time is obtained by a programming technique,
care should be taken to avoid as much interference as possible between the
end of the previous record and the initiation of the reselect. For example,
put the intercept of the reselect just after the reselection has taken place. To
obtain the time of the end of the previous record, it may be necessary for the
analyst to take such expedient steps as counting from a static trace the number
of instructions between the end of record operation and the reselect.

If hardware monitor techniques are used, the analyst can set a latch
when an end of record occurs and reset the latch when the reselect occurs.
These signals can be obtained at the channel or the control unit of the device.
This time duration and a time of day reading would then be readout by a

dynamic device. (An alternative would be to use an event distribution analyzer.)

The final consideration for magnetic tape performance which we will take into account is any data formatting and packing differences between the observed units and the projected units. A classical example of this type of difference would be the conversion from "7 track" tape to "9 track" tape. The first tape has in each bit frame provision for 6 data bits plus 1 parity bit. The second has provision for 8 data bits and 1 parity bit. When converting from 7 track to 9 track, the packing considerations are that alphameric characters are converted on a 1:1 basis, decimal digits on a 2:1 basis, and binary information on a 4:3 basis. However, the overall requirements of the application may cause either decimal representation or binary representation to be converted on a 1:1 basis. This would be especially true when emulation is being used.

To take this characteristic into account, the analyst must determine not only record lengths of the observed system, but also the data formats of the observed data. Since the distinction of the type of the data may not be known to the channel at the time the data are being transmitted, we usually have to look into the format of the data at an earlier point. If the application is written in a higher level source language, the data formats are usually specified as part of the program. Similarly, many operating systems require the programmer to specify explicitly the format of the data. In either of these events, the analyst can determine the data formats for the individual data sets by investigating the original programming of the application. If neither of the programming practices are used, the analyst has to get the required information by either an interview with the programmer or investigating the application program in detail. Fortunately, there are more sources of information than one might expect. For example, primary input and output information may be determined through instructions for operators concerning the creation or printing of data. Additionally, some of the files used in the application under study may be used by other programs in the installation. These programs may have explicitly provided the required information.

Another attribute of formatting and packing is concerned with not the explicit data content of the record, but the error detection and correction facility associated with the data. The simple parity bit for a frame of data has been mentioned. This is used for error detection of information recorded on the magnetic tape.

There are many other approaches which use more error detection and correction coding. Depending on the approach used by the designers, the physical record length in terms of number of frames recorded is increased by one or more additional frames of information. Without going into detail, consideration should also be given to the various error detection and correction facilities. For example, if the tape subsystem had the facility to correct "single" errors (the addition or dropping of a single bit) without invoking a special error routine in the system, the performance could be considerably improved.

There are still other attributes of magnetic tape such as mode switch time and skip characteristics which have not been addressed here. The purpose in dwelling on magnetic tape is to demonstrate that even such a simple media has many complexities which should be considered by the analyst.

10.3. DIRECT ACCESS DEVICE PROJECTIONS

The direct access device generically includes those rotating devices with or without movable access mechanisms; both disk files and drums. Since many of the points of evaluating these devices were covered in previous chapters, only a few notes will be given in this section. Although the direct access device has a distinct set of characteristics to consider, any projection is highly dependent upon the application of the devices and the facilities available in the control units and channels which attach the device to the system.

The complete data organization associated with the device must be defined for evaluation purposes. The data organization includes the access methods used to control the flow of data, the file organization in terms of volume extents and sequence of key fields, and the record organization within the files. Record organization includes more than data length alone. Although a device may have many records on a track, or one record which spans many tracks, some of the recorded information may have special meaning.

In Figure 10.21, four different methods of laying out data are shown.

The track length record or "full track mode" record is a format in which the entire contents of the track are read or written by the system. If the infor-

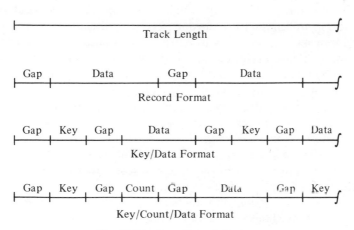

Fig. 10.21   Record organizations.

mation on the track contains more than one logical record for the application program, the CPU must break out the records either before or after the track has been written or read. This format is generally very efficient for the storage subsystem, but obviously requires more CPU activity when multiple logical records are involved. This format is especially efficient for "read only" files, or sequentially increased files. This type of file use tries to avoid the problem of record insertion to be discussed later. (Even this mode of recording has gaps which are not shown, e. g., "home address.")

The second format shown is that of a record mode operation. In this case, the track is split into record areas of predetermined lengths. The length of the records may be variable within a device or may be set in a fixed mode throughout the device. The objective of record mode is to have only the desired record transmitted rather than a full track. This tends to shorten record fetch time by reducing the transmission portion. Access and rotational characteristics would generally remain the same unless the data organization takes advantage of the geometry of the devices and the requirements of the application program. Again, there may be more than one logical record in the physical record transmitted.

The third format shows a short identification record which preceeds the regular data record. Such a short record would normally be used as a search argument when there is a requirement for the application program to search through a set of sequential records for a particular record to process. Such an argument can also be used as a point of confirmation when using update in place techniques. The fourth example merely shows two heading records preceeding the data record. In addition to a key field, there may be a field to describe the number of bytes in the data record. Such an approach would allow a variable record format within a file organization.

Either of the last two formats are closely coupled to the ability of the CPU or channel or control unit to utilize the information. The purpose of separating key field identification from the data record itself is to reduce the amount of record transmission necessary to perform an application. However, if the control unit or channel is locked up for the amount of time that would have been taken by reading the record, there may be little or no improvement in job performance. Consider the following comparison.

Assume that it was necessary to search through five records on a track in order to find the desired record for transmission. If we further assume that the control unit/channel/CPU complex were not fast enough to compare the identification field of a record in time to read the next record, it would take five revolutions of the device for the system to search through the five records. Of course, if the complex were fast enough, then all five records would have been read within a portion of a revolution. To help overcome the speed requirements of matching the search key, a separate record is utilized for the key field. This field may or may not be duplicated within the data record itself. The assumption is that there will be sufficient time for the complex to compare the argument with the search key and cause a read of the next key field within the same revolution. In this way, the five arguments can be examined within a portion of a revolution. To actually read the data record may require an additional revolution.

The presence of such precursor records in a file can compound the measurement activity for the analyst. If the measurement technique does not distinguish between the precursor records and the normal data records, an extremely low average record length may be calculated. Although such a calculation would represent what actually took place, it would not recognize the bi-modal nature of the data. Furthermore, since search techniques can vary for a given file and format, the analyst will be better equipped to take various search techniques into account if precursor records are measured separately from the data records.

Measurement information can be further complicated by the presence of additional records not yet inserted into their proper place in the file. The record insertion problem occurs when a new record is generated which must be logically placed in sequence in a previously established file. Imagine the processing necessary to add one logical record into the first track of a file which is formatted in full track mode. Every subsequent record in the file must be pushed down to allow room for the new record. In this case, insertion requires restructuring the complete file. Methods may be used to overcome this particular problem. One method is simply not to allow insertion of new records until a sufficient number have accumulated to make the file restructuring worthwhile. In the system these records are then handled on an exception basis during the processing of the application. Another method is to not utilize the total space available in each track, but to save at least one record's length just in case an insertion is necessary on that track. This approach can be used on each track or on some small number of tracks. This in effect defers the time when a file restructure is necessary, but achieves this at a cost of reduced utilization of space available, which in turn may cause reduced performance.

Yet another method to defer the restructuring of a file is to utilize the track "overflow" concept. In this case, a relatively small amount of space is set aside to indicate to the process program that although a record should have been found within the boundaries of a track or cylinder of tracks, it will be found in an overflow area of the file. This approach is similar to processing un-inserted records on an exception basis. The difference is that the exception table on the first approach must be examined for every record referenced whether it had been inserted or not. The overflow method enters the exception routine only when a record reference is made to an un-inserted record.

Whatever file or record format is used, there may come a time when it is necessary to restructure the file. In many cases, the incidence of this happening is such that it is scheduled in the installation just like any other application. As such, the analyst may determine the characteristics of this application and apply projective calculation to this portion of the work load.

Since the direct access storage device is extremely versatile, some investigation should be made concerning its principal function in the system. The scope of application can be broken down into four general types or classes of function as follows:

System Residence Function including all process queues

Input/Output Function for removable media

Utility/Scratch/Intermediate Storage Function

Data Base Function.

Within any given function level, various access methods may be used on different data sets on a given device. Furthermore, since there can be multiple data sets on a single device, it is possible to have more than one function, as described above, on a single device. It is common to find such situations in many installations. For example, a single device could have both part of the system residence function and utility functions.

The system residence function varies from installation to installation, but normally contains the various elements of the master control program and language compilers used in the installation. The additions to these two principal elements are almost unlimited. Various libraries of routines are held on the device awaiting a call from the control program. Typically, error routines are held on the device rather than in storage. Various process tables may be stored on the device by the control program while jobs are being processed. The reason for storing the tables on the device rather than retaining them in processor storage may be due to a lack of space in processor storage or the ability to recover easily in case of a system error, or both. The various process queues may be stored on the device. This would include not only the primary input and output queues, but also intermediate queues generated within the system.

Because the system residence function is expandable, there is usually provision to distribute the various sub-functions over more than one device or type of device. Therefore, a mixture of drums and disk files could be utilized to perform the system residence function. The analyst would then treat each sub-function (or perhaps a group of sub-functions) as individual data sets in the course of his analysis.

The input/output function for removable media is similar in concept to changing reels for magnetic tape. However, the utilization of a particular access method may introduce some problems. For example, if a large data set of information were too large for a single disk pack (whatever its volume capability), multiple disk packs could be utilized to store the data set. If the information on the disk packs is processed in a straightforward sequential manner, like tape, then one pack at a time could be placed on a device with pack changes as necessary. To overcome pack changing time, two devices could be used with logical switching whenever necessary. However, if the entire data set were accessed by a random access method, then there would be a requirement for all disk packs of the data set to be mounted on individual devices before the application could proceed. When assessing the effects of pack changing, the analyst should also consider the requirements of the access method to be used on the data.

The utility/scratch/intermediate storage function is used to store temporary data sets that are created during the processing of programs. These data sets are usually purged at the end of the application. The control program itself may create temporary data sets in addition to any that may be created by such functions as language compilation or program editing. The temporary data sets could include not only the process tables which were mentioned earlier, but also the temporary storage of active programs and/or their associated data. This is typically found in multiprogramming systems, where a job forces another job of lower priority temporarily out of the system. In systems which involve virtual memory concepts, "pages" of the virtual memory could be created and held on direct access storage during the execution of the associated job. Normally, we would find a device such as a drum, uniquely allocated as the "paging" device. In addition to these functions, the system may cause a temporary data set to be created which contains sufficient program information and data to allow a "restart" if some unrecoverable error occurs before the next "checkpoint." As new checkpoints are reached, the old checkpoint information may be totally or partially purged, depending on the requirements of the application and operating system.

The data base function is really more of a total system concept than an individual function within the classes of device operation. There are many requirements of data organization in the implementation of a data base. The general requirement is to have many different application programs operating on a common data set in such a way as to allow each of the applications to be performed while also ensuring that a program does not obtain unauthorized information. There must also be provision to ensure that through error a program does not destroy information or prevent other programs from performing their tasks.

When there is a "small" data base used by one application, that data base may be contained in one direct access device. As the data base grows larger, and as more applications are concurrently using it, the analysis problems become more complex. To the analyst, the data base implies the use of additional tables and indices, multiple access methods, and various queue facilities involved in the transmission of data. Where in simpler operations, a reference to a particular physical device implied through a one-to-one correspondence the presence and/or execution of a particular function, the identity of the function will be lost in a data base system. This means that more sophisticated measurement techniques and projective techniques will have to be used to assess the performance of the devices in this environment.

Device	Channel/Control Unit
Data Rate	Read/Write Selection
Rotational Period	Search Techniques
Unit/Track Capacity	Disconnect Capability
Gap Characteristics	
Head Switching Time	
Seek Characteristics	
Pack Change Characteristic	

Fig. 10.22   Direct access device characteristics.

In Figure 10.22 the general characteristics of a direct access device are listed, along with some of the relevant characteristics of the control unit and channel which should be taken into consideration. In projecting the effects of rotational time and transmission rate, the basic system profile can be used, although there can be quite a wide confidence range to the result. In Section 4.3, an overall average record length was used to project performance improvement. Involved in the procedure was a simple check on observed or calculated average rotational delay time on the observed system. If the observation does approximate the device's average rotational delay, there would be good confidence in using profile conversion. If there were a wide variation in the observed average and the theoretical average, it was indicated that other techniques should be invoked, such as simulation.

A slight refinement that can be applied to profile conversion is the separation of record transmission for the purposes of searching key fields and record transmission involving the data records themselves. For the measurement technique this would involve taking two record counts, two fetch times, two character counts, etc. Ignoring seek activity for the moment, the basic system profile which separates search/key field activity from data record activity is shown in Figure 10.23.

In the profile, the region B to C represents the portion of data fetching which is overlapped with CPU activity, and the region E to F represents the portion which is active during wait state. Similarly, the region C to D represents the search/key fetch time which is overlapped with CPU activity and the region D to E the portion during wait state. Again, remember that the profile is merely a summary presentation and that the regions have no ordinal implications. Therefore, when calculating the effects during data fetching, the two regions are first added together to determine an improvement factor.

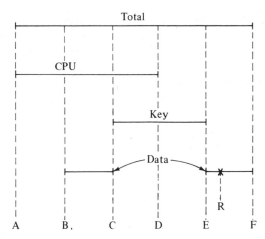

Fig. 10.23 Separation of key field.

Assuming that the measurement technique provided total data transmission times for each category in addition to total fetch times and record counts, there would be a point, R, which indicates the separation of rotational delay time from byte transmission time. In the case of data fetching the diagram could be as shown in Figure 10.23. Here we see that the point R falls in the region E to F. (It could just as well have been in the region B to C.) To calculate the effect of a projected device in these two regions, we again first check the observed average access time against the observed device's theoretical average access time to determine confidence. And, again, if the observed average access time varies greatly from the theoretical, the analyst should probably plan on utilizing some other technique to do the evaluation. A new rotational delay time is calculated by multiplying the projected device's average rotational delay by the number of records transmitted. The projected transmission time is obtained by multiplying the observed byte transmission time by the ratio of the projected device's transmission rate to the observed device's transmission rate, i.e.,

$$t(p) = (R_p/R_o)*t(o).$$

Separating the search/key field from the rest of the data transmission allows the analyst to approximate the effect of varying the number of search fields utilized to locate a particular record.

10.4. PROGRAMMING COMPONENTS

Because of the very wide divergence of programming improvements, little can be said in the general case. We have seen a programming component improve one characteristic, say speed, at the expense of another characteristic, say storage space. On the other hand, we have seen programming components increase speed as well as decrease storage requirements because of some new approach. Given the latter situation, there is almost no evaluation called for. However, even in the latter case, there may be a cost in time and effort as well as the cost of the component to insert the new program into the system. If this cost is considerable, then there may be a place for evaluation.

In the general case, the evaluation of a new programming component will involve the determination of the incidence of use of the facility and also the job load characteristics which may influence the component's improvement factor. The simple case is that of compilation. In previous chapters, a method of expressing the performance of a compiler was demonstrated by the timing formula. The formula was a function of the two job characteristics, number of source cards and number of additional subprograms. In order to assess the direct effect of adopting a new compiler, data would be obtained on the number of jobs using the particular language of the compiler as well as information concerning source cards and subroutines on each of the jobs in the set. This would provide sufficient information to calculate direct savings due to a compiler replacement.

However, in the case of a compiler, there is not only the direct effect during the execution of the compiler, but also the indirect effect due to the efficiency of the object code which it produces. Perhaps the best way to evaluate this effect is to try some typical jobs under the new compiler to obtain an estimate of the improvement. Various techniques may be used to determine the job or jobs which would be used as benchmarks for the exercise. Job stream analysis will aid in the selection of the jobs. Once the benchmark is chosen, its profile can be determined for comparison with the entire computing load's profile. If it is seriously out of line, adjustments can be made to the benchmark in order for it to be more representative of the load on the system.

The benchmark should be executed in such a way as to distinguish carefully between the act of compilation and other pre-production activities, and the act of execution. This should be done in order to assist the analyst in mapping back the results to the actual load on the system. As mentioned earlier, an easy error in benchmarking is to select from a system load that has characteristics of 20 percent compilation and 80 percent production a benchmark that has 80 percent compilation and 20 percent production.

If the replacement program component is not available for actual execution, then the method of determining its effect on the installation would be to use some projective technique. Depending on the functional dependency of the component, any of the techniques which have been presented could be used. Simple dependencies could utilize incidence analysis or profile conversion. The more complex dependencies may require either synthetic or simulative techniques in order to assess their improvement. Again, through the use of job stream and profile analysis, a small subset of the actual work-load can be chosen for processing through the more complex techniques.

10.5. MULTIPROGRAMMING CONSIDERATIONS

The general incentive to go into multiprogramming is to utilize unused facilities in the computing system. Many times, the primary implementation of a multiprogramming system is to improve the utilization of the CPU and processor storage. Therefore, when progressing from a control program which processes a single batch stream to a multiprogramming control program, one of the first things to examine is the present utilization of the CPU and processor storage.

In simple terms, there are three general levels of multiprogramming. The first level provides for the simultaneous transcription of input and output data concurrently with other processing. (This facility is known as "SPOOL," Simultaneous Peripheral Operations, On-Line.) This activity requires a minimum of CPU activity and processor storage. Its purpose is to maintain the transcription of data between unit record equipment such as cards and printers and auxiliary devices of the system such as disk files. As an individual job, it has the characteristics of being I/O bound with very little CPU activity. It would be the perfect candidate to operate concurrently with a "number cruncher."

The second level of multiprogramming utilizes a philosophy which divides processor storage into separate partitions on a preassigned basis. For example, processor storage may be divided up into a supervisor partition and six problem program partitions. If there are more than six jobs available, the excess will have to wait. If there are less than six jobs available, then some of the partitions may be inactive. This philosophy is easier to implement than the general case, but does allow for inefficient use of processor storage when portions are unused.

The third level of multiprogramming utilizes a philosophy which allocates processor storage to jobs (job steps and/or tasks) as needed. There is usually some maximum number of discrete events which can take place (sixteen, thirty-two or so) under the control program. Up to the maximum amount of storage or maximum number of activities, the control program allocates resources as required. It has the advantage of fully utilizing its resources, but the disadvantage of becoming more complex in itself. Because it is more complex, it generally takes more time and space to perform its function.

Starting with an installation which is processing a work load under a single batch stream environment, the analyst is faced with increasing levels of complexity as he considers the performance effects of the various multi-programming philosophies. Unfortunately, there is no panacean answer to expected performance under multiprogramming. This is because the multi-programming system is sensitive to not only the type of jobs performed, but the sequence in which the jobs are performed. As an example of this situation, consider the following experience. A particular job with well defined input and output characteristics was submitted for processing, three times in one day, on a multiprogramming system. The measure of time considered was the time that the job was actually in processor storage, contending for CPU time. At 8 AM, the job took 10 minutes. At 10 AM, it took 16 minutes. At 2 PM, it took 22 minutes. The reason for the variation was that there were less buffers available to the job as the day went on. The reason for the diminished number of buffers was the increasing number of jobs being processed in the system. Although this single job suffered in its processing characteristics, the system, as such, improved in its performance. At 8 AM, this was the only job being processed. At 10 AM, about ten other jobs were being processed concurrently; and at 2 PM, about forty other jobs were being processed.

This highlights a main consideration of multiprogramming. The incentive of such a philosophy is to optimize the system's performance for a complete work load, not just an individual job. Therefore, the evaluation of multi-programming should be taken across a work load as opposed to individual jobs.

To approach an evaluation of a multiprogramming system, the analyst should determine not only job characteristics, but also the incidence and arrival time of the various jobs. The performance of a multiprogramming system may have a wide range of results depending on such things as arrival time. Assume that a set of jobs were selected for evaluation. The system may be sensitive (and probably is) to the sequence A, B, C, D, E, as opposed to the sequence D, C, B, A, E. Given a set of jobs for evaluation, the analyst should vary the arrival sequence through whatever technique is used for evaluation to determine sensitivity to sequence. In fact, best case and worst case deter-mination should be integral to the study.

The tool which is generally used to evaluate the performance of multi-programming systems is the simulator. The particular implementation may be either probabilistic or deterministic, depending on the characterization of the present work load. If it is determined that the arrival time and type of job is completely random in an installation, then a probabilistic simulation should be used. If, on the other hand, there is a well defined pattern of recurring types of jobs, a trace drive simulator can be employed.

The chief adversary of multiprogramming is two or more jobs contending for the same facility. We normally think of contention in terms of compute bound or I/O bound. However, the point of contention may be the facility of the system residence device for a series of compilations. The analyst should be especially cautious when there is contention for auxiliary devices. For example, if the system input stream and the system output stream utilized the same physical device, the operation of the two programs under multi-programming could be much longer than the time it would take to run the two jobs sequentially. This is due to the inordinate movement of a disk arm between the two data sets. Through class and priority assignments to the various jobs, it is possible to avoid having contentious jobs active at the same time.

Since the purpose of multiprogramming is to optimize a complete work load rather than just a single job, it is possible to evaluate improvements due to component replacement in a relatively simple manner. Where the evaluation of augmenting a disk drive or changing CPUs was evaluated on a job basis for the simple control program, the same techniques can be used for a multiprogramming monitor on a work load basis. The inherent assumption is that the characteristics of the total work load will not change appreciably. The major exception to this is the consideration of increasing processor storage.

The evaluation of increasing processor storage in a multiprogramming environment is similar to the evaluation of progressing from a simple batch stream to multiprogramming. In the general case, a system simulator would be used to assess the performance. Such a study can be avoided if intuitive results are accepted. Measurements can be taken of the operating multiprogramming system to determine if, in fact, processor storage is the limiting factor. If it is not, then there is little value in simulating the effect of adding more storage. If it does appear to be the limiting factor, then there would be reason for going into a system simulation.

10.6. INTERACTIVE SYSTEMS CONSIDERATIONS

An interactive system can be one of two types. One type interacts with physical phenomena such as contact sense points, analog to digital conversions, etc.; and the other type deals with human beings. The former type falls under the generic heading of data acquisition and process control while the latter falls under the generic heading of communications and time sharing. Except for the tolerance at the end of the interaction, the systems are similar. In one case, if the system is not responsive, it may lose data. In the other case, if the system is not responsive, the operator may lose patience.

The general attribute which concerns the analyst is response time of the system versus loading on the system. Whether in the process control environment or time sharing environment, there is given a critical response time target which must be met for the system to perform its intended function. The loading on the system is generally expressed as an arrival rate of various transactions. This loading may be best case, average case, or worst case. In any event, a response calculation must be performed.

The techniques generally used are either synthetic techniques for well defined applications, or simulative techniques. Because an interactive system tends to have random input, a probabilisitic simulation is generally used. The necessary ingredient in either case is the knowledge of incidence of use and duration of various programming modules which will be used by the actual system.

When investigating interactive systems, an iterative process can be used by the analyst. On the first pass of investigation, he should determine the incidence of use of major sections of the system. Following this, he should determine the response of those sections if and when they are invoked. As the analyst goes into more detail, he can separate, initially, the response of a facility when invoked from the incidence of requests for the facility. This is really a tradeoff on the analyst's time. It could well be that the requirement for a particular routine is completely random. If that is the case, time is better spent in determining the response to the "if and when" rather than determining the incidence. On the other hand, there is little point in spending an extensive amount of time determining the exact variation of response in a particular routine if that routine is seldom called for.

The main difference between projecting response versus load between process type activities and time sharing type activities is the certainty of what the projected load would be. In a process application, the user would probably want to add repeated functions of the present type. If this were not the case, he probably has in mind a well defined application. In either event, one may derive an expected load from the physics of the application. In time sharing, however, the addition of merely terminals may be secondary to the type of work being performed on the terminals.

In time sharing, it is reasonable to distinguish between the act of creating a program and the execution of previously developed programs. The projection of response versus load could then have a wide range as shown in Figure 10.24.

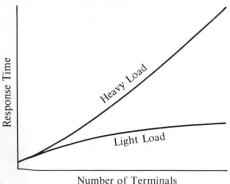

Number of Terminals   **Fig. 10.24** Response vs. load.

In this case, the upper curve represents the response to a *particular* action on a terminal assuming all other terminals are in a mode of extreme load on the system. The lower curve represents the response to the same transaction assuming all other terminals are in a mode of very light load on the system. We can plot on the same curve experience to date on the system, but the real question is whether that curve is indicative of the type of load to be found in the future. A terminal system, like any computing system, has the general attribute that in the early days of installation there is a high proportion of program development with little execution of developed programs. This is natural, because in the early days there are not that many programs developed for execution. As the system matures, the developed load increases in proportion to development activity. A knowledge of the installation will assist in determining which migration curve should be used.

BIBLIOGRAPHY

APPLE, C. T., "The Program Monitor—A Device for Program Performance Measurement," *ACM Proceedings of 20th National Conference*, 1965, pp. 66–75.

ARBUCKLE, R. A., "Computer Analysis and Thruput Evaluation," *Computers and Automation*, Vol. 15, No. 1, 1966, pp. 12–15.

ARNDT, F. R., and G. M. OLIVER, "Hardware Monitoring of Real-Time Computer System Performance," *Digest of 1971 IEEE International Computer Society Conference*, 1971, pp. 123–124.

ASCHENBRENNER, R. A., L. AMIOT, and N. K. NATARAJAN, "The Neurotron Monitor System," *AFIPS Conference Proceedings*, Vol. 39, 1971, pp. 31–37.

BALDWIN, F. R., W. B. GIBSON, and C. B. POLAND, "A multiprocessing approach to a large computer system," *IBM Systems Journal*, Vol. 1, No. 1, 1962, pp. 64–76.

BARD, Y., "Performance criteria and measurement for a time sharing system," *IBM System Journal*, Vol. 10, No. 3, 1971, pp. 193–216.

BAZOVSKY, I., *Reliability Theory and Practice*. Englewood Cliffs, N. J.: Prentice-Hall, Inc., 1961.

BEMER, R. W., and A. L. ELLISON, "Software Instrumentation Systems for Optimum Performance," *Proceedings of IFIP Congress*, 1968, pp. 520–524.

Bibliography on Simulation. IBM Publication 320-0924-0, 1966.

BONNER, A. J., "Using system monitor output to improve performance," *IBM Systems Journal*, Vol. 8, No. 4, 1969, pp. 290–298.

BUCHHOLZ, W., "A Selected Bibliography on Computer System Performance Evaluation," *IEEE Computer Group News*, Vol. 2, No. 8, 1969, pp. 21–22.

———, "A synthetic job for measuring system performance," *IBM Systems Journal*, Vol. 8, No. 4, 1969, pp. 309–318.

BUSSELL, B., and R. A. KOSTER, "Instrumenting Computer Systems and their Programs," *AFIPS Conference Proceedings*, Vol. 37, 1970, pp. 525–534.

CALINGAERT, P., "System Performance Evaluation: Survey and Appraisal," *Communications of the ACM*, Vol. 10, No. 1, 1967, pp. 12–18.

CAMPBELL, D. J., and W. J. HEFFNER, "Measurement and Analysis of Large Operating Systems during System Development," *AFIPS Conference Proceedings*, Vol. 33, 1968, pp. 903–914.

CANTRELL, H. N., "Designing for Measurement," *Digest of 1971 IEEE International Computer Society Conference*, 1971, pp. 125–126.

————, and A. L. ELLISON, "Multiprogramming System Performance Measurement and Analysis," *AFIPS Conference Proceedings*, Vol. 32, 1968, pp. 213–221.

CHANG, W., "A queuing model for a simple case of time sharing," *IBM Systems Journal*, Vol. 5, No. 2, 1966, pp. 115–125.

CHENG, P. S., "Trace-driven system modeling," *IBM Systems Journal*, Vol. 8, No. 4, 1969, pp. 280–289.

COLLMEYER, A. J., and J. E. SHEMER, "Analysis of Retrieval Performance for Selected File Organization Techniques," *AFIPS Conference Proceedings*, Vol. 37, 1970, pp. 201–210.

Computer Characteristics Quarterly. Adams Associates, Inc.

CONTI, C. J., "System Aspect: System/360 Model 92," *AFIPS Conference Proceedings*, Vol. 25, 1964, pp. 81–95.

DENISTON, W. R., "SIPE: A TSS/360 Software Measurement Technique," *ACM Proceedings of 24th National Conference*, 1969, pp. 229–245.

DOHERTY, W. J., "Scheduling TSS/360 for Responsiveness," *AFIPS Conference Proceedings*, Vol. 37, 1970, pp. 97–111.

DRUMMOND, M. E., Jr., "Turnaround, Thru-put, and Multiprocessing," IBM Technical Report TR 00.1110, March 30, 1964.

————, "A perspective on system performance evaluation," *IBM Systems Journal*, Vol. 8, No. 4, 1969, pp. 252–263.

ESTRIN, G., D. HOPKINS, B. COGGAN, and S. D. CROCKER, "Snuper Computer: A Computer in Instrumentation Automation," *AFIPS Conference Proceedings*, Vol. 30, 1967, pp. 645–655.

————, and L. KLEINROCK, "Measures, Models, and Measurements for Time-Shared Computer Utilities," *ACM Proceedings of the 22nd National Conference*, 1967, pp. 85–96.

FENICHEL, R. R., and A. J. GROSSMAN, "An Analytic Model of Multiprogrammed Computing," *AFIPS Conference Proceedings*, Vol. 34, 1969, pp. 717–721.

FERDINAND, A. E., "An analysis of the machine interference model," *IBM Systems Journal*, Vol. 10, No. 2, 1971, pp. 129–142.

GIBSON, J. C., "The Gibson Mix," IBM Technical Report TR00.2043, June 1970.

GORDON, G., "A general purpose systems simulator," *IBM Systems Journal*, Vol. 1, No. 1, 1962, pp. 18–32.

GOSDEN, J. A., and R. L. SISSON, "Standardized Comparisons of Computer Performance," *Proceedings of IFIP Congress*, 1962, pp. 57–61.

GROSCH, H. R. J., "High Speed Arithmetic: The Digital Computer as a Research Tool," *Journal of the Optical Society of America*, Vol. 43, No. 4, 1953, pp. 306–310.

HAHN, S. G., and E. V. HANKAM, "Kernel analysis of elliptic partial differential equations," *IBM Systems Journal*, Vol. 5, No. 4, 1966, pp. 248–270.

HANSSMANN, F., W. KISTLER, and H. SCHULZ, "Modeling for computer center planning," *IBM Systems Journal*, Vol. 10, No. 4, 1971, pp. 305–324.

HARE, V. C., Jr., *Systems Analysis: A Diagnostic Approach.* New York: Harcourt Brace Jovanovich, Inc., 1967.

HART, L. E., and G. J. LIPOVICH, "Choosing a System Stethoscope," *Computer Decisions*, November 1971, pp. 20–23.

HELLERMAN, H., and H. J. SMITH, "Throughput Analysis of Some Idealized Input, Output, and Compute Overlap Configurations," *Computing Surveys*, Vol. 2, No. 2, 1970, pp. 111–118.

HENDRIE, G. C., and R. W. SONNENFELDT, "Evaluating Control Computers," *ISA Journal*, Vol. 10, No. 8, 1963, pp. 73–78.

HERMAN, D. J., "SCERT: A Computer Evaluation Tool," *Datamation*, February 1967, pp. 26–28.

———, and F. C. IHRER, "The Use of a Computer to Evaluate Computers," *AFIPS Conference Proceedings*, Vol. 25, 1964, pp. 383–395.

HILLEGASS, J. R., "Standardized Benchmark Problems Measure Computer Performance," *Computers and Automation*, January 1966, pp. 16–19.

HOLLAND, F. C., and R. A. MERIKALLIO, "Simulation of a Multiprocessing System using GPSS," *IEEE Transactions on System Science and Cybernetics*, Vol. SSC-4, No. 4, 1968, pp. 395–400.

HUESMANN, L. R., and R. P. GOLDBERG, "Evaluating Computer Systems through Simulation," *Computer Journal*, Vol. 10, No. 2, 1967, pp. 150–156.

HULL, T. E., and A. R. DOBELL, "Random Number Generators," *SIAM Review*, Vol. 4, No. 3, 1962.

HUMPHREY, T. A., "Large Core Storage Utilization in Theory and in Practice," *AFIPS Conference Proceedings*, Vol. 30, 1967, pp. 719–727.

HUTCHINSON, G. K., and J. N. MAGUIRE, "Computer Systems Design and Analysis through Simulation," *AFIPS Conference Proceedings*, Vol. 27, 1965, pp. 161–167.

IHRER, F. C., "Computer Performance Projected through Simulation," *Computers and Automation*, April 1967, pp. 22–27.

INTERNATIONAL BUSINESS MACHINES CORP., *Throughput Evaluations ... IBM 7090/7094 Data Processing Systems* (1963).

JOSLIN, E. O., "Application Benchmarks: The Key to Meaningful Computer Evaluations," *ACM Proceedings of 20th National Conference*, 1965, pp. 27–37.

———, *Computer Selection.* Reading, Mass.: Addison-Wesley Publishing Company, Inc., 1968.

———, and J. J. AIKEN, "The Validity of Basing Computer Selections on Benchmark Results," *Computers and Automation*, January 1966, pp. 22–23.

———, and M. J. MULLIN, "Cost-Value Technique for Evaluation of Computer System Proposals," *AFIPS Conference Proceedings*, Vol. 25, 1964, pp. 367–381.

KATZ, J. H., "Simulation of a Multiprocessor Computer System," *AFIPS Conference Proceedings*, Vol. 28, 1966, pp. 127–139.

KEEFE, D. D., "Hierarchical control programs for systems evaluation," *IBM Systems Journal*, Vol. 7, No. 2, 1968, pp. 123–133.

KERRY, D. W., "Choosing Computers for the Post Office," *The Computer Bulletin*, March 1967, pp. 12–16.

KLEINROCK, L., "Time-Shared Systems: A Theoretical Treatment," *Journal of the ACM*, Vol. 14, No. 2, 1967, pp. 242–261.

KOLENCE, K. W., "A Software View of Measurement Tools," *Datamation*, January 1, 1971, pp. 32–38.

KNIGHT, K. E., "Changing Computer Performance," *Datamation*, September 1966, pp. 40–54.

———, "Evolving Computer Performance 1963–1967," *Datamation*, January 1968, pp. 31–35.

LEHMAN, M. M., and J. L. ROSENFELD, "Performance of a Simulated Multiprogramming System," *AFIPS Conference Proceedings*, Vol. 33, 1968, pp. 1431–1442.

LUCAS, H. C., JR., "Performance Evaluation and Monitoring," *Computing Surveys*, Vol. 3, No. 3, 1971, pp. 80–91.

LUM, V. Y., H. LING, and M. E. SENKO, "Analysis of a Complex Data Management Access Method by Simulation Modeling," *AFIPS Conference Proceedings*, Vol. 37, 1970, p. 211.

MCGREW, M. J., "Measuring for Design," *Digest of 1971 IEEE International Computer Society Conference*, 1971, pp. 121–122.

MARGOLIN, B. H., R. P. PARMELEE, and M. SCHATZOFF, "Analysis of free-storage algorithms," *IBM Systems Journal*, Vol. 10, No. 4, 1971, pp. 283–304.

MARKOWITZ, H. M., B. HAUSER, and H. W. KARR, *SIMSCRIPT: A Simulation Programming Language.* Englewood Cliffs, N. J.: Prentice-Hall, Inc., 1963.

MATTSON, R. L., J. GECSEI, D. R. SLUTZ, and I. L. TRAIGER, "Evaluation techniques for storage hierarchies," *IBM Systems Journal*, Vol. 9, No. 2, 1970, pp. 78–117.

MERIKALLIO, R. A., and F. C. HOLLAND, "Simulation Design of a Multiprocessing System," *AFIPS Conference Proceedings*, 1968, pp. 1399–1410.

MEZGER, R. A., "The Use of Simulation for Design Analysis of an On-Line Financial Application in a Multi-Programmed Environment," *ACM Proceedings of 24th National Conference*, 1969, p. 11.

MURPHEY, J. O., and R. M. WADE, "The IBM 360/195 in a World of Mixed Job Streams," *Datamation*, April 1970, pp. 72–79.

MURPHY, R. W., "The System Logic and Usage Recorder," *AFIPS Conference Proceedings*, Vol. 35, 1969, pp. 219–229.

NIELSEN, N. R., "The Simulation of Time Sharing Systems," *Communications of the ACM*, Vol. 10, No. 7, 1967, pp. 397–412.

———, "Computer Simulation of Computer System Performance," *ACM Proceedings of the 22nd National Conference*, 1967, pp. 581–590.

OPLER, A., "Measurement of Software Characteristics," *Datamation*, July 1964, pp. 27–30.

RAICHELSON, E., and G. COLLINS, "A Method for Comparing the Internal Operating Speeds of Computers," *Communications of the ACM*, Vol. 7, No. 5, 1964, pp. 309–310.

ROEK, D. J., and W. C. EMERSON, "A Hardware Instrumentation Approach to Evaluation of a Large System," *ACM Proceedings of 24th National Conference*, 1969, p. 351–367.

ROSIN, R. F., "Determining a Computing Center Environment," *Communications of the ACM*, Vol. 8, No. 7, 1965, pp. 463–468.

SCHATZOFF, M., R. TSAO, and R. WIIG, "An Experimental Comparison of Time Sharing and Batch Processing," *Communications of the ACM*, Vol. 10, No. 5, 1967, pp. 261–265.

SCHERR, A. L., "Time Sharing Measurement," *Datamation*, Vol. 12, No. 4, 1966, pp. 22–26.

———, *An Analysis of Time-Shared Computer Systems*. Cambridge, Mass.: MIT Press, 1967.

SCHULMAN, F. D., "Hardware Measurement Device for IBM System/360 Time Sharing Evaluation," *ACM Proceedings of 22nd National Conference*, 1967, pp. 103–109.

SCHWARTZ, E. S., "Computer Evaluation and Selection," *Journal of Data Management*, Vol. 6, No. 6, 1968, pp. 58–62.

SEAMAN, P. H., and R. C. SOUCY, "Simulating operating systems," *IBM Systems Journal*, Vol. 8, No. 4, 1969, pp. 264–279.

SEDGEWICK, R., R. STONE, and J. W. McDONALD, "SPY—A Program to Monitor OS/360," *AFIPS Conference Proceedings*, Vol. 37, 1970, pp. 119–128.

SHEDLER, G. S., and S. C. YANG, "Simulation of a model of paging system performance," *IBM Systems Journal*, Vol. 10, No. 2, 1971, pp. 113–128.

SHEMER, J. E., and D. W. HEYING, "Performance Modeling and Empirical Measurements in a System Designed for Batch and Time-Sharing Users," *AFIPS Conference Proceedings*, Vol. 35, 1969, p. 17–26.

SMITH, E. C., Jr., "A directly coupled multiprocessing system," *IBM Systems Journal*, Vol. 2, No. 3, 1963, pp. 218–229.

———, "Simulation in systems engineering," *IBM Systems Journal*, Vol. 1, No. 1, 1962, pp. 33–50.

SMITH, J. M., "A Review and Comparison of Certain Methods of Computer Performance Evaluation," *The Computer Bulletin*, May 1968, pp. 13–18.

SOLOMON, M. B., Jr., "Economies of Scale and the IBM System/360," *Communications of the ACM*, Vol. 9, No. 6, 1966, pp. 435–440.

STANG, H., and P. SOUTHGATE, "Performance Evaluation of Third Generation Computing Systems," *Datamation*, November 1969, pp. 181–190.

STANLEY, W. I., "Measurement of system operational statistics," *IBM Systems Journal*, Vol. 8, No. 4, 1969, pp. 299–308.

———, and H. F. HERTEL, "Statistics gathering and simulation for the Apollo real-time operating system," *IBM Systems Journal*, Vol. 7, No. 2, 1968, pp. 85–102.

STATLAND, N., "Methods of Evaluating Computer Systems Performance," *Computers and Automation*, Vol. 12, No. 2, 1964, pp. 18–23.

STEVENS, D. F., "System Evaluation on the Control Data 6600," *Proceedings of IFIP Congress 1968*, pp. 542–547.

STIMLER, S., and K. A. BRONS, "A Methodology for Calculating and Optimizing Real-Time System Performance," *Communications of the ACM*, Vol. 11, No. 7, 1968, pp. 509–516.

STRAUSS, J. C., "A Simple Thruput and Response Model of EXEC 8 under Swapping Saturation," *AFIPS Conference Proceedings*, Vol. 39, 1971, pp. 39–49.

Teleprocessing systems design. IBM Systems Journal, Vol. 5, No. 3, 1966.

WALTER, E. S., and V. L. WALLACE, "Further Analysis of a Computing Center Environment," *Communications of the ACM*, Vol. 10, No. 5, 1967, pp. 266–272.

WARNER, C. D., "Monitoring: A Key to Cost Efficiency," *Datamation*, January 1, 1971, pp. 40–49.

WHITE, P., "Relative Effects of Central Processor and Input-Output Speeds Upon Throughput on the Large Computer," *Communications of the ACM*, Vol. 7, No. 12, 1964, pp. 711–714.

WILLIAMS, Q. N., R. S. PERROTT, J. WEITZMAN, J. A. MURRAY, and J. A. SHOBER, "A Methodology for Computer Selection Studies," *Computers and Automation*, May, 1963, pp. 18–22.

WOOD, D. C., and E. H. FORMAN, "Throughput Measurement using a Synthetic Job Stream," *AFIPS Conference Proceedings*, Vol. 39, 1971, pp. 51–56.

INDEX